PMP EXAM PREP

The Ultimate Guide to Passing the Exam on Your First Try. Elevate Your Project Management Expertise and Propel Your Career to New Heights

Nexus Prep Editions

Access your exclusive bonus content by scanning the QR code found at the end of this book. Enjoy additional resources designed to enhance your exam preparation and success!

Introduction to PMP Certification

Overview of PMP and Its Importance

The Evolution of PMP Certification - Let's dive into the fascinating journey of the PMP certification, a voyage that has not just shaped but *revolutionized the landscape of project management* across the globe. Imagine a world where project managers navigated their tasks relying solely on instinct and personal experience. Enter the PMP certification, *introduced by the PMI*, which brought a wave of *standardization*, much like a compass in the hands of a seasoned captain steering through uncharted waters.

From its inception in the 1980s, the PMP certification was more than just a badge of honor; it was a beacon calling out to professionals seeking validation of their skills and knowledge in project management. But it didn't stop there. As the business world evolved, so did the PMP certification, embracing not just the traditional waterfall methodologies but also the dynamic, flexible *Agile and hybrid approaches*. This evolution mirrored the changing tides of project management, acknowledging that the one-size-fits-all approach was a relic of the past.

The certification's journey has been marked by periodic updates, each version more inclusive and encompassing than the last, ensuring that it remains relevant in the fast-paced, ever-changing world of project management. These updates have expanded the certification's appeal, making it a sought-after credential in various industries worldwide. It's not just about leading projects; it's about leading them successfully, efficiently, and innovatively.

What's truly remarkable about the PMP certification is its global recognition. It speaks a universal language of excellence, understanding, and adaptability, bridging cultural and geographical divides. This global appeal has made it a passport to career advancement, opening doors to opportunities that span continents.

The eligibility criteria and examination process have also evolved, becoming more inclusive and reflective of the diverse experiences of professionals in the field. This inclusivity has enriched the PMP community, bringing together a vibrant mosaic of insights, experiences, and perspectives.

In essence, the evolution of the PMP certification is a testament to the enduring importance of project management and its critical role in the success of projects and organizations alike. It's a narrative of growth, **adaptation**, and continuous improvement, inspiring project managers to aim for the stars while keeping their projects firmly grounded in best practices and proven methodologies.

So, as we look back at the journey of the PMP certification, it's clear that it's more than just a series of updates; it's a reflection of the profession's growth and the increasing recognition of the value that skilled project managers bring to the table. It's a story of how a certification can evolve to meet the needs of the modern world, preparing project managers not just to navigate but to thrive in the complexities of today's project environments.

Value to Professionals - Achieving PMP certification is a *game-changer for professionals* in project management. It's not just a *mark of excellence*; it's a testament to your dedication to the profession, showcasing your skills and knowledge on a global stage. This certification can open doors to *higher salary brackets*, with PMP holders often earning significantly more than their non-certified peers. It also enhances your *marketability*, making you a preferred candidate for employers seeking top-tier project management talent. Furthermore, the journey to certification enriches your understanding of both *traditional and agile methodologies*, equipping you with versatile tools to tackle complex projects. Beyond the immediate professional benefits, PMP certification fosters a culture of continuous learning and improvement, connecting you with a global network of professionals and opportunities for career advancement. It's a commitment to your professional growth, signaling to the world that you're serious about project management. Furthermore, actively participating in forums, conferences, and workshops organized by the global PMP community can further enrich your professional experience and open new doors in the field of project management.

Value to Organizations - The value of PMP certification extends significantly to organizations by not only *enhancing project success rates* but also by introducing a *standardized approach to project management*. This standardization ensures projects are completed on time, within budget, and according to their defined scope. Such uniformity is crucial for reducing risks and increasing efficiency, which directly impacts an organization's bottom line in a positive manner.

Moreover, the PMP certification instills a continuous improvement mindset, fostering a culture of professional growth and innovation within organizations. Employing PMP-certified project managers is a clear signal of an organization's commitment to quality and excellence, thereby enhancing its reputation in the market.

Adding to this, PMP-certified professionals are instrumental in implementing new project management techniques that lead to improved project outcomes and increased efficiency. Organizations often find that having PMP-certified employees may be a prerequisite for winning new projects, indicating that this credential can significantly aid in business growth. Customer satisfaction tends to increase as projects managed by certified professionals are more likely to be completed on time and within budget. This, in turn, fosters improved relationships with clients.

The certification also contributes to a positive work culture, elevating employee morale and leading to higher levels of productivity. The international recognition of the PMP certification further means that organizations can compete more effectively on a global scale, implementing best practices in project management that are acknowledged and respected worldwide.

By incorporating these aspects, organizations not only demonstrate their dedication to project management excellence but also position themselves favorably for future opportunities and challenges, leveraging the comprehensive skill set and knowledge base of PMP-certified managers to navigate the complexities of modern projects successfully.

Current Trends in Project Management - The current landscape of project management is characterized by a swift adoption of *Agile and hybrid methodologies*, reflecting the need for flexibility in today's fast-paced environment. *Digital transformation* initiatives are at the forefront, driving the integration of *AI and data analytics* into project management processes for enhanced decision-making and efficiency. The emphasis on *soft skills*, such as leadership and communication, has also risen, acknowledging their critical role in project success. *Sustainability and social responsibility* are becoming increasingly important, influencing project objectives and execution strategies.

To this foundational understanding, it's essential to add real-world applications of these trends. Agile methodologies, for instance, have proven to be a game-changer in how organizations approach project execution, promoting iterative development, and responding swiftly to changes. An illustrative example of Agile's impact can be seen in the way companies have navigated the challenges presented by the pandemic, demonstrating increased resilience and adaptability. Organizations have leveraged Agile and cloud technologies to quickly adjust to new working conditions, maintain productivity, and continue delivering value to customers.

Moreover, the Agile framework, such as Scrum and Kanban, has allowed businesses to streamline their operations, fostering environments where small, interdisciplinary teams can thrive, ensuring rapid delivery of high-quality outputs. This shift towards Agile has not only improved internal processes but also enhanced customer satisfaction by ensuring projects meet their ever-evolving needs.

In the context of PMP certification and exam preparation, these trends underscore the importance of understanding and applying Agile principles. The evolution of the PMP certification to include Agile methodologies reflects the industry's acknowledgment of these critical skills for today's project managers. Aspiring PMP candidates must therefore equip themselves with knowledge of Agile practices, understanding their application in enhancing project outcomes and organizational success. This alignment with industry trends ensures that PMP certification remains relevant and valuable in preparing project managers to thrive in complex project environments.

Exam Eligibility and Application Process

Understanding Eligibility Requirements - Understanding the eligibility requirements for the PMP exam involves a detailed assessment of both educational background and project management experience. The PMI outlines specific criteria: for those **with a four-year degree**, 4,500 hours leading and directing projects plus 35 hours of project management education are required. **Without**

a four-year degree, *7,500 hours in a leadership role and 35 hours of education in the field are necessary.* This structure ensures candidates have a solid foundation of practical experience and theoretical knowledge, preparing them for the complexities of modern project management. This delineation ensures the PMP certification maintains its status as a benchmark for project management excellence, aligning with the profession's evolving standards and practices.

The Application Process Explained - The application process for the PMP exam is structured yet straightforward, designed to validate your qualifications and readiness. Here's a step-by-step guide:

- **Registration**: Begin by registering on the PMI website.

- **Application Details**: Fill out an application detailing your educational background, project management experience, and training.

- **Project Experience**: Be prepared to support your experience with specific examples, including project dates, roles, and responsibilities.

- **Audit Preparation**: Maintain an organized archive of your project and training documents for a potential audit.

- **Submission Review**: Once submitted, your application will be reviewed for completeness.

- **Audit Process**: If selected for audit, provide the required additional documentation.

- **Exam Scheduling**: Upon approval, you'll receive authorization to schedule your exam at a testing center or online.

This process ensures that all candidates meet the high standards set by PMI, preparing them for the complexities of modern project management.

Exam Fees and Scheduling - PMP exam fees and scheduling are critical steps in your certification path. The fee structure differs for *PMI members and non-members*, with members enjoying discounted rates of $**405**, compared to $**555** for non-members. Once your application is approved and fees are paid, you'll receive authorization to take the exam. If you need to retake the exam, members can do so at a reduced fee of $**275**, while non-members will pay $**375**. Joining PMI can be cost-effective, as the $**150** discount on the exam fee essentially covers the annual membership fee of $**139**. It's important to note that some candidates may have access to *financial assistance or discounts*, which is worth considering if you're concerned about exam costs. Additionally, it's advisable to schedule the exam in advance due to potential high demand at testing centers. This flexibility allows candidates to align their exam with their study schedule, ensuring they're at their best on test day.

Preparing Your Application - Preparing your application for the PMP exam involves meticulous documentation of your project management experience and education. To streamline this process:

- **Detail Your Project Roles**: Start by documenting your project roles, responsibilities, and the hours you've dedicated to leading and directing projects, aligning everything with PMI's criteria.

- **Collect Education Evidence**: Gather and organize evidence of your 35 hours of project management education, ensuring all your documents are clear and verifiable.

- **Use a Tabular Format**: For effective organization, consider using a tabular format to list projects, including dates, roles, outcomes, and hours, accompanied by corresponding certificates or letters for your educational credits.

A well-prepared application not only streamlines the review process but also facilitates a smoother approval path, reducing the likelihood of audit-related delays. This thorough preparation demonstrates your dedication to meeting the stringent standards of PMP certification, highlighting your commitment and readiness for the examination.

Navigating Audits - Navigating the *audit process* for the PMP exam application can seem daunting initially, but with careful preparation, it becomes a straightforward step. If selected for an audit, you'll be asked to provide evidence supporting the education and experience detailed in your application. This includes obtaining *signatures from your supervisors* or managers on the projects listed and documentation of your 35 hours of project management education. To effectively gather these signatures, consider drafting a concise and polite request via email, outlining the PMI audit requirements and how their verification supports your application. **Organizing your records in advance** can expedite this process. Approach the audit as an opportunity to validate your qualifications, maintaining open and professional communication with PMI for any clarifications. This proactive stance underscores the importance of readiness and a positive approach to fulfilling audit requirements.

Understanding the PMBOK Guide

Key Concepts of Project Management

Project Management Fundamentals - At the core of the PMBOK Guide are the project management fundamentals, essential for effective project leadership. This begins with understanding projects as temporary endeavors to create unique products, services, or results. Key elements to consider in project management include:

- **Defining the Project Scope**: Clearly outlining what the project aims to achieve, including the development of innovative products that meet market needs.

- **Resource Planning**: Coordinating the necessary resources to execute the project efficiently.

- **Cost Estimation**: Using estimation techniques to define the budget, ensuring financial resources are allocated wisely.

- **Risk Management**: Identifying potential obstacles such as supply chain delays and developing strategies to mitigate these risks.

Consider managing the launch of a new technological product. Here, applying project management fundamentals starts with a clear definition of the project's scope. During planning, estimation techniques are used to define the budget and timelines. Effective risk management enables the identification and mitigation of potential obstacles. Similarly, organizing a professional conference involves coordinating resources, schedules, and stakeholder expectations. This foundational knowledge equips professionals for successfully initiating, planning, executing, monitoring, and closing projects, ensuring alignment with goals and constraints.

Process Groups and Knowledge Areas - The PMBOK Guide organizes project management into five Process Groups and ten Knowledge Areas, creating a comprehensive framework for managing projects. These include:

- **Process Groups**:
  - *Initiating*: Defining a new project or phase by obtaining authorization.
  - *Planning*: Establishing the scope, objectives, and procedures.
  - *Executing*: Completing the work defined in the project plan.
  - *Monitoring & Controlling*: Tracking, reviewing, and regulating progress.
  - *Closing*: Finalizing all activities to formally close the project.
- **Knowledge Areas**:
  - *Integration Management*: Ensuring that project components are coordinated.
  - *Scope Management*: Defining and managing the project's scope.

- *Schedule Management*: Managing the project timeline.

- *Cost Management*: Planning and controlling the project budget.

- *Quality Management*: Ensuring project deliverables meet requirements.

- *Resource Management*: Managing the project team and physical resources.

- *Communications Management*: Ensuring timely and appropriate project information is shared.

- *Risk Management*: Identifying, analyzing, and responding to project risks.

- *Procurement Management*: Acquiring goods and services from outside the project team.

- *Stakeholder Management*: Engaging all project stakeholders.

This structure facilitates a holistic approach, enabling project managers to achieve excellence and efficiency across all aspects of a project. For example, in the Planning process, imagine developing a project plan for launching new customer management software. Similarly, the Risk Management Knowledge Area applies practical strategies in various scenarios, demonstrating how these groups and areas interact to guide a project to success.

Integration of Process Groups and Knowledge Areas - The integration of Process Groups and Knowledge Areas in the PMBOK Guide is pivotal for a seamless and effective project management approach, ensuring that each project phase is informed by all relevant knowledge areas. For example:

- **During Project Initiation**: Integrating stakeholder management with initiating processes ensures all potential impacts and expectations are considered from the start.

- **In the Planning Phase**: The integration of schedule management with planning processes helps in developing a timeline that aligns with the project's scope and resource availability.

- **During Execution**: Applying quality management principles within the executing processes ensures the project's deliverables meet the required standards.

- **In Monitoring and Controlling**: Risk management integration allows for proactive identification and mitigation of potential issues, ensuring project objectives remain achievable.

This holistic approach ensures decisions in one area support the project's overall objectives, crucial for navigating complex challenges and achieving project goals.

Importance of Standards and Practices - Adhering to global standards and practices in project management, as highlighted in the PMBOK Guide, is crucial for project success. These standards provide a tested framework, ensuring consistency and quality across projects. Benefits of following these standards include:

- **Resource Optimization:** Efficient allocation of personnel and equipment.
- **Data Accuracy Improvement:** Enhancing the reliability of project data.

- **Career Advancement:** Increasing professional growth opportunities through recognition of adherence to global standards.

Consider the impact in various sectors: In the energy sector, applying PMBOK resource management standards optimized personnel and equipment allocation in a wind turbine installation project, overcoming logistical challenges and finishing early. In healthcare, employing PMBOK quality management practices in digitizing patient records improved data accuracy and patient safety. These examples underscore the universal applicability and importance of PMBOK standards in modern project management, enhancing career prospects through continuous professional development.

Overview of Knowledge Areas and Process Groups (6th and 7th Editions)

Comparison of 6th and 7th Editions - The transition from the 6th to the 7th edition of the PMBOK Guide signifies a pivotal shift in project management practices, endorsing a more agile and adaptable approach. This evolution from a process-based perspective to a principle-based framework emphasizes critical aspects such as value delivery and adaptability, catering to the diverse requirements of modern projects by blending agile, waterfall, and hybrid methodologies. It equips professionals to adeptly navigate the complexities of contemporary project environments, ensuring project success through a more flexible and inclusive approach.

In detail, the 7th edition of the PMBOK Guide introduces several key principles designed to underscore the importance of adaptability, stakeholder engagement, and value delivery:

- **Adaptability**: Encouraging a flexible approach to project management that can respond swiftly to changes.

- **Stakeholder Engagement**: Prioritizing active involvement of all stakeholders to ensure their needs and expectations are met.

- **Value Delivery**: Focusing on providing real benefits and value to stakeholders throughout the project.

- **Holistic Thinking**: Promoting an integrated view of project management to ensure coherence and alignment with organizational goals.

- **Leadership and Teamwork**: Emphasizing the role of strong leadership and cohesive team effort in achieving project objectives.

These principles guide project managers in applying flexible, value-driven approaches to project delivery across various methodologies, including agile, waterfall, and hybrid models. For example, in a software development project, employing a principle-based approach might involve iterative development with regular stakeholder feedback, contrasting with the more rigid process steps outlined in the 6th edition. This shift ensures project managers are better prepared to implement strategies that effectively meet project goals.

While the shift to a principle-based framework presents numerous advantages, such as increased adaptability and a stronger focus on stakeholder value, it also introduces challenges, particularly in adapting to a less prescriptive approach to project management. Project professionals may initially face uncertainties in how to apply these broad principles to specific project contexts. Overcoming these challenges involves engaging in continuous learning and professional development, such as participating in workshops and seminars focused on the 7th edition's principles, to gain a deeper understanding and practical knowledge of applying these principles effectively.

Let's review the main differences between the 6th and 7th editions of the PMBOK Guide to better understand the evolution in project management standards:

Comparison of PMBOK 6th and 7th Editions

Feature	6th Edition	7th Edition	Implications
Framework Emphasis	Process-based	Principle-based	Shift from doing to thinking
Knowledge Areas	10 Knowledge Areas	8 Performance Domains	Broader focus areas
Process Groups	5 Process Groups	No direct mapping; focus on value delivery	More flexibility
Approach	Mainly predictive	Integrates predictive, agile, and hybrid	Greater adaptability
Planning Scope	Detailed early planning	Continual re-planning and adjustment	More dynamic planning
Stakeholder Engagement	One of the Knowledge Areas	Emphasized across value delivery	Increased importance
Measurement of Success	Based on project constraints	Based on value delivery and outcomes	Focus on benefits realization
Agile and Hybrid Methods	Supplementary (Agile Practice Guide)	Embedded in the standard	Agile is a central approach

Detailed Overview of the 10 Knowledge Areas - The 10 Knowledge Areas are fundamental to project management, each offering unique insights and strategies for handling various aspects of project work. These areas are:

- **Integration Management**: Acts as the project's backbone, harmonizing its various elements to work towards a unified goal.

- **Scope Management**: Defines what is and is not included in the project, ensuring all efforts align with defined objectives.

- **Schedule Management**: Works closely with Cost Management to devise and oversee timelines, optimizing the use of time.

- **Cost Management**: Focuses on budgeting and expenditure, working alongside Schedule Management to ensure financial efficiency.

- **Quality Management**: Guarantees that project outcomes meet or surpass stakeholder expectations, upholding high standards.

- **Resource Management**: Allocates human and material resources wisely, crucial for meeting strategic project and organizational goals.

- **Communications Management**: Facilitates effective information exchange, keeping all stakeholders informed and aligned.

- **Risk Management**: Identifies, assesses, and mitigates potential project risks, protecting both project and organizational interests.

- **Procurement Management**: Manages the acquisition of goods and services from outside the project team, aligning these efforts with project objectives.

- **Stakeholder Management**: Ensures stakeholder needs and expectations are met, fostering satisfaction and engagement.

Each Knowledge Area provides a lens through which project managers can view and address the specific needs of their project, from inception through to completion. By effectively leveraging these areas, project managers can steer their projects towards success, navigating through challenges and optimizing resources to meet and exceed organizational and stakeholder expectations.

Exploration of the 5 Process Groups - The 5 Process Groups underpin successful project management, guiding projects from inception to completion. Each group plays a crucial role in the project lifecycle:

- **Initiating**: This phase involves starting the project by defining its scope and goals, exemplified by stakeholder meetings in a new software development project to ensure alignment from the outset.

- **Planning**: Key for establishing the project's roadmap, including schedules, budgets, and resources. For instance, in a construction project, detailed planning is crucial for setting a clear path forward.

- **Executing**: The phase where the project plan is put into action, as seen in software development through coding and feature integration, highlighting the importance of teamwork and coordination.

- **Monitoring & Controlling**: Involves regular checks against the plan to make necessary adjustments, similar to adapting marketing strategies based on consumer feedback to stay on course.

- **Closing**: The final phase marks the project's conclusion, ensuring all objectives have been met and outcomes are documented, akin to summarizing a conference's successes in a post-event report.

By providing a comprehensive framework, these Process Groups enable project managers to effectively navigate complexities, adapt to changes, and achieve goals across various sectors

Practical Application - The PMBOK Guide's principles serve as a comprehensive blueprint for project management, catering to a diverse array of project environments through **agile, traditional, and hybrid methodologies**. Agile methodologies shine in software development projects, where the market's volatility demands rapid responses. **Agile practices** empower teams to embrace change, making iterative adjustments based on ongoing feedback, ensuring the product remains relevant and competitive.

In contrast, **traditional project management methods** offer a structured approach ideal for construction projects. These projects benefit from detailed planning and phased execution, where predictability and stability are paramount. The sequential nature of traditional practices ensures that each phase is meticulously planned and executed, minimizing risks and ensuring timely delivery within budget constraints.

Hybrid models blend the best of both worlds, offering adaptability alongside structured planning. Such models are particularly effective in product launch projects, where the market's unpredictability requires flexibility, while the need for detailed budgeting and scheduling demands a structured approach. Hybrid methodologies enable project managers to plan strategically while remaining agile enough to respond to market feedback swiftly.

Applying *the PMBOK Guide's principles allows project managers to navigate the complexities of modern projects*, from managing stakeholder expectations in multifaceted environments to addressing resource limitations under stringent timelines. The essence of successful project management lies in the **holistic integration of these methodologies**, ensuring that every decision is informed, strategic, and aligned with the overarching project and organizational goals.

This integrated approach does not only equip project managers to overcome challenges effectively but also empowers them to anticipate and adapt to changes rapidly. By adhering to the **PMBOK Guide's framework**, project managers can ensure the successful delivery of projects, irrespective of the industry, by marrying the principles of flexibility, structure, and adaptability.

In essence, the PMBOK Guide offers a versatile toolkit for project managers, enabling them to tailor their approach to meet the unique demands of each project. Whether navigating the fast-paced changes of a tech project, ensuring the precision and safety of a construction project, or launching a new product in a competitive market, the PMBOK Guide's methodologies provide the foundation for success. Through its application, project managers are better positioned to lead their teams toward achieving project objectives, ultimately driving organizational growth and success in today's dynamic project environments.

Agile Practice Guide Essentials

Introduction to Agile Methodologies - Agile methodologies emphasize flexibility, customer satisfaction, and iterative development, rooted in the Agile Manifesto. They prioritize individuals and interactions over processes and tools, working solutions over comprehensive documentation, customer collaboration over contract negotiation, and responding to change over following a plan. Agile focuses on adapting to change, continuous improvement, and delivering high-quality products that meet customer needs. Frameworks like Scrum and Kanban encourage frequent reflection on becoming more effective, fostering a dynamic, collaborative environment aimed at efficiently achieving project goals.

Agile aligns with PMBOK® Guide areas such as stakeholder management, communication, and risk, highlighting the value of continuous stakeholder engagement and iterative risk management. Real-world Agile applications across software development, marketing, and product management demonstrate its efficiency and adaptability. For instance, a software development company implementing Scrum reduced product release cycles from 12 to 4 months, enhancing customer satisfaction through quicker releases and feedback.

Comparing Agile to traditional (predictive) methodologies, Agile's flexibility and adaptability stand out against the detailed planning and strict adherence to predefined plans of traditional methods. Agile excels in rapidly changing environments or projects with uncertain or evolving requirements, allowing teams to respond more effectively to changes, thereby reducing risk and increasing the final product's value to the customer. This integration into the subsection will enrich the content with practical details and direct comparisons, maintaining consistency, fluidity, and addressing the needs and preferences of the target audience for the PMP exam preparation manual.

Key Agile Frameworks - Within Agile methodologies, key frameworks like Scrum, Kanban, and Lean stand out. Each framework has distinct methodologies and principles that offer unique advantages to project management, aligning with various aspects of the PMBOK® Guide's knowledge areas and process groups.

- **Scrum** is a project management methodology that organizes work into fixed-length periods known as sprints, typically lasting from one to four weeks. Within Scrum, specific roles are defined: the Scrum Master facilitates the process, ensuring obstacles are removed and the team can work efficiently; the Product Owner represents the project's stakeholders, prioritizing the work to be done based on business value. Scrum incorporates ceremonies like daily stand-ups, where the team shares progress and impediments, and sprint reviews, which evaluate the work done. This iterative approach is designed to accommodate rapid changes through feedback loops, aligning with the PMBOK® Guide's focus on timely stakeholder engagement and project time management.

- **Kanban** is a visual project management method that uses boards and cards to represent work items and their progress through different stages of the development process. It emphasizes improving workflow, reducing time delays, and applying just-in-time production, allowing teams to manage work more flexibly and efficiently. By visualizing tasks, teams can easily identify bottlenecks and prioritize tasks, aligning with the PMBOK® Guide's principles on quality management and continuous process improvement.

- **Lean** project management seeks to maximize value to the customer by eliminating waste and optimizing process efficiency. Originating from Toyota's manufacturing principles, Lean focuses on removing unnecessary activities, optimizing resource use, and improving project outcomes. By concentrating on value creation and efficient resource utilization, Lean practices support the PMBOK® Guide's emphasis on effective cost management and resource allocation, ensuring projects deliver maximum value with minimal waste.

Case Studies and Applications:

- A technology startup adopted **Scrum** to manage the development of a new software product. The use of sprints enabled the team to adapt to changing customer requirements rapidly, with regular sprint reviews facilitating stakeholder feedback and ensuring the product met market needs.

- A marketing agency implemented **Kanban** to manage its creative projects. The visualization of tasks on a Kanban board allowed for better workflow management and reduced project delivery times, with the team able to adjust quickly to new client requests or changes in project scope.

- A manufacturing company applied **Lean** principles to its project management processes, focusing on eliminating non-value-added activities. This resulted in significant cost savings and a faster time-to-market for new products, aligning project outcomes more closely with strategic business objectives.

By integrating these frameworks into project management practices, organizations can enhance team collaboration, project adaptability, and efficient delivery. Connecting these Agile frameworks with the PMBOK® Guide's knowledge areas ensures a holistic approach to project management, marrying traditional principles with modern, flexible methodologies to meet the complex demands of today's project environments.

Agile Practices and Tools - To effectively integrate Agile practices and tools, expanding on foundational practices like daily stand-ups, sprints, and retrospectives is essential. These practices, rooted in continuous improvement and collaboration, are pivotal in Agile's effectiveness. For instance, a software development team at a tech startup may utilize daily stand-ups to quickly address emerging issues, ensuring that the development process remains agile and responsive to client feedback. Sprints allow for the rapid delivery of product features, facilitating a competitive edge in fast-paced markets.

Digital Kanban boards and Agile project management software, such as Trello or Jira, are instrumental in maintaining productivity and adaptability. A marketing team, for example, might use Trello to visually organize campaign tasks, enabling seamless transitions between different stages of project development and enhancing team coordination.

When selecting Agile tools, the key is to consider the specific needs of your project. For smaller teams, a simple Kanban board might suffice, streamlining workflow without overwhelming users with complex features. In contrast, larger projects with more intricate requirements may benefit from the robust functionalities of Agile project management software like Jira, which offers detailed analytics and reporting tools to track progress comprehensively. This nuanced approach to tool selection ensures that Agile practices are not just implemented, but optimized to meet the unique demands of each project, thereby enhancing overall outcomes.

Integrating Agile with Traditional Project Management - Integrating Agile with traditional project management methods, such as Waterfall, creates a versatile, hybrid approach that harnesses the strengths of both methodologies. This integration is particularly beneficial in projects that require the upfront, detailed planning characteristic of Waterfall, alongside the flexibility and rapid iteration of Agile practices.

For instance, in the development of a new software application, a company might use Waterfall to establish clear, upfront requirements and design specifications. However, recognizing the need for adaptability in development and testing phases, the company could then implement Agile sprints, allowing for iterative testing, feedback, and modifications. This hybrid approach ensures that while the project's scope, budget, and timeline are well-defined from the outset, there's also room for refinement and adjustment as work progresses, enhancing the final product's quality and relevance.

Challenges in integrating these methodologies often revolve around reconciling the rigid structure of Waterfall with the fluid nature of Agile. Teams may struggle with shifting mindsets and adapting to a more flexible approach during the project's lifecycle. Overcoming these challenges requires clear communication, comprehensive training, and a shift towards a culture that values both planning and adaptability.

A real-world example of this successful integration can be seen in the construction and IT sectors, where projects start with detailed planning phases under Waterfall to secure budget approvals and define scope, followed by Agile's implementation in execution phases to adapt to emerging requirements and stakeholder feedback. This strategy has enabled projects to stay on track with their strategic objectives while ensuring the end product is responsive to user needs.

In conclusion, the hybrid model offers a pragmatic solution for managing complex projects, providing a structured framework for planning and execution that still allows for flexibility and iterative improvement. By carefully selecting which aspects of Agile and Waterfall to combine, organizations can optimize their project management approaches, catering to the unique demands of each project and maximizing outcomes in diverse operational environments.

Benefits of Agile Practices - The adoption of Agile practices significantly enhances project management across various dimensions. One of the foremost benefits is **enhanced flexibility**; Agile methodologies allow teams to adapt swiftly to changes, which is particularly crucial in today's fast-paced market environments. This flexibility is achieved through iterative development cycles or sprints, enabling projects to pivot as requirements evolve.

Agile also **fosters a collaborative environment** by integrating customer feedback throughout the project lifecycle. This continuous loop of feedback ensures that the final product is more closely aligned with customer needs and expectations. For instance, a software development team could utilize sprints to incorporate user feedback after each iteration, thereby enhancing the software's user-friendliness and functionality.

Moreover, **Agile methodologies improve project visibility and tracking**, facilitating more informed decision-making. Tools like digital Kanban boards and daily stand-ups provide teams with real-time insights into project progress, allowing for immediate adjustments. This visibility ensures that all team members are aware of their responsibilities, the project's current state, and areas requiring attention.

This approach leads to **higher productivity and efficiency**, as teams are focused on delivering value incrementally. Each sprint delivers a potentially shippable product increment, enabling teams to measure progress in terms of completed features. This incremental delivery model ensures continuous improvement and leverages feedback effectively, leading to a product that truly meets the end users' needs.

Ultimately, the cumulative effect of these practices is **increased customer satisfaction and project success**. An illustrative example could be a product development team that uses Agile to launch a new app. By engaging with users throughout the development process, the team can make necessary adjustments based on user feedback, leading to a highly successful app that meets users' actual needs and preferences.

In summary, Agile practices offer a robust framework for managing projects with an emphasis on flexibility, collaboration, customer engagement, and efficiency. These benefits collectively contribute to improved project outcomes, ensuring that projects not only meet but exceed customer expectations, thereby enhancing overall project success.

Challenges and Considerations - Adopting Agile practices indeed introduces challenges, including resistance to change, the necessity of continuous customer involvement, and the demand for effective self-management by teams. These hurdles can be navigated through a steadfast commitment to Agile principles, fostering open and effective communication, and nurturing a supportive organizational culture.

- **Resistance to Change**: Teams accustomed to traditional methodologies might view Agile as too radical or uncertain. To mitigate this, organizations can introduce Agile through pilot projects, demonstrating its benefits in a controlled, low-risk environment. Training sessions and workshops that emphasize Agile's advantages for both the team and the end product can also help in reducing resistance.

- **Continuous Customer Involvement**: Agile requires ongoing customer or stakeholder engagement, which can be challenging. To address this, developing clear channels of communication and setting regular intervals for feedback can ensure stakeholders are engaged but not overwhelmed. Tools like sprint reviews and demos can facilitate this process, making it part of the Agile routine.

- **Effective Self-Management**: Agile teams often struggle with self-management, especially if they are used to being closely directed. Encouraging autonomy and responsibility can be fostered through clear expectations, trust-building, and empowerment. Regular retrospectives allow teams to reflect on their performance and self-organize more effectively over time.

- **Overcoming Obstacles**: A commitment to Agile values is foundational. This includes embracing change, focusing on delivering value, and maintaining simplicity. Effective communication is equally vital, ensuring that all team members are aligned and that there is a clear understanding of goals and progress. Finally, establishing a supportive culture that encourages experimentation, learning from failures, and celebrating successes is crucial for a smooth transition to Agile.

By addressing these challenges head-on with specific strategies, organizations can not only make a successful transition to Agile but also maximize its benefits, leading to more responsive, efficient, and successful project outcomes.

Understanding Development Life Cycles in Project Management

Introduction to Development Life Cycles - Development life cycles in project management are indispensable frameworks guiding the phases of a project from initiation to completion. Understanding these cycles is crucial for grasping how a project unfolds over time, influencing the team's approach to planning, executing, and delivering work. By categorizing projects into distinct life cycles—predictive (waterfall), agile, or hybrid—project managers can customize their management practices to suit the project's unique requirements, enhancing both efficiency and adaptability.

- **Predictive (Waterfall) Life Cycle** The predictive life cycle, often referred to as Waterfall, is characterized by its sequential phase approach where each step must be completed before moving on to the next. This model is particularly effective for projects with well-defined requirements and minimal expected changes. For example, a construction project for a new bridge would benefit from a Waterfall approach due to its fixed scope, budget, and timeline requirements.
- **Agile Life Cycle** Agile methodologies prioritize flexibility and customer involvement, with iterative cycles known as sprints. This approach is ideal for projects requiring adaptability and continuous feedback, such as software development. An illustrative example is the development of a mobile application where requirements and user preferences evolve rapidly, necessitating frequent reassessments and adjustments to the project plan.
- **Hybrid Life Cycle** The hybrid model merges elements of both predictive and agile methodologies, offering a solution that benefits from the structured planning of Waterfall and the adaptability of Agile. This approach suits projects that start with a clear set of requirements but also need to accommodate changes as the work progresses. A digital marketing campaign for a new product launch exemplifies the hybrid life cycle, combining upfront strategic planning with the agility to adapt to market responses.

This detailed exploration of development life cycles underscores their significance in tailoring project management strategies to meet specific project demands, ensuring projects are delivered successfully and aligned with stakeholders' expectations.

Types of Development Life Cycles - The types of development life cycles in project management include:

- **Predictive (Waterfall) Life Cycle**: This traditional approach, where tasks are completed one after another in a linear sequence, is most suitable for projects with well-defined scopes and where changes are unlikely. For example, consider a construction project for a commercial building. The project's scope, budget, and timeline are established early, making the predictive model ideal for managing such endeavors efficiently.
- **Agile Life Cycle**: Agile's flexibility and emphasis on customer feedback make it perfect for projects with uncertain or evolving requirements, like software development. Imagine a startup developing a new app; Agile allows for rapid iterations based on user feedback, ensuring the final product truly meets user needs.
- **Iterative Life Cycle**: This approach focuses on developing a project through repeated cycles, making it beneficial for projects where the end goal is not clear from the beginning. An example could be the development of a new technology where each iteration builds on the previous one, refining the technology as understanding improves.
- **Incremental Life Cycle**: Building the project piece by piece allows for portions of the project to be delivered and become operational even as the project is still underway. This can be seen in the phased rollout of a new software platform, where each increment adds functionality and value.
- **Hybrid Life Cycle**: Combining elements of both predictive and agile, the hybrid model is adaptable to projects that require the stability of the Waterfall approach for certain phases and the flexibility of Agile for others. A digital marketing campaign for a new product might start with a comprehensive market analysis (predictive) but use Agile to adapt marketing strategies based on ongoing consumer feedback.

Aligning these life cycles with the PMBOK® Guide involves understanding the project's scope, quality, schedule, cost, resources, communication, risk, procurement, and stakeholder engagement. For instance, an Agile life cycle might focus more on stakeholder engagement and communications management, ensuring constant collaboration and feedback, while a predictive life cycle may emphasize scope and cost management, with detailed planning upfront.

Each life cycle offers unique advantages and can be aligned with PMBOK® processes to enhance project management practices, ensuring project managers can select the most suitable approach based on the project's specific needs, stakeholder requirements, and environmental factors.

Choosing the Right Life Cycle - Choosing the right development life cycle for a project is a critical decision that impacts its execution and success. It involves evaluating the project's scope, stakeholder needs, and environmental factors. Here's an expanded overview:

- **Predictive (Waterfall)** life cycles are linear and sequential, best for projects with well-defined requirements and low change expectations. For example, constructing a bridge where specifications are clear and alterations are minimal.

- **Agile** life cycles emphasize flexibility and rapid adaptation, suitable for projects with evolving requirements. A software development project, for instance, can greatly benefit from Agile methodologies due to changing customer demands and technological advancements.

- **Iterative** life cycles focus on repetitive development cycles, allowing for refinements at each iteration. This can be ideal for research and development projects where initial concepts need validation through continuous testing and refinement.

- **Incremental** life cycles involve building the project piece by piece, which can be effective for large-scale software implementations that are rolled out in phases to manage risks and incorporate feedback progressively.

- **Hybrid** models combine elements of both predictive and Agile approaches, offering flexibility and structured planning. An example might be a product development project that requires a clear initial design phase followed by flexible development and testing stages.

Aligning these life cycles with the PMBOK® Guide processes involves mapping the chosen life cycle to the project's knowledge areas and process groups. This ensures that the project management approach is comprehensive and cohesive, covering all aspects from integration to stakeholder management.

Life Cycles in the PMBOK Guide - The PMBOK Guide underscores the pivotal role of selecting an appropriate development life cycle for project success, a choice deeply intertwined with the project's inherent characteristics and stakeholder expectations. This decision shapes the project's trajectory, impacting its planning, execution, monitoring, and closure phases. The Guide delineates various life cycles—predictive, agile, and hybrid—each suited to different project environments and requirements.

Predictive (Waterfall) Life Cycles are sequential, progressing through stages with defined objectives and deliverables. Ideal for projects with clear requirements and minimal scope changes, this approach offers a structured framework that facilitates meticulous planning and control.

Practical Application: In the realm of infrastructure development, the Predictive (Waterfall) Life Cycle stands as a paragon of efficiency and predictability, particularly exemplified in the construction of the 'Riverway Bridge.' This monumental project was characterized by its well-defined objectives, scope, and stringent compliance requirements, making it an ideal candidate for the Waterfall approach.

- **Project Planning and Execution**: The 'Riverway Bridge' project was meticulously planned in sequential phases, starting with a comprehensive feasibility study that outlined the project's scope, budget, and timeline. Following this, detailed design documents were prepared, specifying every architectural and engineering requirement down to the minutest detail.
- **Stakeholder Engagement and Milestone Reviews:** Key milestones were established to review progress and ensure alignment with the original plan. Stakeholder meetings at the end of each phase facilitated clear communication and provided opportunities for feedback, albeit within a structured framework that minimized deviations from the plan.
- **Challenges and Solutions:** One of the primary challenges encountered was the rigidity in scope management. Mid-project, geological surveys revealed unforeseen subterranean obstacles, necessitating adjustments in the bridge design. The project team addressed this by meticulously documenting the required changes and obtaining stakeholder approval in a manner that adhered to the Waterfall model's sequential nature, ensuring the project remained on track.
- **Outcome:** The 'Riverway Bridge' was completed on schedule and within budget, serving as a testament to the effectiveness of the Predictive Life Cycle in managing large-scale, complex projects with well-defined requirements. This example underscores the value of thorough planning, disciplined execution, and rigorous stakeholder engagement in achieving project success.

Agile Life Cycles Agile life cycles are characterized by their flexibility and responsiveness to change, making them ideal for projects with undefined or evolving requirements. This approach emphasizes continuous feedback, iterative development, and stakeholder involvement throughout the project lifecycle.

Key Features:

- **Iterative Development**: Short cycles of work allow for rapid adjustments based on stakeholder feedback.
- **Stakeholder Collaboration**: Close, ongoing collaboration between project teams and stakeholders ensures that the project remains aligned with user needs and expectations.

- **Adaptability**: Agile methodologies are designed to accommodate changes in project scope and requirements with minimal disruption.

Practical Application: In the dynamic sector of software development, the Agile life cycle has proven itself as a beacon of adaptability and responsiveness. A prime illustration of this is 'Tech Innovate's' journey in developing 'FinTrack,' a groundbreaking personal finance application. The project was earmarked for its ambitious goal to offer real-time financial tracking and advice, leveraging the latest in AI technology. The inherent uncertainties of consumer preferences and the fast-evolving tech landscape necessitated a flexible and iterative approach.

Agile Implementation in 'FinTrack':

- **Initial Planning and Stakeholder Engagement:** 'Tech Innovate' commenced with a series of workshops to align the project's vision with stakeholder expectations, setting the stage for a collaborative Agile journey.

- **Sprint Planning and Execution:** The team adopted two-week sprints, each culminating in a sprint review with stakeholders. This allowed for the rapid integration of feedback, ensuring that each iteration of 'FinTrack' was closer to the target user's needs.

- **Continuous Improvement:** Regular retrospectives enabled the team to refine their process, enhancing efficiency and teamwork with each sprint.

Challenges and Solutions:

- **Managing Rapid Changes:** The volatile nature of user requirements posed a significant challenge. 'Tech Innovate' addressed this by embedding flexibility in their sprint planning, allowing for mid-sprint adjustments when necessary.

- **Stakeholder Engagement:** Ensuring consistent stakeholder involvement was crucial. The project utilized demo days at the end of each sprint, showcasing new features and functionalities to gather direct feedback.

- **Team Training and Mindset Shift:** To cultivate an Agile mindset, 'Tech Innovate' organized regular Agile training sessions and team-building activities, fostering a culture of open communication and continuous improvement.

The 'FinTrack' project stands as a testament to the Agile life cycle's efficacy, with the application not only meeting but exceeding market expectations upon launch. The iterative development approach, coupled with stakeholder collaboration and adaptability to change, underscored the project's success, highlighting the Agile life cycle's pivotal role in navigating the complexities of modern software development

Hybrid Life Cycles merge elements of predictive and agile approaches, offering a balanced solution that leverages the strengths of both. This life cycle is advantageous for projects requiring upfront planning and flexibility for change during execution. Product development initiatives, which commence with defined market analyses and evolve through customer feedback, illustrate the hybrid model's effectiveness.

Selecting the right life cycle involves a nuanced evaluation of the project's scope, complexity, stakeholder needs, and environmental context. This decision is not merely a procedural step but a strategic determination that influences project management practices, communication plans, risk management strategies, and ultimately, project success.

The PMBOK Guide facilitates this selection process by providing a framework for mapping life cycles to specific project characteristics and requirements. It encourages project managers to consider factors such as project size, complexity, regulatory compliance needs, and stakeholder engagement levels in their decision-making. For example, a project with high uncertainty might warrant an agile or hybrid approach to accommodate changes and facilitate stakeholder input throughout the project lifecycle.

In applying these life cycles within the PMBOK framework, it's crucial to integrate them with the knowledge areas and process groups. This integration ensures a holistic approach to project management, where decisions regarding the life cycle are informed by a comprehensive understanding of project management principles and practices. For instance, an agile life cycle might emphasize continuous stakeholder engagement and iterative planning, aligning with the PMBOK's stakeholder management and planning process groups.

Practical Application: In the innovative sphere of technology startups, navigating the development and launch of new products demands a versatile project management approach. 'TechVenture', a startup aiming to disrupt the home automation market, exemplifies the strategic application of a Hybrid Life Cycle in their flagship product's journey from concept to market.

Initial Conceptualization with a Predictive Approach: 'TechVenture' began its project with a predictive approach to solidify the product's concept and scope. This phase involved extensive market research, feasibility studies, and the development of a comprehensive project plan. The goal was to establish a clear blueprint for the product that included defined features, budget, and timelines.

Transition to Agile for Development and Feedback Integration: As the project moved into the development phase, 'TechVenture' transitioned to an Agile approach to foster flexibility and rapid iteration. This shift was driven by the need to adapt to real-time market feedback and emerging technological trends. The development team adopted Scrum, working in sprints to develop, test, and refine the product iteratively. Stakeholder and customer feedback were integral at this stage, guiding each iteration's direction.

Hybrid Integration for Market Launch: Approaching the market launch, 'TechVenture' integrated elements of both predictive and Agile approaches. The predictive component ensured that strategic marketing and distribution channels were well-planned and executed, while the Agile aspect allowed the team to continue refining the product based on beta testing feedback and early adopter responses.

Challenges and Solutions: The hybrid approach presented unique challenges, particularly in aligning team capabilities with the shifting project management styles and managing stakeholder expectations through the transition. 'TechVenture' addressed these challenges by:

- Conducting cross-functional training sessions to ensure all team members were adept in both predictive and Agile methodologies.

- Implementing a transparent communication strategy that kept stakeholders informed about the rationale behind the methodological shift and the benefits it brought to the product's success.

Outcome: The result was a highly adaptable project execution strategy that allowed 'TechVenture' to launch a product that was not only technically sound but also highly attuned to market needs and customer preferences. The hybrid life cycle facilitated a balance between structured planning and adaptability, enabling 'TechVenture' to navigate the complexities of product development and launch with agility and strategic foresight.

In conclusion, the choice of development life cycle is a cornerstone of project management that significantly influences a project's direction and outcomes. The PMBOK Guide offers valuable insights and frameworks for making this choice, emphasizing the need for alignment with project requirements and environmental factors. By carefully selecting and applying the appropriate life cycle, project managers can enhance their project's success potential, navigating the complexities of modern project environments with agility and strategic foresight.

Best Practices for Implementing Life Cycles - Implementing the right project life cycle is crucial for efficient project management, ensuring alignment with objectives and stakeholder expectations. This process involves:

- **In-depth Understanding**: Start with a clear grasp of the project's goals and stakeholder expectations to select a suitable life cycle.

- **Team Engagement**: Engaging the project team in the life cycle selection leverages diverse insights and secures team commitment.

- **Clear Documentation and Communication**: Documenting and communicating the chosen life cycle ensures clarity and alignment across the team and stakeholders.

- **Provision of Training**: Offer training to team members unfamiliar with the life cycle to ensure effective implementation.

- **Regular Review and Adaptation**: Continuously evaluate the life cycle's effectiveness and remain open to adjustments based on project evolution.

Practical Examples:

- In software development, agile life cycles accommodate rapid requirement changes through iterative development and stakeholder feedback, leading to continuous alignment and improvement.

- Construction projects benefit from predictive life cycles with clear phases and milestones, enhancing efficiency through regular stakeholder meetings and team training.

Overcoming Challenges includes addressing resistance to change, bridging knowledge gaps, and staying adaptable to project evolution through regular reviews and stakeholder engagement.

By strategically selecting and implementing the appropriate life cycle, and being prepared to tackle common challenges, project managers can significantly improve project success rates, delivering value and maintaining alignment with the dynamic project environment.

Navigating Life Cycle Transitions in Evolving Projects - Understanding when and how to transition between life cycles is crucial for managing projects that undergo significant evolution. This strategic flexibility can be the key to project success, particularly in environments where initial conditions or stakeholder needs change.

For instance, in the early stages of a new software development project, a predictive approach may be employed to establish a clear framework and scope. However, as the project progresses and user feedback is integrated, a shift towards an agile or hybrid approach may become necessary to accommodate evolving requirements and ensure the product remains aligned with market needs.

Considerations for Transition:

- **Assessment of Current Project Status**: Regularly review project progress against its objectives and stakeholder feedback to determine if the current life cycle still fits the project's needs.

- **Stakeholder Communication**: Engage with stakeholders to discuss potential benefits and implications of transitioning to a different life cycle, ensuring their support and alignment.

- **Preparation and Training**: Prepare the project team for the transition by providing training and resources needed to adapt to a new project management approach effectively.

Example of Transitioning Between Life Cycles: A tech startup initially employs a predictive life cycle for developing a new digital platform, focusing on detailed upfront planning. As the project progresses, market analysis reveals a shift in consumer behavior, prompting the need for more flexible and iterative development processes. The project manager decides to transition to an agile life cycle, allowing for rapid iterations and adjustments based on ongoing user feedback, ultimately leading to a more successful product launch.

This strategic maneuvering between life cycles, guided by a thorough understanding of project management principles and the specific demands of the project, exemplifies the dynamic nature of modern project management. By carefully selecting and applying the appropriate life cycle, and being prepared to navigate transitions, project managers can significantly enhance their project's success potential.

Deep Dive into Each Knowledge Area

Detailed Chapters on Each of the 10 Knowledge Areas

Integration Management - Integration Management stands as a pivotal knowledge area within project management, encapsulating essential processes and activities necessary to identify, define, unify, and coordinate the various processes and activities across all the Project Management Process Groups. It involves crucial decision-making regarding resource allocation, harmonization of competing demands, and assimilation of solutions to achieve the project objectives. Mastery of Integration Management ensures that the project components are coordinated effectively, leading to a cohesive, unified, and consistent project perspective.

- **Project Charter Development:** The Project Charter is the cornerstone of any project, marking the official start. It provides the project manager with the authority to allocate organizational resources to project activities. The development of the Project Charter involves defining the project's purpose, objectives, and constraints. It also identifies the main stakeholders and establishes the authority level of the project manager. Understanding how to create and utilize the Project Charter is crucial, as it sets the stage for all subsequent project activities and decisions.

- **Project Management Plan Creation:** This is the process of developing a comprehensive blueprint for managing and executing the project. The Project Management Plan is dynamic and integrates all subsidiary plans and baselines, detailing how the project will be executed, monitored, and controlled. It covers aspects such as scope, schedule, cost, quality, resource, communication, risk, procurement, and stakeholder engagement plans. Mastery of this area involves understanding how to compile and harmonize various components into a coherent document that guides project execution and control.

- **Directing and Managing Project Work:** This entails carrying out the project plan by performing the activities included within it. Directing and Managing Project Work involves leading the team, implementing approved changes, and ensuring that project deliverables are completed as planned. This process requires a hands-on approach to guide the team, manage stakeholders, and ensure that the project remains aligned with its objectives and business environment.

- **Monitoring and Controlling Project Work:** Monitoring and controlling project work is critical for identifying performance variances from the project management plan. This process involves measuring project activities, managing changes, and ensuring that project objectives are met with the approved plan. It includes collecting, measuring, and disseminating performance information, and assessing measurements and trends to effect process improvements.

- **Performing Integrated Change Control:** Integrated Change Control is a vital process where all requests for changes are reviewed, approved, or denied. It's pivotal in ensuring that changes are systematically processed and only approved changes are incorporated into the project baseline. This area demands an understanding of how to manage and control changes to the project scope, schedule, costs, and quality, ensuring all changes are aligned with overall project objectives.

- **Closing the Project or Phase:** The closing process formalizes the completion of project deliverables to the customer's satisfaction and formally concludes the project or a project phase. Understanding how to effectively close a project or phase includes finalizing all activities, transferring the completed work, obtaining formal acceptance, and ensuring that project documents are archived and lessons learned are documented.

Real-World Application Scenario: Consider a large-scale infrastructure project aimed at enhancing urban mobility. Integration Management in this context would involve coordinating between different segments of the project such as design, construction, and stakeholder engagement. This requires developing a robust project charter, outlining clear objectives, and integrating diverse functional areas and processes to ensure that all aspects of the project align with the overarching goals.

Challenges and Solutions: A major challenge in Integration Management is maintaining a cohesive approach among cross-functional teams. This challenge can be addressed through regular, integrated planning sessions, ensuring that all team members understand the project objectives and are aligned with the project status. Additionally, effective change control processes are vital in adapting to scope changes while ensuring the project remains on track.

Practical Example: In our urban mobility project, Integration Management facilitated the synchronization of various project elements, such as aligning the construction timelines with regulatory approvals and community outreach programs. Regular, integrated planning sessions ensured that changes in one segment, like a delay in obtaining permits, were addressed within the broader project framework, thereby maintaining alignment with overall objectives.

Conlcusion: Effective Integration Management requires strategic oversight, meticulous planning, and flexible coordination. By treating the project as a holistic entity and maintaining open communication channels, project managers can steer complex, multifaceted projects towards successful completion. This integrated approach not only adheres to PMBOK® guidelines but also ensures that project deliverables meet or exceed stakeholder expectations, thereby delivering genuine value.

Scope Management - Scope Management is indispensable for defining and achieving project objectives, ensuring that all necessary work is included while excluding tasks that are not essential. Proper scope management lays the groundwork for project success, ensuring that resources are allocated efficiently and objectives are met effectively.

Requirement Collection: Effective Scope Management starts with the meticulous collection of project requirements. This stage is critical because it sets the foundation for all subsequent project planning and execution. Techniques used in this phase include:

- **Interviews**: Conduct one-on-one discussions with stakeholders to understand their needs and expectations.

- **Surveys and Questionnaires**: Distribute these to a larger audience to gather a broad range of requirements and preferences.

- **Focus Groups**: Bring together stakeholders and subject matter experts to discuss and refine project requirements.

- **Observations and Market Research**: Understand user behavior and market trends which can influence project requirements.

Collaborative sessions with stakeholders are crucial to ensure every aspect of the project is covered. These meetings help in aligning project goals with stakeholder expectations, ensuring a unified understanding and agreement on project objectives.

Scope Definition and Documentation: Once requirements are collected, defining and documenting the project scope becomes essential. The project scope statement is a vital document that should detail:

- **Project Objectives**: Clear, measurable outcomes that the project is expected to achieve.

- **Deliverables**: Tangible or intangible products or services produced as a result of project activities.

- **Boundaries**: Defines what is included and excluded from the project.

- **Acceptance Criteria**: Conditions under which project deliverables will be accepted.

Creating a detailed project scope statement helps in preventing misunderstandings and provides a baseline for future project decisions. This clarity ensures that all project participants, from team members to stakeholders, understand the project's limits and expectations.

Work Breakdown Structure (WBS): The WBS is a fundamental tool in Scope Management. It breaks down the total scope of work into smaller, more manageable components, typically displayed in a hierarchical format. The creation of an effective WBS involves:

- **Understanding Project Scope**: Clearly define and understand the project's scope before beginning the WBS.

- **Dividing Tasks**: Break down the project deliverables into smaller tasks until they are manageable and assignable.

- **Assigning Responsibility**: Clarify each team member's responsibilities by associating them with specific elements of the WBS.

The WBS aids in resource allocation, scheduling, and the identification of potential risks. It ensures each team member knows their specific responsibilities, contributing to overall project efficiency and clarity.

Scope Verification: Verifying the scope involves ensuring that all stakeholders agree on the project's defined scope. This process typically includes formal reviews and approval processes. Techniques for scope verification include:

- **Review Meetings**: Conduct meetings with stakeholders to go through the scope document and confirm that it meets all requirements and expectations.

- **Inspection**: Formal inspection of deliverables to ensure they meet the acceptance criteria outlined in the scope statement.

Managing scope changes through a formal change control process is vital to maintaining project direction and preventing scope creep. This process ensures that any changes to the project scope are thoroughly evaluated for their impact on the project's time, cost, and quality before being approved.

Practical Example: In a city's public transportation upgrade project, effective Scope Management was crucial. The project initially focused on enhancing bus services but was expanded to include subway improvements following stakeholder feedback. Utilizing a detailed WBS allowed the project team to manage these expanding requirements systematically, ensuring each new element was integrated seamlessly without disrupting the original project scope.

Challenges and Solutions: Projects often face challenges such as scope creep and misaligned stakeholder expectations. Implementing a strict change control process is essential for managing these issues. This involves formal approval for all changes and regular scope review meetings to ensure ongoing alignment with project objectives. Adjusting the WBS as needed helps in accommodating scope changes while keeping the project on track.

Integrating Scope Management with Other Knowledge Areas: Effective project management requires integrating Scope Management with other areas, such as Time Management and Cost Management. For example, any changes in the project scope can significantly impact the project's schedule and budget. Coordinating adjustments across these areas is crucial for maintaining overall project viability and success.

In summary, a detailed approach to Scope Management, focusing on comprehensive requirement collection, precise scope definition, structured WBS creation, and rigorous scope verification, equips project managers with the necessary tools to navigate complex projects. This approach aligns with PMBOK® principles and enhances the probability of project success, meeting or exceeding stakeholder expectations.

Schedule Management - Schedule Management is a vital component in project management, focusing on the effective planning, structuring, and controlling of project timelines to ensure project objectives are met within the designated timeframe. This expanded section delves deeper into the facets of Schedule Management, crucial for PMP exam preparation and practical project management application.

Activity Identification: The foundation of effective Schedule Management lies in identifying all tasks required to complete the project. This involves a detailed analysis of the project's objectives, breaking them down into actionable activities. Techniques such as brainstorming with the project team, stakeholder interviews, and the Decomposition method are instrumental. The goal is to create a comprehensive list of activities without overlooking essential tasks. Be wary of ambiguities; clearly defined activities form the backbone of a reliable project schedule.

Activity Sequencing: Once activities are identified, the next step is sequencing them in logical order based on dependencies. The Precedence Diagramming Method (PDM) and Critical Path Method (CPM) are key methodologies here. PDM helps in visualizing dependencies through a flowchart, facilitating better understanding and communication among team members. CPM, on the other hand, identifies the longest sequence of dependent activities (critical path) and calculates the minimum project duration. Understanding these concepts is crucial as they directly impact the project's timeline and flexibility.

Estimating Activity Durations: A key part of Schedule Management is accurately estimating how long each project activity will take. Several estimation techniques can be used:

1. **PERT (Program Evaluation and Review Technique)**: PERT is a statistical tool used to estimate the duration of activities in a project. The formula for calculating the estimated duration (TE) is:

$$TE=(O+4M+P)/6$$

where:

- O = Optimistic duration

- M = Most likely duration

- P = Pessimistic duration

This weighted average accounts for uncertainty in activity duration estimates.

2. **Three-point Estimation**: Similar to PERT, this technique uses different estimates to calculate an average duration. It helps in accommodating uncertainty and variability in activity durations.

By applying these techniques, project managers can create more accurate and realistic project schedules.

Critical Path Method (CPM) and Float Calculation: Understanding and applying the Critical Path Method (CPM) is crucial for developing an efficient project schedule. The critical path determines the shortest time possible to complete the project and identifies which activities are critical (i.e., any delay in these activities will delay the project).

Calculating the Critical Path:

1. List all activities required to complete the project.

2. Determine the sequencing of these activities.

3. Estimate the duration of each activity.

4. Identify the longest path through the project, which is your critical path.

Additionally, calculating the float or slack for each activity helps in identifying the leeway available without affecting the project schedule.

Total Float Calculation:

The total float for an activity can be calculated as:

- **Total Float (TF) = Late Start (LS) - Early Start (ES) or Late Finish (LF) - Early Finish (EF)**

Understanding CPM and float is essential for managing project timelines effectively, allowing project managers to prioritize tasks and allocate resources where they are most needed.

Schedule Development: With activities sequenced and durations estimated, develop the project schedule. This step consolidates all your planning into a visual timeline, typically represented through Gantt charts. These charts display activities, their start and end dates, and overlap, offering a clear overview of the project lifecycle. Ensure this schedule is detailed yet flexible, accounting for all known factors while providing buffer zones for unforeseen events.

Schedule Control: Monitoring the project's adherence to the set schedule is continuous and involves making necessary adjustments to keep the project on track. Effective schedule control requires a defined process for managing and approving changes. Regularly compare actual progress with planned progress, identify variances, and implement corrective actions promptly. Communication is key; all schedule changes should be transparent and communicated to all stakeholders to maintain trust and alignment.

Integration with Other Knowledge Areas: Schedule Management does not operate in isolation. It is intricately connected with other areas such as Cost and Risk Management. For example, any changes to the schedule may impact the project budget and introduce new risks. Understanding these interdependencies is essential for holistic project management and for navigating the complexities of real-world projects.

Practical Example: Consider a community center construction project. The project manager employed the WBS for task breakdown and utilized the CPM for establishing critical paths. This meticulous planning allowed for resource adjustments ensuring the project remained on schedule despite unforeseen challenges like weather delays. This example highlights the practical application of Schedule Management techniques and the importance of adaptability and proactive planning.

Practical Tips:

- Regularly review and update the project schedule to reflect real-time progress and adjustments.

- Clearly communicate any changes in the schedule to all project stakeholders to ensure transparency and alignment.

- Use project management software tools for more efficient schedule creation, monitoring, and control.

Conclusion: A well-managed schedule is a hallmark of successful project management. By understanding and applying the principles and techniques outlined in this section, project managers can ensure that projects are delivered on time, within scope, and to the satisfaction of all stakeholders. This comprehensive approach not only prepares candidates for the PMP exam but also equips them with the knowledge and skills necessary for effective real-world project management.

Remember, the key to successful Schedule Management is not just in meticulous planning but also in flexible execution and clear communication. These elements, combined with a deep understanding of project dynamics and stakeholder needs, are what make a project manager truly effective.

Cost Management - Cost Management is a vital component of project management, focusing not just on maintaining expenses within the budget but also on implementing a comprehensive financial strategy that aligns with the project's objectives and delivers value. This multifaceted approach encompasses everything from initial planning to the final review of expenditures, ensuring projects are completed within the allocated budget while still achieving their goals.

Planning for Financial Success

The foundation of effective Cost Management is the development of a detailed Cost Management Plan. This plan outlines procedures for managing project costs, from estimation and budgeting to controlling expenses. It should address:

- How costs will be estimated, budgeted, and controlled
- Roles and responsibilities in managing costs

- Reporting formats and frequency

- Thresholds for action, particularly with cost variances

Mastering Cost Management Formulas

Understanding and applying key formulas is essential in managing and controlling project costs efficiently. Below are the crucial formulas every PMP candidate must know:

1. **Earned Value (EV)**: This represents the value of work performed expressed in terms of the budget authorized for that work. It's calculated based on the percentage of completed work.
2. **Planned Value (PV)**: This is the total cost of work planned to be completed by a set date. It's the budget for the work scheduled as of the reporting date.
3. **Actual Cost (AC)**: This is the total cost incurred for the work completed to date. It reflects the actual cost of work done as of the reporting date.
4. **Schedule Variance (SV) = EV - PV**: This formula calculates the difference between the amount of work actually completed and the amount of work planned to be completed. A positive number indicates a project ahead of schedule, while a negative number indicates a delay.
5. **Cost Variance (CV) = EV - AC**: This measures the cost performance of the project. A positive CV indicates that the project is under budget, while a negative CV indicates it is over budget.
6. **Schedule Performance Index (SPI) = EV / PV**: This index measures the efficiency of time utilized on the project. An SPI greater than 1 indicates the project is ahead of schedule, while an SPI less than 1 indicates the project is behind schedule.
7. **Cost Performance Index (CPI) = EV / AC**: This index measures the cost efficiency of the project. A CPI greater than 1 indicates the project is under budget, while a CPI less than 1 indicates the project is over budget.
8. **Estimate at Completion (EAC)**: There are different ways to calculate EAC depending on the conditions of the project. One common formula is EAC = BAC / CPI, used when current variances are seen as typical for the future.
9. **Estimate to Complete (ETC) = EAC - AC**: This calculates how much more is expected to complete the project.
10. **Variance at Completion (VAC) = BAC - EAC**: This estimates the expected budget surplus or deficit.

Understanding these formulas and how to apply them will significantly enhance your ability to manage project costs effectively.

Mastering the Art of Estimation

Accurate cost estimation prevents budget overruns and sets the stage for successful project completion. Key techniques include:

- **Bottom-up Estimating**: Breaking down project components into smaller sections for more detailed estimation.

- **Analogous Estimating**: Using historical data from similar projects as a basis for estimates.

- **Parametric Estimating**: Utilizing statistical relationships between historical data and other variables to estimate costs.

- **Three-Point Estimating**: Considering the most optimistic, pessimistic, and most likely costs to provide a more comprehensive view.

Budgeting with Precision

With estimates in hand, the next step is establishing a budget that reflects the project's financial constraints and objectives. This involves creating a Cost Baseline against which financial performance can be measured. Key components include:

- Direct and indirect costs

- Fixed and variable costs

- Contingency reserves to address project risks

Navigating the Financial Waters – Cost Control

Effective cost control is essential for keeping a project financial track. Earned Value Management (EVM) is a critical tool in this effort, enabling project managers to measure project performance and progress in monetary terms. Key EVM metrics include:

- **Cost Performance Index (CPI)**: Measures cost efficiency on the project.

- **Schedule Performance Index (SPI)**: Measures how well the project is performing against the schedule.

Practical Application

Consider a large-scale construction project for a new community center. The project manager establishes a thorough Cost Management Plan, employs various estimating techniques to forecast expenses accurately, and sets a detailed budget. As the project unfolds, EVM is used to track and control costs, with regular updates to stakeholders on financial performance.

Overcoming Common Financial Obstacles

Projects often encounter financial challenges such as unexpected cost increases or scope creep. Strategies to mitigate these risks include:

- Establishing a contingency reserve for unforeseen costs.

- Employing a formal change control process to assess and approve changes to the project scope and costs.

- Conducting regular cost performance reviews to detect variances early and adjust strategies accordingly.

Integration with Other Knowledge Areas

Effective Cost Management is closely linked with other areas of project management. Changes in project scope or schedule can significantly impact the project's costs. Therefore, a collaborative approach, integrating Scope, Schedule, and Cost Management, is crucial for maintaining project alignment and ensuring financial success.

Practical Tips

To ensure effective Cost Management:

- Regularly update and review the project budget against actual expenses.

- Communicate any financial changes or concerns with stakeholders promptly.

- Utilize project management software to track costs and forecast financial trends.

By adhering to these principles and practices, project managers can navigate the complexities of Cost Management, ensuring projects are completed within budget while still achieving desired outcomes.

Quality Management - Quality Management in project management transcends mere compliance with specifications; it signifies a deep commitment to excellence and ensuring stakeholder satisfaction. This crucial discipline is interwoven throughout the project lifecycle, assuring that deliverables not only meet but often surpass the required standards, leading to enhanced stakeholder contentment and project success.

- **Defining Quality Policies and Objectives:** The journey towards quality starts with the establishment of clear, concise quality policies that mirror the project's vision and the expectations of stakeholders. Objectives defined under this umbrella should be SMART: Specific, Measurable, Achievable, Relevant, and Time-bound. These set a clear benchmark for project success and ensure that everyone involved has a clear understanding of what constitutes 'quality' on the project. Engage stakeholders in defining these quality metrics to ensure alignment with overall project goals.

- **Planning for Quality:** Quality planning involves identifying relevant quality standards and determining how they will be achieved. It is not an isolated activity but an integral part of the overall project plan. This could involve conducting a Failure Mode and Effects Analysis (FMEA) to anticipate potential quality issues before they occur, or adopting methodologies such as Six Sigma to reduce variability and improve quality. The Quality Management Plan developed during this phase should detail the quality control, quality assurance, and continuous improvement processes, making sure they are integrated seamlessly with other project processes.

- **Performing Quality Assurance:** Quality assurance is about ensuring that the project's processes are adequate to achieve the project's quality objectives. This involves systematic activities like regular audits and methodical reviews to affirm that the project is following established quality processes and standards. Quality assurance serves as a proactive measure, designed to instill confidence in the project's direction and adherence to quality standards.

- **Controlling Quality:** Quality control entails the operational techniques and activities undertaken to fulfill quality requirements. This practical aspect involves inspecting deliverables to identify any defects and taking corrective action as necessary. Employing tools such as Control Charts and Pareto Diagrams can be instrumental in this phase, allowing project teams to monitor defect occurrences and identify their root causes effectively.

- **Integration with Other Knowledge Areas:** Quality Management does not exist in a vacuum; it must be integrated with other knowledge areas such as Scope, Schedule, and Cost Management. This interconnection ensures that quality considerations are made not just in the context of the deliverable itself but in how the project is managed as a whole. For instance, any changes in project scope should trigger a review of the quality plans to ensure that new requirements are met without compromising established quality standards.

Practical Application: Consider a software development project employing Agile methodologies, where quality is integrated into every sprint. The team uses automated testing and peer reviews to ensure high-quality outcomes, addressing issues promptly. This adaptive approach, combined with regular stakeholder engagement, helps the project meet all quality benchmarks within time and budget constraints.

Overcoming Quality Challenges: Projects often face hurdles like limited resources or unclear quality expectations. Addressing these challenges can involve allocating a dedicated quality budget, conducting stakeholder workshops to clarify quality expectations, and maintaining flexibility to adjust quality plans as the project evolves.

In conclusion, effective Quality Management is paramount in delivering projects that exceed stakeholder expectations. By weaving rigorous quality processes with comprehensive planning and continuous improvement, project managers can assure that every project component upholds the highest standards, thereby ensuring project success and boosting customer satisfaction.

Resource Management - Resource Management is a pivotal aspect of project management, focusing on the strategic deployment of organizational resources to achieve project objectives efficiently and effectively. This encompasses not just the allocation but also the identification and management of both human and material resources, critical for the successful execution of any project. By understanding and optimizing the use of these resources, project managers can significantly enhance project performance and outcome.

Strategic Resource Planning

Effective resource management begins with a comprehensive assessment, identifying all necessary resources for the project. This entails distinguishing between human resources (such as team members and contractors) and physical resources (like materials and equipment). The Resource Management Plan, developed from this assessment, serves as a blueprint, outlining the methodologies for acquiring, utilizing, and eventually releasing resources. This plan should align seamlessly with the project's timelines and goals, ensuring that every resource contributes optimally towards the project's success.

- **Human Resources**: Identify the number, skills, and roles required. Consider factors like project phase, complexity, and geographical location.

- **Physical Resources**: Assess the necessary materials, equipment, and technology. Determine quantities, timeframes, and storage requirements.

In-depth Resource Estimation

Resource estimation requires meticulous methods to evaluate the type and quantity of resources needed. Utilizing techniques such as bottom-up estimating ensures a granular and accurate assessment. This step involves breaking down project activities into smaller tasks and analyzing the resources necessary for each, considering availability, skill levels, and potential project constraints.

- **Resource Breakdown**: List resources required for each task, considering quality and regulatory requirements.

- **Availability and Constraints**: Assess resource availability, including potential scheduling conflicts and market availability for materials.

Effective Team Acquisition and Development

Building the right team is crucial. This involves matching individual skills and competencies with project requirements, fostering a collaborative environment, and focusing on professional development. Acknowledge and address the diverse needs and motivations of team members, implementing recognition and rewards systems to boost morale and productivity.

- **Team Composition**: Align team member skills with project tasks and milestones. Consider cultural and interpersonal dynamics.

- **Development and Training**: Identify skill gaps and provide necessary training. Promote continuous learning and knowledge sharing.

Meticulous Management of Physical Resources

Managing physical resources involves more than just procurement; it requires strategic planning to ensure timely availability and optimal use. Coordinate with suppliers, manage inventory effectively, and apply techniques like Just-In-Time (JIT) to reduce costs and eliminate waste.

- **Procurement Strategy**: Develop relationships with suppliers and establish clear contracts. Consider lead times and quality requirements.

- **Inventory Management**: Implement tracking systems, schedule regular audits, and adapt to project changes promptly.

Dynamic Resource Control

Continuously monitor resource utilization against the project plan, making adjustments as necessary. Implement resource leveling and smoothing techniques to address imbalances, ensuring that resources are available when needed without overburdening the team or budget.

- **Monitoring and Adjustments**: Use software tools and regular check-ins to track resource allocation and performance.

- **Response Strategies**: Develop contingency plans for resource shortages or conflicts, ensuring alternative solutions are readily available.

In conclusion, effective Resource Management is vital for the success of any project. By strategically planning, accurately estimating, efficiently acquiring, and dynamically controlling both human and physical resources, project managers can ensure that their projects are well-equipped to meet their objectives and deliver significant value.

Communications Management - Communications Management is an essential facet of project management that focuses on the timely and appropriate generation, collection, distribution, storage, retrieval, and ultimate disposition of project information. This process ensures all stakeholders are kept informed and that the project's objectives are aligned with the organization's goals.

Strategic Communications Planning: Effective Communications Management begins with creating a comprehensive Communications Management Plan. This plan should:

1. Align communication goals with the project's objectives.

2. Identify all stakeholders' information needs.

3. Determine the methods and technologies for information dissemination.

The plan should be well-structured to guarantee that all team members and stakeholders receive pertinent information when they need it, thus ensuring informed decision-making and stakeholder satisfaction.

Executing the Communications Plan: This involves more than dispatching updates; it demands active engagement strategies like:

- Establishing feedback loops for continuous improvement.

- Holding regular status meetings to ensure all stakeholders are aligned.

- Tailoring communications to fit the project environment and stakeholder preferences.

Utilizing a mix of communication tools, from traditional face-to-face meetings to modern digital platforms, can significantly enhance the effectiveness of information exchange.

Monitoring and Controlling Communications: The key focus here is to ensure that the communication strategy remains effective throughout the project lifecycle. This involves:

- Monitoring the effectiveness of communication efforts and making necessary adjustments.

- Addressing any information gaps or misunderstandings in a timely manner.

Regular assessments and adaptations of the communication approach can help in maintaining stakeholder engagement and project alignment.

Practical Application and Challenges: Consider the example of a multinational project with diverse teams across different geographical locations. The project manager could face significant communication challenges due to cultural and time zone differences. To address these challenges, a robust Communications Management Plan that incorporates regular virtual meetings, culturally sensitive communication practices, and collaborative tools can be crucial in fostering a culture of open and effective communication.

Overcoming Communication Barriers: Projects can face communication hurdles such as cultural differences, language barriers, and technological constraints. Strategies to surmount these obstacles include:

- Gaining an understanding of cultural nuances to foster better relations and communication.

- Using clear, concise, and simple language to avoid misunderstandings.

- Ensuring all team members have access to and are proficient with the chosen communication technology.

Regular training and team-building activities can also help bridge communication gaps and promote a more cohesive team environment.

Integration with Other Knowledge Areas: Effective Communications Management is interconnected with all other project management knowledge areas. It ensures that updates and changes regarding project scope, schedule, and costs are effectively communicated, which supports informed decision-making and maintains project alignment.

In conclusion, mastering Communications Management is crucial for any project manager aspiring to lead successful initiatives. By ensuring clear, effective, and timely communication, misunderstandings can be minimized, stakeholder engagement maximized, and project success enhanced. This comprehensive approach, when integrated with other knowledge areas, forms the foundation of effective project management, facilitating the achievement of project objectives and boosting overall productivity and satisfaction.

Risk Management - Risk Management is an essential discipline in project management, focusing on identifying, analyzing, and responding effectively to project risks. This discipline ensures that projects are less susceptible to unforeseen challenges, enabling smooth execution and adaptability.

Identifying Risks: The initial step in Risk Management involves systematically identifying potential project risks. This process includes:

1. Conducting brainstorming sessions with the project team and stakeholders to gather diverse perspectives on potential risks.

2. Consulting with experts or conducting expert interviews to leverage specialized knowledge in identifying unique project risks.

3. Utilizing SWOT analysis to understand strengths, weaknesses, opportunities, and threats associated with the project.

4. Developing a comprehensive Risk Register that lists all identified risks, along with their characteristics and potential impact on the project.

Analyzing Risks: Once risks are identified, the next step is to analyze them to prioritize their attention:

1. Use qualitative analysis methods to prioritize risks based on their likelihood of occurrence and impact. Employ tools such as risk matrices to facilitate this analysis.

2. For significant risks, undertake quantitative analyses, such as Monte Carlo simulations, to understand the potential impacts on project objectives more thoroughly.

Planning Risk Responses: Develop appropriate strategies for each identified risk, which can include:

1. Avoidance: Changing project plans to eliminate the threat.

2. Mitigation: Taking steps to reduce the likelihood or impact of the risk.

3. Transfer: Shifting the impact of the risk to a third party.

4. Acceptance: Acknowledging the risk without taking steps to alter its course.

Each strategy should include specific action plans outlined in the project management plan.

Monitoring and Controlling Risks: Risk Management is an ongoing process:

1. Continuously monitor the risk environment for changes and new risks.

2. Update risk assessments and response strategies as the project progresses.

3. Implement risk audits and regular reviews to ensure the effectiveness of the risk management process.

Practical Application: Consider an infrastructure project threatened by seasonal flooding. Through early risk identification and analysis, the team could develop contingency plans, allowing them to manage the risk effectively, avoid delays, and ensure project continuity.

Overcoming Common Risk Challenges: Projects may encounter challenges such as scope changes or external uncertainties. Effective strategies to address these challenges include:

1. Establishing a risk-aware culture within the team.
2. Conducting regular risk reassessment.
3. Maintaining open communication channels for risk reporting and discussion.

Integration with Other Knowledge Areas: Risk Management is interconnected with all other project management areas:

1. Ensure that risk management strategies are aligned with the project's scope, schedule, and cost management plans.
2. Recognize that changes in these areas may introduce new risks or alter existing ones.

Conclusion: A robust Risk Management process enables project managers to minimize negative impacts and steer projects toward successful outcomes, even in the face of uncertainty. By identifying, analyzing, responding to, and monitoring risks, project managers can ensure that projects remain aligned with their objectives and are prepared to handle unforeseen events.

Procurement Management: Procurement Management is a critical facet of project management that involves the strategic acquisition of products, services, or results necessary to complete the project but which are outside the project team. Effective procurement management ensures that projects are equipped with the required external resources, maintaining both budget and schedule integrity while fostering productive relationships with vendors and suppliers.

Strategic Procurement Planning: The journey begins with strategic planning, which lays the foundation for successful procurement. A detailed Procurement Management Plan is essential, delineating the procedures for procurement execution and control. This plan addresses several critical areas:

- **What to Procure:** Define the specific products, services, or results needed.
- **When and How to Procure:** Outline the timeline and methods for procurement.
- **Vendor Selection Criteria:** Establish the criteria for evaluating and selecting vendors.
- **Contract Types:** Decide on the types of contracts that best suit the project's needs, considering factors like risk, cost, and timeline.

Executing Procurements: The execution phase involves several key activities:

- **Vendor Solicitation:** Conduct an open and transparent process to solicit bids, proposals, or quotes, ensuring all potential suppliers have a fair chance to participate.

- **Proposal Evaluation:** Assess proposals against predefined criteria, ensuring the selection process is fair and transparent.
- **Contract Awarding:** Finalize negotiations and award contracts to the chosen vendors, ensuring agreements align with project objectives and comply with legal requirements.

Vendor Relations and Contractual Oversight: Maintaining a strong relationship with vendors and conducting thorough contractual oversight are pivotal for smooth project progression:

- **Vendor Management:** Develop and maintain a positive relationship with all vendors, ensuring clear communication and mutual understanding.
- **Contract Management:** Monitor contract performance, manage changes, and address issues promptly to mitigate procurement risks and ensure contractual compliance.

Monitoring and Closing Procurements: Continuous monitoring and proper closing are crucial:

- **Performance Monitoring:** Regularly assess contract performance against the project's objectives and requirements.
- **Procurement Closure:** Conclude procurements once all contractual obligations are satisfied, ensuring all deliverables are accepted and all administrative tasks are completed.

Overcoming Procurement Challenges: Effective strategies to tackle common procurement challenges include:

- **Robust Risk Management:** Develop strategies to manage risks associated with procurement activities.
- **Clear Communication:** Establish clear communication channels between the project team, vendors, and stakeholders.
- **Flexible Approaches:** Adopt flexible, solution-oriented approaches to manage and adapt to procurement challenges.

Integration with Other Knowledge Areas: Procurement Management is interconnected with other project management areas, particularly Cost, Risk, and Schedule Management. This integration ensures that procurement activities support the overall project objectives and contribute to its success.

In conclusion, effective Procurement Management requires comprehensive planning, execution, and oversight. By adopting strategic practices, project managers can ensure that external procurements align with project needs, thereby safeguarding project timelines, budgets, and quality standards and ultimately enhancing project outcomes. This integrative approach, coupled with proactive vendor and contract management, paves the way for successful project completion.

Stakeholder Management - Stakeholder Management is vital in ensuring that all parties affected by the project are identified, understood, engaged, and satisfied throughout the project lifecycle. This process ensures the alignment of project objectives with stakeholder expectations and fosters a foundation of trust and support essential for project success.

Comprehensive Stakeholder Identification: Begin with a systematic approach to identify all potential stakeholders. Employ tools such as stakeholder analysis matrices and power-interest grids.

This crucial step ensures a complete overview of all individuals, groups, or organizations that may impact or be impacted by the project outcomes.

In-depth Stakeholder Analysis: Conduct detailed analyses to understand each stakeholder's interests, level of influence, and potential project impact. Use this analysis to categorize stakeholders by their interest and power levels and develop engagement strategies tailored to address their unique needs and concerns.

Strategic Engagement Planning: Formulate a Stakeholder Engagement Plan, detailing communication methods, frequency, and content tailored to various stakeholder groups. This plan should align with overall project objectives and ensure consistent, effective engagement.

Effective Stakeholder Engagement Execution: Implement your engagement strategies with a focus on maintaining open, two-way communication. Encourage feedback and collaboration, addressing concerns and adapting your approach as needed to suit project evolution and stakeholder dynamics.

Ongoing Monitoring and Relationship Management: Regularly evaluate the effectiveness of your stakeholder engagement efforts. Adjust strategies as needed to enhance cooperation and maintain project support. Utilize feedback mechanisms to monitor satisfaction and identify areas for improvement.

Real-World Application: Consider a regional airport expansion affecting diverse stakeholders. Early stakeholder analysis led to targeted community meetings addressing specific concerns, such as noise control, resulting in reduced opposition and smoother project advancement.

Navigating Stakeholder Challenges: Address common challenges like conflicting interests by employing negotiation skills, transparency, and finding common ground. Regular meetings and clear communication channels are essential in reconciling differing viewpoints.

Integration with Other Project Management Areas: Recognize that effective Stakeholder Management interacts closely with Communications, Risk, and Change Management. Ensuring stakeholders are informed and involved helps mitigate misunderstandings and fosters a supportive project environment.

Practical Tips:

- Regularly update your stakeholder analysis to reflect changes.

- Use a variety of communication channels to reach different stakeholders effectively.

- Develop a clear understanding of stakeholder expectations and measure engagement success against these benchmarks.

Conclusion: Mastering Stakeholder Management is crucial for project leaders aiming for success. By identifying, understanding, and engaging stakeholders effectively, project managers can ensure project objectives and stakeholder expectations are aligned, leading to enhanced project outcomes and stakeholder satisfaction.

Integration of Agile Practices in Each Area

Introduction to Agile Integration - In today's dynamic project environments, integrating Agile practices into traditional project management methodologies is not just beneficial—it's becoming essential. Agile's adaptive and iterative approaches offer a complementary counterbalance to the structured, predictive frameworks traditionally employed in project management. This section introduces the foundational principles of Agile methodologies and sets the stage for their integration into each of the PMBOK®'s ten Knowledge Areas.

Core Agile Principles: At the heart of Agile methodologies lie four fundamental principles: valuing individuals and interactions over processes and tools, preferring working solutions over comprehensive documentation, collaborating with customers over contract negotiation, and responding to change over following a set plan. These principles guide the Agile mindset, promoting a flexible, collaborative, and customer-focused approach to project management.

The Value of Agile Integration: By blending Agile practices with traditional project management approaches, teams can leverage the strengths of both worlds. This hybrid, or 'Agilified', approach allows for greater flexibility in planning and execution while maintaining the oversight and direction provided by a structured framework. The result is a more resilient project management strategy that can adapt to change, meet stakeholder needs more effectively, and deliver value continuously and incrementally.

Preview of Agile Application Across Knowledge Areas: As we delve deeper into each Knowledge Area, we will explore how Agile methodologies can enhance and enrich traditional project management practices. From fostering collaborative scope definition using user stories in Scope Management to applying iterative planning in Schedule Management, each section will provide specific strategies for integrating Agile principles.

- In Integration Management, we'll discuss how Agile methodologies can enhance project charter development and adaptive project governance.

- Scope Management will explore collaborative approaches to defining and managing project scope, emphasizing flexibility and customer value.

- Schedule Management will illustrate how Agile practices create adaptable, iterative schedules responsive to project evolution.

- In Cost Management, the focus will be on value-driven spending and applying lean principles to manage project budgets effectively.

- Quality Management will detail continuous integration and testing to maintain high standards throughout the project lifecycle.

- Resource Management will examine Agile's impact on team dynamics and cross-functional collaboration.

- Communications Management will highlight the role of transparency and regular feedback loops in maintaining effective communication channels.

- Risk Management will explain how Agile practices aid in proactive risk identification and management.

- Procurement Management will address integrating Agile practices in procurement, emphasizing flexible contracts and supplier collaboration.

- Finally, Stakeholder Management will describe how Agile fosters continuous engagement and satisfaction through early and continuous value delivery.

By integrating Agile practices into these areas, project teams can achieve better outcomes, characterized by collaborative efforts, effective communication, and dynamic responses to project challenges and opportunities.

Conclusion: This introduction sets the groundwork for a comprehensive understanding of Agile integration within traditional project management frameworks. As we move forward, each section will delve into specific applications of Agile practices, offering actionable insights and strategies for effectively managing modern, complex projects.

Agile in Integration Management - In the realm of Integration Management, incorporating Agile methodologies shifts the paradigm towards a more dynamic, flexible governance, and adaptive planning approach. This integration is crucial in today's fast-paced project environments where adaptability can significantly influence project success.

- **Adaptive Project Charters and Management Plans:** Traditional project charters and management plans often serve as static documents. However, in an Agile-infused process, these documents are living, breathing entities, continuously updated to reflect changes in project scope, stakeholder needs, or market conditions. This adaptive approach ensures that project governance remains relevant and responsive to external and internal shifts, fostering an environment where iterative planning is not only accepted but encouraged.
- **Continuous Stakeholder Engagement:** Agile methodologies underscore the importance of regular stakeholder involvement. Unlike traditional methods where stakeholder engagement may occur at key milestones, Agile insists on continuous collaboration. This ensures that stakeholder needs and feedback are integrated into the project from inception to closure, enhancing satisfaction and alignment with project outcomes.
- **Iterative Review and Adaptation:** In line with Agile principles, Integration Management becomes an ongoing process of review and adjustment. Regular sprint reviews and retrospectives allow for the assessment of current project status against objectives, enabling timely adaptations. This iterative process ensures that the project remains on track, aligned with stakeholder expectations, and responsive to any arising challenges or opportunities.
- **Bridging Agile with Traditional Practices:** While Agile offers a framework for flexibility and rapid response, integrating these practices within traditional project management structures requires careful balancing. The key lies in leveraging Agile's strengths—such as its iterative nature and focus on collaboration—while maintaining the overarching governance and strategic direction provided by traditional methodologies.

Practical Application: Consider a software development project employing a hybrid approach. Initial project planning follows traditional lines with a clear project charter and baseline plan. However, as development progresses, Agile practices such as Scrum are introduced for task management and execution, facilitating rapid iterations and feedback incorporation. This blend ensures that while the project benefits from Agile's flexibility and stakeholder engagement, it remains guided by a structured management framework.

Conclusion: Integrating Agile into Integration Management offers a pathway to more responsive, stakeholder-centered project execution. By adopting flexible charters, engaging stakeholders continuously, and embracing iterative review, projects can achieve greater adaptability without sacrificing clear governance. This approach not only aligns with modern project demands but also enhances the ability to navigate complexities and deliver value effectively.

Agile in Scope Management - Agile Scope Management emphasizes a collaborative and evolutionary approach, ensuring the project scope is defined, managed, and refined through active stakeholder collaboration. This dynamic practice adapts to changes and integrates stakeholder feedback, enhancing value delivery and meeting project objectives effectively.

- **Collaborative Scope Definition:** The process begins with stakeholders and project teams working together to define the scope. Using Agile tools like user stories and product backlogs, the scope is detailed in a manner that is both comprehensive and adaptable. This collaboration ensures that all perspectives are considered and that the project scope reflects actual user needs and expectations.
- **Evolutionary Development and Prioritization**: Unlike the fixed scope outlines in traditional project management, Agile adopts an iterative approach to scope development. Changes in business environments, stakeholder needs, or technology are embraced, with the scope evolving through continuous refinement and prioritization. This ensures the project remains relevant and focused on delivering maximum value.
- **Continuous Stakeholder Engagement:** A cornerstone of Agile Scope Management is the ongoing involvement of stakeholders. This approach contrasts with traditional methods that might limit stakeholder interaction to specific milestones. In Agile, regular communication and collaboration ensure that the project aligns with stakeholder expectations and can swiftly adapt to feedback or changes.

Practical Application: An e-commerce platform update project provides a practical example. The project began with a broad scope encompassing several new features. As development progressed, regular feedback sessions with users and stakeholders led to the reprioritization of features and adjustments to the scope based on user demand and technical feasibility.

Challenges and Solutions: Implementing Agile Scope Management can present challenges such as managing evolving requirements without scope creep. Effective solutions include maintaining a prioritized backlog, setting clear iteration goals, and employing rigorous change control processes. Regularly revisiting the backlog and scope with stakeholders helps in managing expectations and ensuring alignment with project goals.

Integration with Other Knowledge Areas: Agile Scope Management interacts closely with other areas such as Communications and Risk Management. Effective communication ensures stakeholders are informed and engaged, while an Agile approach to risk management enables the project to anticipate and respond to scope-related risks proactively.

In conclusion, integrating Agile practices in Scope Management enables projects to be more adaptive and responsive. By fostering a collaborative environment and prioritizing iterative development, projects can better meet stakeholder needs and navigate the complexities of modern project demands.

Agile in Schedule Management - In the dynamic world of project management, Agile in Schedule Management stands out for its innovative approach to handling project timelines. Unlike traditional methods that adhere to rigid schedules, Agile introduces iterative work cycles and flexibility, crucial for adapting to the evolving landscape of project demands and stakeholder needs.

Iterative Work Cycles and Flexibility: Agile Schedule Management is characterized by its division of projects into smaller, more manageable segments, typically known as sprints or iterations. This segmentation allows project teams to focus on delivering specific sets of features or project components within short, predetermined timeframes. This approach not only boosts focus and productivity but also ensures that the project can swiftly adapt to changes without overhauling the entire schedule.

Practical Application: Consider a scenario where a software development team employs the Scrum framework. They organize their project work into two-week sprints, with each sprint targeting a set of predetermined deliverables. This clear, concise framework enables the team to reassess and reprioritize tasks continuously, ensuring alignment with evolving customer expectations and project objectives. Another example is the use of Kanban boards, which help visualize workflow and task progress, enabling teams to adjust priorities in real-time based on immediate project needs.

Common Challenges and Solutions: Transitioning to Agile Schedule Management can present several challenges. Team members accustomed to conventional scheduling might resist the shift towards more fluid timelines. Strategies to overcome these challenges include:

- **Gradual Implementation**: Introducing Agile practices incrementally can help ease the transition, allowing team members to acclimate to new processes.

- **Comprehensive Training**: Providing detailed training sessions and workshops can demystify Agile concepts, fostering a more accepting and cooperative environment.

- **Open Communication**: Establishing clear channels for feedback and discussion encourages team members to voice concerns and contribute ideas, facilitating smoother adoption of Agile practices.

Integration with Other Knowledge Areas: Agile Schedule Management does not exist in isolation; it deeply intertwines with other project management disciplines. For instance, changes in project scope directly impact the schedule under Agile frameworks. Regular sprint planning and review sessions ensure that any modifications in scope are immediately accounted for in the schedule. Additionally, Agile's flexible nature allows for rapid reallocation of resources, addressing emerging tasks or challenges efficiently, thereby maintaining the project's momentum.

Tools and Techniques: Key to Agile Schedule Management are specific tools and techniques that enhance visibility and control:

- **Burndown Charts**: These visual tools track remaining work versus time, providing a clear picture of progress and helping teams stay on target.

- **Velocity Tracking**: By measuring the amount of work completed in each sprint, teams can forecast future performance more accurately, ensuring realistic and achievable scheduling.

Measuring Success: In Agile, success is measured by the team's ability to meet customer expectations and adapt to changing conditions while maintaining productivity. Indicators of successful Agile Schedule Management include:

- **On-Time Feature Delivery**: Meeting deadlines for feature releases or project milestones.

- **Positive Stakeholder Feedback**: Receiving affirmative responses from clients or stakeholders regarding the project's progress and outcomes.
- **Adaptability to Changes**: Demonstrating the ability to adjust plans and priorities efficiently in response to new information or challenges.

Conclusion: Adopting Agile in Schedule Management empowers teams with greater flexibility, responsiveness, and efficiency. By embracing iterative planning, engaging stakeholders continuously, and utilizing Agile-specific tools, project teams can navigate the complexities of modern projects more adeptly. This approach not only aligns with the rapid pace of change in today's project environments but also ensures that projects deliver substantial value at every stage of their lifecycle, culminating in more successful and satisfying project outcomes.

Agile in Cost Management - In the realm of Agile methodologies, Cost Management shifts from traditional, rigid budgeting frameworks to a more dynamic, value-driven approach. This section delves into how Agile practices are integrated into Cost Management, focusing on maximizing project value and ensuring efficient resource utilization.

Value-Driven Expenditure: Agile Cost Management emphasizes spending based on value rather than merely adhering to a fixed budget. This approach encourages teams to continuously evaluate and prioritize spending based on the direct benefits to the project and stakeholders. Instead of allocating funds at the outset with little flexibility, Agile methodologies advocate for a more adaptive financial strategy, where budget decisions are made iteratively, reflecting current project needs and objectives.

Continuous Prioritization and Reassessment: Under Agile, cost management is not a one-time task but a continuous process. Teams are encouraged to regularly reassess project activities, considering both value and cost implications. This ongoing evaluation ensures that resources are allocated efficiently, funding high-priority tasks that deliver significant value while deferring or eliminating lower-value activities. This constant realignment with project goals helps in minimizing waste and optimizing the use of available resources.

Regular Cost Reviews and Iterative Decisions: Agile practices introduce regular cost reviews within each iteration or sprint. These reviews allow teams to reflect on expenditures, understand cost drivers, and make informed decisions on future spending. By analyzing actual spending against planned budgets in short cycles, teams can quickly identify variances and adjust course as necessary, ensuring financial management is tightly aligned with project progress and outcomes.

Integrating Agile Cost Management with Project Goals and Stakeholder Value: The ultimate aim of Agile Cost Management is to align financial decisions with project goals and stakeholder expectations. This alignment is achieved by involving team members and stakeholders in budget discussions and decisions, ensuring transparency and shared understanding of financial constraints and priorities. Regular stakeholder engagement ensures that budget adjustments are made with a clear understanding of their implications on project value and stakeholder satisfaction.

Challenges and Strategies: Implementing Agile Cost Management can present challenges, particularly in organizations accustomed to traditional budgeting practices. Resistance to change, difficulty in shifting from fixed to variable budgeting, and challenges in tracking costs in a fast-paced Agile environment are common. Strategies to address these challenges include:

- **Education and Training:** Providing comprehensive training on Agile principles and practices to all team members and stakeholders.

- **Incremental Implementation:** Gradually introducing Agile cost management practices, allowing teams to adapt to the new approach.

- **Clear Communication**: Ensuring transparent communication about the reasons behind budget adjustments and their expected impact on project value.

- **Effective Tooling:** Utilizing software and tools that support Agile budget tracking and reporting, enabling real-time insight into financial performance.

Practical Application: A practical example of Agile Cost Management could involve a tech start-up developing a new mobile application. Instead of allocating a fixed budget for the entire project, the team uses an Agile approach, setting budgetary guidelines for each two-week sprint based on prioritized features. Regular cost reviews enable the team to adjust spending in response to feedback and market changes, ensuring that investment is focused on features that deliver maximum value to users and stakeholders.

Conclusion: Agile in Cost Management represents a paradigm shift towards more flexible, responsive, and value-focused financial planning and control. By embracing this approach, teams can ensure that project expenditures directly contribute to key objectives and stakeholder satisfaction, leading to more successful and sustainable project outcomes. This dynamic approach to cost management, grounded in Agile principles, fosters a culture of continuous improvement and effective resource utilization, crucial for navigating the complexities of modern projects.

Agile in Quality Management - Agile Quality Management redefines traditional approaches by embedding quality directly into the iterative development process. This section explores how Agile methodologies enhance quality through continuous feedback, iterative testing, and a steadfast focus on meeting customer needs.

Incorporating Continuous Feedback and Iterative Testing: Agile methodologies distinguish themselves by integrating feedback loops and testing phases into every stage of development, ensuring that quality is not an afterthought but a fundamental aspect of the product lifecycle. By engaging customers and stakeholders in frequent reviews and applying iterative testing, Agile teams can identify and resolve issues promptly, preventing minor defects from evolving into major problems.

Practical Application Consider a software development project utilizing the Agile framework. The team conducts daily stand-up meetings to discuss progress and challenges, including quality concerns. They employ test-driven development (TDD), where tests are written before the actual code, ensuring each feature meets the required standards before moving forward. At the end of each sprint, the team showcases the increment to the stakeholders in a sprint review, gathering feedback that directly informs the next cycle of work.

Addressing Common Challenges: Transitioning to an Agile approach can pose challenges, particularly in environments accustomed to traditional quality assurance methods. Teams may struggle with the shift from end-of-cycle testing to continuous testing, or they may find it difficult to balance rapid iteration with thorough quality checks. Here are key strategies to address these challenges effectively:

- **Fostering an Agile Mindset**: Encourage a cultural shift where all team members prioritize quality throughout the development process, not just at the end.

- **Continuous Testing**: Integrate testing into every phase of the project, ensuring issues are identified and resolved early.

- **Training and Education**: Provide comprehensive training on Agile practices and tools to enhance the team's understanding and implementation of continuous quality checks.

- **Balancing Speed and Quality**: Educate teams on managing the balance between rapid delivery and maintaining high quality, reinforcing the concept that speed should not compromise product integrity.

By implementing these strategies, teams can overcome common challenges associated with Agile Quality Management, leading to improved product quality and increased project success.

Integration with Other Knowledge Areas: Agile Quality Management does not operate in isolation. It intersects significantly with other areas such as Scope, Schedule, and Cost Management. For example, the iterative refinement of product backlogs impacts the scope and ensures that quality considerations are aligned with project priorities. Similarly, the Agile approach to scheduling, which allows for regular adaptations, supports the integration of quality management activities without disrupting the project timeline.

Tools and Techniques: Agile teams utilize a variety of tools and techniques to maintain quality, such as automated testing suites, continuous integration pipelines, and pair programming. These practices enable rapid identification and correction of defects, streamline the development process, and maintain high-quality standards throughout the project lifecycle.

Measuring Success: In Agile Quality Management, success is gauged by the ability to deliver products that not only meet but exceed customer expectations. Key metrics include defect rates, customer satisfaction scores, and the frequency of iterations required to reach the desired quality level. Regular retrospectives provide a platform for reflecting on quality practices, allowing teams to celebrate successes and identify areas for improvement.

By integrating quality management principles into every aspect of the Agile process, teams can ensure that the final product is of the highest possible quality, meets customer needs, and achieves project objectives efficiently. This commitment to quality and continuous improvement underpins the Agile philosophy, contributing to enhanced customer satisfaction and overall project success.

Agile in Resource Management - Agile in Resource Management revolutionizes the traditional approach by emphasizing flexibility, efficiency, and empowerment in managing both human and material resources. In Agile environments, resource management extends beyond simple allocation, fostering an ecosystem where cross-functional teams collaborate effectively, adapt rapidly, and are empowered to make decisions that best serve project objectives.

Flexibility and Efficiency: Agile methodologies promote an adaptable framework for resource management, where team members with diverse skills come together to form dynamic, cross-functional units. This setup allows for a seamless shift of roles and responsibilities, tailored to meet the evolving demands of the project. Efficiency is achieved as these teams self-organize, minimizing bottlenecks and enhancing the flow of work through continuous communication and collaboration.

Practical Application: Consider a tech startup transitioning to Agile methodologies. Initially, developers, testers, and designers worked in silos, leading to delays and communication gaps. By adopting Agile, the company formed cross-functional teams, where each member could contribute across different domains. This shift not only improved project turnaround times but also enhanced innovation as diverse perspectives were brought into every stage of product development.

Common Challenges and Solutions: Transitioning to Agile Resource Management can present challenges, such as resistance to new roles or misunderstanding Agile principles. To overcome these:

- **Structured Onboarding**: Introduce clear onboarding for new Agile roles to clarify expectations and responsibilities.

- **Agile Training**: Offer comprehensive Agile training programs to deepen understanding of Agile methodologies.

- **Feedback Sessions**: Conduct regular feedback sessions, allowing team members to express concerns and adapt to Agile practices more comfortably.

- **Team-Building Activities**: Engage in activities that promote team cohesion, enhancing collaboration and a unified approach to project goals.

These strategies facilitate smoother transitions to Agile Resource Management, ensuring team adaptability and cohesion.

Integration with Other Knowledge Areas: Effective Agile Resource Management interacts seamlessly with other project management disciplines. For example, in Agile Communications Management, open channels of communication within cross-functional teams enhance clarity and ensure that resources are aligned with current project needs. Similarly, Agile Risk Management benefits from the adaptive nature of resource management, as teams can quickly reassign resources to address emerging risks or capitalize on new opportunities.

Tools and Techniques: In Agile settings, tools like Kanban boards and Scrum boards provide visual representations of work progress, facilitating better resource planning and allocation. Capacity planning during sprint planning sessions ensures that team workloads are manageable and that expectations are realistic, contributing to higher productivity and job satisfaction.

Measuring Success: Success in Agile Resource Management is measured by the team's ability to remain adaptable, maintain high productivity levels, and meet project goals within the constraints of time and budget. Key performance indicators might include the percentage of tasks completed within sprints, resource utilization rates, and stakeholder satisfaction levels. Regular retrospectives allow the team to assess these metrics, identify areas for improvement, and refine resource management practices accordingly.

By embracing the principles of Agile in Resource Management, organizations can create a more responsive, cohesive, and efficient approach to managing project resources. This not only aligns with the dynamic nature of modern projects but also ensures that the right resources are available at the right times, ultimately driving project success and stakeholder satisfaction.

Agile in Communications Management - Agile Communications Management revolutionizes traditional communication protocols by emphasizing transparency, frequency, and adaptability. This section delves into how Agile practices foster a culture where open communication underpins every activity, ensuring that project objectives, status, and requirements are clearly understood by all team members and stakeholders.

Principles of Effective Agile Communication: In Agile environments, communication is continuous and multidirectional. Daily stand-ups, sprint reviews, and retrospectives are not mere meetings but essential forums for dialogue, feedback, and collaborative problem-solving. This open communication strategy ensures that team members stay aligned with the project's goals and adapt swiftly to any changes or challenges.

Practical Application: Consider a digital marketing project employing Agile methodologies. The team begins each day with a stand-up meeting to discuss current tasks, challenges, and strategies. This daily communication keeps the project aligned with client needs and allows for immediate adjustments. During sprint reviews, the team presents completed work, receiving direct feedback from stakeholders, which informs the planning for the next cycle. This iterative process of communication and feedback ensures that the project remains on track and aligned with strategic goals.

Addressing Common Challenges: Agile Communications Management can face obstacles such as cultural barriers or resistance to open dialogue. Here are strategies to navigate these challenges:

- **Cultural Adaptation:** Encourage an environment where speaking up is valued. Implement training sessions to highlight the importance of open communication in Agile practices.

- **Tool Utilization:** Leverage communication tools like chat platforms or project management software to facilitate clear, continuous dialogue among remote or distributed teams.

- **Feedback Mechanisms:** Establish clear channels and regular schedules for feedback to ensure it is constructive, timely, and integrated into the project workflow.

Integration with Other Knowledge Areas: Effective communication in Agile extends beyond the confines of the team to encompass all project stakeholders. It aligns closely with Resource Management, ensuring that team dynamics and resource allocation support project goals. Additionally, Agile communication practices integrate with Risk Management by providing a framework for identifying and addressing issues as they arise, ensuring that risks are managed proactively.

Tools and Techniques: Agile teams employ various tools to enhance communication, including Kanban boards for visualizing workflow and digital dashboards for real-time project tracking. These tools, combined with regular Agile ceremonies, support a robust communication framework that underpins successful project execution.

By adopting Agile principles in Communications Management, teams can ensure more effective collaboration, faster problem resolution, and improved project outcomes. This approach not only streamlines information flow but also builds a foundation for sustained project success in the dynamic landscape of modern project management.

Agile in Risk Management - Agile Risk Management revolutionizes traditional risk management by embedding continuous identification, assessment, and mitigation of risks directly into the Agile workflow. This proactive approach ensures risks are managed dynamically, allowing projects to adapt swiftly and efficiently.

Incorporating Continuous Risk Identification and Assessment: Agile methodologies integrate risk management into daily activities, ensuring that risks are not only identified early but are also assessed continuously throughout the project lifecycle. This integration occurs through regular team meetings, sprint planning, and retrospectives, where potential risks are discussed, evaluated, and prioritized based on their potential impact on the project.

Practical Application: Consider a technology upgrade project in an IT department utilizing Agile methodologies. The project team employs sprint planning sessions to identify potential risks associated with technology integration and compatibility. Risk mitigation strategies, such as prototype testing and early user feedback, are implemented to address these risks proactively. The team revisits these risks in daily stand-ups and sprint reviews, adjusting their strategies based on the latest information and feedback, ensuring that risk management is an ongoing process.

Addressing Common Challenges: Adopting Agile Risk Management can present challenges, especially in transitioning from a traditional risk management approach. Here are strategies to address these challenges effectively:

- **Cultivating an Agile Mindset:** Encourage teams to view risk management as an integral part of their daily activities, not as a separate or isolated process.

- **Empowering Teams:** Enable team members to identify and assess risks, fostering a sense of ownership and responsibility towards mitigating them.

- **Frequent Communication:** Hold regular discussions on risks and their mitigation strategies, ensuring transparency and collective understanding.

Integration with Other Knowledge Areas: Agile Risk Management intersects significantly with other project management disciplines, including Scope, Schedule, and Communications Management. For instance, changes in project scope identified through Agile processes can introduce new risks, requiring immediate reassessment and adjustment of risk management plans. Similarly, effective communication ensures that all stakeholders are aware of potential risks and the strategies in place to mitigate them, fostering a collaborative approach to risk management.

Tools and Techniques: Agile teams leverage various tools and techniques for effective risk management, including risk burndown charts to visually track the elimination of risks over time and risk registers updated in real-time during Agile ceremonies. These tools support the Agile team's ability to manage risks proactively and transparently.

Measuring Success: Success in Agile Risk Management is measured by the team's ability to minimize the impact of risks on project objectives. Metrics such as the number of risks mitigated, the time taken to respond to new risks, and stakeholder satisfaction with risk management practices can provide insights into the effectiveness of the Agile risk management approach.

By embedding risk management into the Agile framework, teams can ensure that they are prepared to deal with uncertainties more effectively, leading to improved project outcomes and enhanced stakeholder confidence. This dynamic approach to risk management supports the Agile commitment to flexibility, adaptability, and continuous improvement.

Agile in Procurement Management - Agile Procurement Management modifies traditional procurement processes to align with the flexible, dynamic nature of Agile project environments. This section will delve into how adopting Agile methodologies transforms procurement activities to support the project's evolving needs effectively.

Adapting Procurement Practices: In the Agile framework, procurement extends beyond mere transactional interactions with vendors and suppliers. It encompasses establishing partnerships that are conducive to the Agile spirit of collaboration and flexibility. Contracts under Agile procurement often include clauses allowing for changes in scope or deliverables, accommodating the project's iterative nature. Early engagement with suppliers ensures that they are aligned with the project's goals and prepared to respond to changes swiftly.

Practical Application: Imagine a scenario in a tech startup where the procurement process is guided by Agile principles. Instead of locking in rigid contracts, the company negotiates agreements with suppliers that allow for adjustments in order volumes or project specifications. Regular check-ins and feedback sessions with these partners ensure that any necessary changes are made promptly, keeping the project on track without sacrificing quality or timelines.

Addressing Common Challenges: Transitioning to Agile Procurement Management can bring about several challenges:

- **Resistance to Change:** Overcome this by educating stakeholders about the benefits of Agile procurement, such as increased flexibility and improved supplier relationships.

- **Finding Suitable Partners:** Identify vendors who understand and are willing to work within an Agile framework.

- **Maintaining Clear Communication:** Ensure that all changes and requirements are communicated clearly and promptly to avoid misunderstandings.

Integration with Other Knowledge Areas: Agile Procurement Management does not operate in a vacuum. It significantly intersects with areas like Scope, Schedule, and Resource Management. For instance, changes in project scope directly impact procurement needs, while the Agile scheduling approach allows for adjustments in resource allocation and procurement planning to be made seamlessly.

Tools and Techniques: Leverage Agile tools such as Kanban boards and backlog lists to manage procurement activities, track supplier performance, and ensure timely delivery of resources. Regular sprint planning and review meetings should include discussions on procurement needs and supplier performance to ensure alignment with project objectives.

Measuring Success: Success in Agile Procurement Management is measured by the ability to maintain project momentum through efficient resource allocation, timely delivery of products and services, and the establishment of mutually beneficial supplier relationships. Key indicators include the speed of response to change, satisfaction levels of both project teams and suppliers, and the overall impact on project delivery and quality.

By incorporating Agile principles into procurement practices, organizations can enhance the adaptability and efficiency of their procurement activities, ensuring that they contribute effectively to project success. This approach fosters a more collaborative, responsive, and value-driven procurement environment, ultimately supporting the Agile project's goals and ensuring stakeholder satisfaction.

Agile in Stakeholder Management - Agile in Stakeholder Management redefines the traditional approach by ensuring active, continuous engagement with all project stakeholders. This part of Agile methodology ensures stakeholders' needs and expectations are consistently met throughout the project lifecycle, fostering a collaborative environment that enhances project outcomes.

Frequent Communication and Collaboration: Stakeholder engagement in Agile is not periodic; it is a constant element of the project management process. This involves setting up regular communication channels and platforms where stakeholders can share their input and feedback. Techniques like sprint reviews, user story mapping sessions, and stakeholder interviews are employed to keep the communication lines open and productive.

Direct Involvement in the Decision-Making Process: Agile practices such as sprint reviews and backlog refinement sessions include stakeholders in the decision-making process. By involving stakeholders in these Agile ceremonies, their requirements and feedback become integral to the product development, ensuring that the final product aligns closely with their expectations.

Practical Application: Consider a scenario where a new product development project employs Agile methodologies to enhance stakeholder engagement. The project team initiates with defining clear personas for each stakeholder category to ensure all needs are captured. Daily stand-ups include discussions on stakeholder feedback received the previous day, and the product backlog is adjusted accordingly. In bi-weekly sprint reviews, stakeholders are invited to provide direct feedback, which is immediately incorporated into the planning for the next sprint. This continuous loop of feedback and adaptation leads to a product that closely aligns with stakeholder expectations, thereby improving satisfaction and project outcomes.

Addressing Common Challenges: Adapting to Agile Stakeholder Management can present challenges, particularly in projects where stakeholders are not accustomed to continuous engagement or are spread across different geographical locations. Here are strategies to address these challenges:

- **Enhanced Communication Tools:** Utilize various communication platforms to facilitate easy and open dialogue with stakeholders. Tools like video conferencing, shared collaboration platforms, and instant messaging can bridge the gap between different locations and time zones.
- **Stakeholder Education:** Conduct orientation sessions to educate stakeholders on Agile processes and their roles within them. Clarify how their feedback becomes integral to project development and the iterative nature of Agile.
- **Regular Feedback Loops:** Establish structured yet flexible feedback mechanisms like scheduled review meetings, feedback forms, and open forums. Ensure stakeholders know their input is valued and taken into consideration.
- **Transparency and Trust:** Build transparency by sharing regular progress updates and being open about project challenges. Trust is fostered when stakeholders see their suggestions being implemented or discussed openly.

Implementing these strategies can help overcome the common hurdles associated with Agile Stakeholder Management, leading to enhanced collaboration and project success.

Integration with Other Knowledge Areas: Agile Stakeholder Management intersects significantly with other project management disciplines like Communications, Risk, and Scope Management. Effective stakeholder engagement ensures that communication is clear, risks are identified and mitigated in collaboration with stakeholders, and the project scope aligns with stakeholder expectations.

By implementing Agile in Stakeholder Management, project teams can ensure that stakeholders remain engaged and invested throughout the project, leading to higher satisfaction levels, better project outcomes, and increased value delivery. This approach not only aligns with the Agile philosophy of collaboration and adaptability but also enhances the overall success of the project.

Process Groups and Project Management Processes

Detailed Overview of the 5 Process Groups

Initiating Process Group - The Initiating Process Group is fundamental in setting the project or phase's trajectory and ensuring alignment with organizational strategies. This initial phase is characterized by several critical actions: obtaining project authorization, defining the initial scope, committing financial resources, identifying key stakeholders, and appointing the project manager if they haven't been already assigned.

Project Authorization and Scope Definition: Every project commences with its formal authorization, generally encapsulated within a project charter. This document, marking the project's inception, delineates the project's vision, objectives, and preliminary scope, acting as an agreement between the sponsoring entity and the project team. In the context of an IT project, this phase might involve setting clear goals for a new software development initiative, like enhancing data security or improving user interface design, with the charter specifying expected outcomes like meeting specific security standards or achieving user satisfaction targets.

Stakeholder Identification: Identifying stakeholders early is crucial. They are individuals or entities impacted by or capable of influencing the project's outcome. The process involves more than listing names; it requires understanding their interests, influence, and potential impact on the project. Effective stakeholder engagement from the onset can significantly influence the project's direction and success. For example, in a construction project, stakeholders may include local government bodies, future tenants, and construction firms, each with unique needs and concerns, from regulatory compliance to design preferences and contractual obligations.

Alignment with Organizational Goals: It's vital to ensure the project aligns with the organization's strategic objectives. This alignment is essential for securing ongoing support and resources. Projects should not only conform to current strategic goals but also adapt to evolving organizational directions. For instance, a company focusing on sustainability might prioritize projects that minimize environmental impact, aligning new initiatives with this overarching goal.

Developing the Business Case and Benefits: The business case underpins the project's rationale, offering an analysis of costs, benefits, risks, and alternatives. It articulates why the project is necessary and the value it will bring to the organization. The project manager, alongside the project sponsor and other stakeholders, often plays a crucial role in shaping this document. In a marketing project, the business case might explain how a new advertising campaign will enhance brand awareness and boost sales, detailing the anticipated return on investment.

Practical Tips and Common Pitfalls:

- **Ensure Clarity in the Project Charter:** A vague charter can lead to misunderstandings and misaligned objectives. Articulate the project's goals, scope, and key stakeholders clearly.

- **Engage Stakeholders Early:** Start with a comprehensive stakeholder analysis to understand their needs and concerns. Early engagement can foster support and mitigate resistance.

- **Align with Organizational Strategies:** Regularly reassess the project's alignment with the organization's goals to ensure continued relevance and support.

- **Don't Overlook the Business Case:** Ensure the business case is robust, justifying the project's need, addressing potential risks, and outlining clear benefits.

By integrating these elements, considering both the structured approach of the PMBOK 6th Edition and the principles and performance domains of the 7th Edition, the Initiating Process Group section will provide project managers with a solid foundation for starting projects effectively. This ensures alignment with organizational objectives and stakeholder expectations, setting the stage for successful project execution.

Planning Process Group - The Planning Process Group is vital in project management, setting the stage for how the project will be executed, monitored, and controlled. This group involves a series of processes that define the project's total scope, refine its objectives, and establish the sequence of actions necessary for achieving project goals.

Scope and Objectives: The planning begins with a clear definition of the project scope and objectives. The scope outlines what will be included in the project and helps prevent scope creep. Objectives should be SMART: Specific, Measurable, Achievable, Relevant, and Time-bound. For example, in a software development project, objectives might include developing a user-friendly application within six months that meets specific performance criteria.

Comprehensive Planning: The heart of the Planning Process Group lies in developing the project management plan and subsidiary plans. This includes:

- **Scope Management Plan:** Outlining how the scope will be defined, validated, and controlled.

- **Schedule Management Plan:** Establishing timelines, milestones, and scheduling methodologies.

- **Cost Management Plan:** Budgeting resources and setting cost control measures.

- **Quality Management Plan:** Defining quality benchmarks and testing methods.

- **Communication Management Plan:** Planning stakeholder communication frequency and formats.

- **Risk Management Plan:** Identifying potential risks and mitigation strategies.

- **Procurement Management Plan:** Outlining procurement strategies and contract management.

- **Stakeholder Engagement Plan:** Identifying all stakeholders and defining engagement levels.

Stakeholder Engagement: Identifying and planning for stakeholder engagement is critical in this phase. Stakeholders' needs and expectations should be understood and managed. Engaging stakeholders early and effectively can lead to greater support and reduced resistance, ultimately contributing to project success.

Progressive Elaboration: The planning process is iterative. As more information becomes available, or as the project environment changes, the project management plan and its components should be revisited and revised as necessary. This concept, known as progressive elaboration, ensures that the plan remains relevant and aligned with project needs.

Integration with Organizational Goals: The project should align with the broader organizational goals and strategies. This alignment ensures that the project contributes to the overall success of the organization and receives the necessary support from key stakeholders.

Practical Application:

- **Software Development Project:** During planning, a tech firm might use Agile sprints within a Predictive framework, defining the product scope in the charter and detailing sprint schedules in the schedule management plan. Stakeholder feedback loops are integrated to refine ongoing development.

- **Construction Project:** A building project might establish detailed architectural plans (scope) and a phased construction timeline (schedule), with cost estimates for materials and labor detailed in the cost management plan. Quality control measures might include regular inspections and compliance checks.

Best Practices:

- Developing a clear and detailed scope statement to guide project execution and prevent scope creep.
- Using a Work Breakdown Structure (WBS) to break down the project scope into manageable components.
- Establishing clear communication channels and protocols to ensure effective information exchange among project stakeholders.
- Implementing a change management process to handle changes systematically and ensure they are properly evaluated and integrated into the project plan.
- Conducting thorough risk management activities to identify, analyze, and plan for potential risks.

Common Pitfalls and How to Avoid Them:

- Failing to involve key stakeholders in the planning process can lead to misunderstandings and lack of support.
- Underestimating the time and resources required can lead to project delays and budget overruns.
- Not establishing clear metrics for success can make it difficult to measure project performance and achieve objectives.

Conclusion: Effective planning is essential for successful project execution. By comprehensively developing and integrating all aspects of the project management plan, and by engaging stakeholders and aligning with organizational goals, the Planning Process Group lays the foundation for project success. Remember, planning is not a one-time effort but an ongoing activity that requires continuous refinement and adjustment as the project evolves.

Executing Process Group - The Executing Process Group is pivotal in project management, translating the project management plan into actionable tasks and tangible results. This phase is the embodiment of execution, where strategies and plans become operational realities.

Coordinating People and Resources: Effective coordination involves aligning team efforts and resources with project tasks. For example, in an IT development project, this could mean assigning developers to specific software features based on their expertise and scheduling resources like testing environments when needed.

Executing Project Plans: This involves implementing the defined strategies for scope, schedule, and cost management. Execution should be in strict adherence to the project management plan but flexible enough to accommodate necessary changes.

Quality Standards and Deliverables: Ensuring deliverables meet predefined quality standards is crucial. For instance, in a manufacturing project, this might involve regular quality checks and adherence to industry standards throughout the production process.

Stakeholder Engagement: Maintaining clear and continuous communication with stakeholders is essential. Engage them through regular updates and involve them in decision-making processes where appropriate. Effective stakeholder engagement ensures that project objectives remain aligned with stakeholder expectations.

Integrating PMBOK Concepts: Adhering to PMBOK principles, the executing phase should seamlessly integrate with other process groups. This ensures a holistic approach, where planning, monitoring, and closing activities support and enhance execution efforts.

Practical Application:

- In a construction project, executing might involve coordinating different contractor schedules, ensuring materials are delivered on time, and maintaining strict adherence to safety standards.

- In a marketing campaign, execution involves launching advertising efforts, tracking engagement metrics, and adjusting strategies based on consumer feedback.

Best Practices:

- Regularly review and adjust execution plans to reflect current project realities and stakeholder feedback.

- Foster a collaborative environment where team members can communicate openly and address issues promptly.

- Implement a robust change management process to evaluate and integrate changes without derailing project objectives.

Common Pitfalls:

- Avoiding communication silos that can lead to misinformed decisions or stakeholder dissatisfaction.

- Preventing resource bottlenecks by ensuring all necessary materials and personnel are available when needed.

- Overcoming resistance to change by ensuring all team members and stakeholders understand the benefits and reasons for modifications to the project plan.

In conclusion, the Executing Process Group is where plans are put into action. By understanding and applying the principles laid out in the PMBOK, project managers can ensure that this phase is managed effectively, leading to successful project outcomes. Remember, successful execution hinges on detailed planning, effective communication, and the dynamic coordination of resources and stakeholders.

Monitoring and Controlling Process Group - The Monitoring and Controlling Process Group plays a pivotal role in the management and oversight of a project. This phase is integral to ensuring that a project's objectives are met by systematically tracking, reviewing, and regulating its progress and performance against the established project management plan.

Key Functions:

This process group encompasses a range of critical functions:

- **Performance Measurement and Analysis:** At its core, Monitoring and Controlling involves the continuous measurement of project performance against the project management plan and baselines. It employs various performance measurement techniques, such as Earned Value Management (EVM), to provide a comprehensive overview of project health, enabling project managers to identify variances between actual and planned performance.

- **Change Management:** Change is inevitable in any project. This group addresses change systematically through a structured change control process, ensuring that all modifications are assessed, approved, and documented. Change requests can stem from various sources, including stakeholder feedback, project risks, or unforeseen obstacles. Effective change management ensures that changes are implemented in a controlled manner, keeping the project aligned with its goals.

- **Risk and Issue Management:** Monitoring and controlling also involve the proactive identification and resolution of risks and issues. This includes the application of risk response strategies and the management of issues that could impact project objectives. Regular risk reassessment and audits are conducted to ensure that the risk management plan remains relevant and effective throughout the project lifecycle.

- **Quality Control:** This involves ensuring that project deliverables meet the required standards and stakeholder expectations. Techniques like inspections, audits, and testing are used to measure quality performance and identify areas for improvement.

- **Information Distribution and Communication:** Effective communication is crucial for project success. This process ensures that all project information, including status reports, performance measurements, and forecasts, is accurately collected, analyzed, and disseminated to relevant stakeholders in a timely manner.

Practical Application: Consider a project aimed at developing a new software application. The Monitoring and Controlling Process Group would involve:

- Regularly assessing project progress through agile sprint reviews and retrospectives, comparing completed work against the sprint backlog.

- Implementing a change control board (CCB) to evaluate and approve changes to the software's features or scope based on user feedback and testing results.

- Conducting code reviews and software testing sessions to ensure the application meets predefined quality standards and user requirements.

- Utilizing communication tools like project dashboards or weekly status meetings to keep stakeholders informed of the project's status, risks, and issues.

Tools and Techniques: Several tools and techniques are essential for effective monitoring and control, including:

- **Dashboards and Performance Reports:** Visual tools that provide a snapshot of project status, key performance indicators (KPIs), and trends.

- **Gantt Charts and Schedules:** Used to track project progress against planned timelines and milestones.

- **Risk Registers and Action Item Lists:** Maintained to document and track the status of identified risks and action items.

Best Practices:

- **Regular Status Reviews:** Conduct weekly or bi-weekly project status meetings to review progress, discuss issues, and align on next steps.

- **Transparent Communication:** Foster an environment of open communication where team members and stakeholders can share updates, concerns, and suggestions.

- **Adaptive Processes:** Be willing to adapt monitoring and control processes to better fit the project's evolving needs and complexities.

In conclusion, the Monitoring and Controlling Process Group is crucial for keeping a project on track, within scope, and aligned with its objectives. By effectively applying these principles and practices, project managers can navigate challenges, implement necessary changes, and steer their projects toward successful completion, all while meeting the specific needs and goals of their target audience.

Closing Process Group - The Closing Process Group is an essential part of the project management lifecycle, signifying the formal completion of the project phases, contractual commitments, and the consolidation of individual project elements. This process group plays a critical role in ensuring that the project's objectives have been met and that all project work has been completed as per the agreed-upon project management plan.

Objective Fulfillment and Deliverables Confirmation: The primary objective of the Closing Process Group is to ensure that the project has successfully met all its objectives and that all deliverables have been accepted by the relevant stakeholders. This involves a systematic review of project outcomes against the initial goals and requirements. It's crucial to confirm that all project scope has been executed and that all deliverables meet the quality standards agreed upon at the project's inception.

Formal Acceptance and Evaluation: Obtaining formal acceptance of the project's outcomes from the client or sponsor is a critical step within this group. This acceptance is the client's acknowledgment that the project has met its objectives and deliverables. Following this, conducting a post-project evaluation allows for the assessment of the project's success against its original benchmarks and the effectiveness of project management practices employed.

Documentation and Lessons Learned: Documenting lessons learned is an invaluable practice within the Closing Process Group. This activity involves recording the project's successes and failures, insights, and unresolved issues to provide valuable information for future projects. These lessons become part of the organizational process assets and are essential for continuous improvement.

Resource Release and Transition: Another key aspect of the Closing Process Group is the release of project resources, ensuring that human, financial, and physical resources are appropriately disbursed or reassigned upon project completion. Additionally, ensuring a smooth transition of deliverables to operations or maintenance teams is crucial for the project's long-term success and sustainability.

Administrative Closure: Administrative closure includes finalizing all project activities, ensuring all documents are signed off, and archiving project documents for future reference. This also involves closing out all project accounts and ensuring that all contractual obligations have been fulfilled.

Stakeholder Communication: Effective communication with stakeholders is crucial during the closing phase. Stakeholders should be informed of the project's closure, its outcomes, and any subsequent steps or actions required. This communication ensures that all parties are aware of the project's status and any changes to the project's products or services.

Integration with PMBOK® Guide Principles: According to the PMBOK® Guide, the Closing Process Group aligns with the principles of project integration management, ensuring that all elements of the project are properly coordinated and unified. This integration ensures that the project's objectives are met efficiently and effectively, aligning with business goals and stakeholder expectations.

Reflection and Improvement: The closing phase is also an opportunity for reflection and improvement. Evaluating what worked well and what could be improved for future projects is a critical component of this process group. This reflective practice contributes to the development of best practices and enhances the efficiency and effectiveness of future projects.

Agile and Adaptive Considerations: In agile and adaptive environments, the Closing Process Group may involve additional considerations, such as retrospective meetings to discuss lessons learned and opportunities for improvement in a more iterative and incremental manner. These considerations ensure that the project remains aligned with changing business needs and project environments.

Conclusion: In conclusion, the Closing Process Group is critical for ensuring that projects are completed successfully, lessons are learned and applied, and resources are released efficiently. By adhering to the practices outlined in the PMBOK® Guide and integrating lessons from both traditional and agile methodologies, project managers can ensure effective project closure and contribute to the continuous improvement of project management practices within their organizations.

Processes Within Each Group with Agile Considerations

Initiating with Agile - In Agile project initiation, the primary focus is on establishing a high-level vision and scope that prioritizes change and flexibility, a concept that diverges from the traditional, more rigid project initiation processes. This phase is crucial as it sets the tone for the entire project, integrating the dynamic nature of Agile methodologies with the foundational principles of project management as outlined in both the 6th and 7th editions of the PMBOK Guide.

Developing an Agile Charter: The Agile Charter serves as a lighter, more flexible version of the traditional project charter. While it outlines the project objectives, key stakeholders, and the overall approach, it intentionally avoids delving into detailed requirements. This document is pivotal as it aligns the team and stakeholders with the project's goals without confining them to a fixed set of requirements, thus accommodating the iterative and evolving nature of Agile projects.

The creation of an Agile Charter involves collaborative workshops or meetings, promoting stakeholder engagement from the outset. This collaborative initiation ensures a shared understanding of project goals and aligns expectations, establishing a solid foundation for iterative development and continuous feedback, which are central tenets of Agile methodology.

Key Components of an Agile Charter:

- Project objectives.

- Key stakeholders.

- Overall approach.

- Note on avoiding overly detailed requirements to maintain flexibility.

Stakeholder Engagement and Collaboration: From the beginning, stakeholder engagement is paramount in Agile project initiation. Unlike traditional methodologies that might involve stakeholders at specific milestones, Agile insists on their continuous involvement. This approach ensures that the project remains aligned with stakeholder needs and expectations, adapting as they evolve throughout the project lifecycle. Techniques such as user story mapping sessions, backlog grooming, and sprint planning meetings are employed to foster this ongoing collaboration.

Setting the Stage for Iterative Development: The initial stage in an Agile project is not about setting in stone what needs to be done; instead, it's about establishing a flexible framework within which the project can evolve. This approach is deeply rooted in the Agile principles of embracing change and focusing on customer value, highlighted in both the PMBOK editions.

Iterative development is the heartbeat of Agile projects. By setting up a project initiation phase that accommodates change, teams are better prepared to respond to new information, stakeholder feedback, and evolving market conditions. This adaptability is what makes Agile particularly suitable for projects in dynamic environments where requirements, scope, and solutions may not be fully understood from the outset.

Continuous Stakeholder Feedback: Continuous stakeholder feedback is integrated from the very beginning, ensuring that the project delivers real value. This involves setting up mechanisms for regular communication and review, such as sprint reviews, demos, and retrospectives. These practices are not only about showing progress but also about soliciting feedback and incorporating it into future iterations of the project.

Conclusion: By initiating projects with an Agile mindset, project managers and teams lay the groundwork for a responsive, flexible, and stakeholder-centered project lifecycle. This approach aligns with the PMBOK Guide's shift towards more adaptive project management practices, recognizing the value of flexibility, stakeholder engagement, and continuous improvement.

Incorporating Agile practices from the outset ensures that projects are well-positioned to adapt to changes, meet stakeholder needs, and deliver value efficiently. As the project management field evolves, as reflected in the transition from the PMBOK 6th to the 7th edition, the integration of Agile principles from the initiation phase becomes increasingly essential for project success in today's fast-paced, ever-changing environment.

Planning with Agile - Agile planning is the backbone of successful Agile projects, emphasizing flexibility, iterative development, and continuous stakeholder engagement. Unlike traditional project management approaches, which may lay out a comprehensive plan upfront, Agile planning adapts to changes and evolves with the project.

Backlog Grooming and Sprint Planning: Backlog grooming, or refinement, is a collaborative effort to review, prioritize, and detail backlog items. For example, a software development team might review their backlog in a grooming session and decide to prioritize a new feature based on recent customer feedback, ensuring that they're always working on the most valuable tasks.

During sprint planning, the team might select items from the groomed backlog to develop over the next two weeks. For instance, they could choose to focus on user stories related to enhancing the checkout process of an e-commerce platform, clearly defining the sprint goal of improving user experience and conversion rates.

Estimating Work Using Story Points: In Agile planning, tasks are estimated using story points rather than hours, focusing on effort and complexity. For example, if a team estimates a login feature as 5 story points and a payment gateway integration as 13 story points, this reflects the relative complexity and effort involved, not the specific time it will take.

Adaptive Scheduling and Incremental Progress Explained: Adaptive scheduling allows the team to remain flexible and responsive. For instance, if midway through a sprint, a critical bug is found, the team can adjust their plan to fix this issue, ensuring the project stays on track and continues delivering value.

Incremental progress is made through regular sprint cycles, with each sprint resulting in a potentially shippable product increment. For example, after each two-week sprint, a tech startup might release a new set of features for their app, gradually building up to a full product launch.

Ensuring Continuous Alignment with Stakeholder Expectations: Continuous alignment with stakeholder expectations is crucial in Agile planning. For example, a marketing team using Agile methods might hold bi-weekly show-and-tell sessions with stakeholders to demo new campaign ideas and gather feedback, ensuring the project remains aligned with the company's strategic goals.

Fostering a Dynamic Project Environment Through Collaboration: A dynamic project environment is fostered through regular collaboration. For instance, a cross-functional project team might hold daily stand-up meetings to discuss progress and obstacles, promoting transparency and teamwork, and adapting the plan as needed based on these discussions.

Practical Application: Imagine a team developing a new mobile application. The project starts with a high-level vision: to create a user-friendly fitness tracking app. During backlog grooming, the team breaks down this vision into smaller, manageable pieces, such as "Implement a step-tracking feature" and "Design a user interface for meal tracking."

In sprint planning, they decide to focus on the step-tracking feature for the first sprint, estimating its complexity at 8 story points. They plan the sprint tasks, from designing the interface to coding the functionality. Throughout the sprint, they adapt their schedule to feedback from beta testers, ensuring that the final product aligns with user needs and expectations.

Conclusion: Incorporating Agile planning practices, such as backlog grooming, sprint planning, and adaptive scheduling, enables teams to navigate project uncertainties effectively. By providing practical examples, such as developing a new feature or adapting to user feedback, this section aims to equip project manager with a solid understanding of how Agile planning operates in real-world scenarios, preparing them for both the exam and practical application in their professional lives.

Executing with Agile - The Executing phase in Agile project management is pivotal for transforming plans into actionable tasks and delivering incremental value. This phase is characterized by high team collaboration, continuous integration, and the rapid delivery of product increments, aligning closely with Agile principles such as transparency, inspection, and adaptation.

Fostering Team Collaboration and Communication: In Agile environments, fostering team collaboration is essential. Implement daily stand-ups or Scrum meetings to encourage open communication and problem-solving. For example, a software development team might use daily stand-ups to address immediate issues affecting the sprint's progress, such as technical blockers or resource needs, ensuring the team remains on track and focused.

Practical Sprint Execution: Sprint execution is the heart of Agile delivery, where teams work on selected backlog items to create a potentially shippable product increment. For instance, a marketing team could execute a sprint dedicated to launching a new campaign, breaking down the campaign into smaller tasks such as content creation, design, and testing, delivering tangible results every two weeks.

Continuous Integration and Delivery: Implement continuous integration practices to ensure that changes are tested and integrated regularly. This could involve automatic build and test sequences each time a team member commits changes, allowing a tech team to detect and address issues early, reducing integration headaches and improving product quality.

Adaptability through Retrospectives and Feedback: Agile emphasizes adaptability and learning. After each sprint, conduct a retrospective to discuss what went well, what didn't, and how processes can be improved. For instance, if a team finds that tasks are consistently underestimated, they can explore new estimation techniques or adjust their planning approach for future sprints.

Practical Application: Consider an e-commerce website project where the team uses Agile execution. The team organizes work into two-week sprints, focusing on high-priority features such as shopping cart functionality and user profile creation. Daily stand-ups help the team stay aligned and address any impediments quickly. Continuous integration tools automate testing and deployment, ensuring that new features are reliably integrated and available for customer feedback. The team's adaptability is demonstrated when unexpected user feedback leads to a pivot in the shopping cart design, which is seamlessly integrated into the next sprint's workload.

Maintaining Project Momentum: Maintaining momentum in Agile projects requires a clear vision and effective backlog management. The product owner prioritizes the backlog items based on customer value and team feedback, ensuring that the team always works on the most impactful tasks. Regular reviews with stakeholders and the demonstration of working software ensure that the project remains aligned with business objectives and customer needs.

Challenges and Solutions in Agile Execution: Executing with Agile presents unique challenges such as managing changing priorities and ensuring team productivity. Address these by fostering a culture of open communication, encouraging team self-management, and maintaining a prioritized and well-groomed backlog. For example, if a team struggles with shifting priorities, implement a more rigorous backlog grooming session to clarify and reassess priorities before each sprint.

Conclusion: Executing with Agile is about more than just doing the work; it's about doing the right work at the right time and adapting to change swiftly and effectively. By focusing on collaboration, continuous delivery, and adaptability, teams can overcome challenges and deliver value consistently. This approach not only aligns with the Agile principles but also prepares candidates for real-world scenarios they may face in their PMP certification journey.

Monitoring and Controlling with Agile - The Monitoring and Controlling phase in Agile project management plays a critical role in ensuring that projects remain on track and aligned with client goals and business objectives. This phase diverges from traditional models by incorporating Agile metrics and visual tools, facilitating a more dynamic and responsive approach to project management.

Utilizing Agile Metrics and Visual Tools: Agile metrics, such as lead time, cycle time, velocity, and cumulative flow, provide teams with a quantitative basis to gauge their efficiency and productivity. For example, velocity, which measures the amount of work a team completes during a sprint, helps in forecasting future sprints and managing stakeholder expectations.

Visual tools like Kanban boards and burn charts offer clear, at-a-glance insights into project progress and workflow. A Kanban board, for instance, can help a team track the status of various tasks and identify bottlenecks in real-time, promoting swift adjustments. Similarly, a burn-down chart visualizes the remaining work versus time, enabling teams to gauge if they are on pace to complete the work in the sprint.

Regular Review Sessions for Continuous Improvement: Agile emphasizes regular review sessions, including sprint reviews and retrospectives, which are pivotal for assessing performance and implementing necessary adjustments. During sprint reviews, teams present completed work to stakeholders, facilitating direct feedback and collaborative decision-making. This practice ensures that the project remains aligned with client needs and expectations.

Retrospectives, on the other hand, focus on the team's working methods. They provide a structured way for teams to reflect on their processes, discuss what worked well and what didn't, and plan for improvements in the next cycle. By continually refining their practices, teams can enhance their efficiency and effectiveness over time.

Real-time Monitoring for Swift Response: Agile projects benefit from real-time monitoring, allowing teams to address issues as they arise. Tools like continuous integration and deployment pipelines facilitate this by automating the testing and integration of changes, ensuring that any defects are caught and addressed early. This capability, combined with regular stand-ups and the use of information radiators, ensures that the entire team has up-to-the-minute information on project status and can respond rapidly to changes.

Challenges in Agile Monitoring and Controlling: Teams may face challenges such as fluctuating stakeholder requirements or team dynamics that can impact the project's direction. Effective monitoring and controlling strategies involve maintaining open channels of communication and fostering a culture of transparency and accountability. For instance, if a team encounters unexpected external dependencies that impact their sprint goals, they should discuss these issues in their stand-up meetings and work collaboratively to find solutions, possibly adjusting their backlog or sprint tasks accordingly.

Engaging Stakeholders and Adapting to Change: Stakeholder engagement is integral to the Agile monitoring and controlling phase. Regular updates, combined with the iterative review and planning sessions, keep stakeholders informed and involved. This continuous engagement helps in managing expectations and ensures that the project adapts effectively to evolving requirements or market conditions.

Conclusion: In summary, monitoring and controlling with Agile is an ongoing, iterative process that emphasizes transparency, adaptation, and continuous improvement. By leveraging Agile metrics, visual tools, and regular review sessions, teams can maintain a clear understanding of their progress, address challenges proactively, and ensure that project outcomes meet stakeholder needs and expectations. This approach not only aligns with Agile principles but also adheres to the PMI's standards for project management excellence, providing a solid foundation for project manager aiming to apply these practices in their professional roles.

Closing with Agile - In the Agile framework, the Closing phase encapsulates more than just the end of a project; it represents a critical reflection point to encapsulate learning, celebrate successes, and integrate improvements for future initiatives. This phase is crucial for Agile teams to ensure that they are not just completing tasks, but also enhancing their processes and delivering real value to the organization.

Finalizing Project Activities: The Closing phase in Agile involves a comprehensive review of all project activities against the initial goals and objectives. This ensures that all deliverables are completed and meet the required quality standards. For instance, in a software development project, this could involve final user acceptance testing, documentation handover, and deployment activities. The project team should ensure that all artifacts are up to date and that there is clear documentation of the project outcomes.

Conducting Sprint Retrospectives: Sprint retrospectives are integral to the Agile Closing phase. Unlike traditional post-mortem analyses that occur at the end of the project, retrospectives happen at the end of each sprint, allowing teams to apply lessons learned in real-time. During these sessions, teams discuss what went well, what didn't, and how processes can be improved. This could involve revisiting the team's definition of done, examining the effectiveness of communication channels, or adjusting the workload for future sprints.

Capturing Lessons Learned: In Agile, capturing lessons learned is a continuous process but becomes more formalized during the Closing phase. This involves documenting insights gained throughout the project and sharing this knowledge across the organization. For example, a development team might create a knowledge base article detailing how they overcame specific technical challenges or a marketing team might document the results of A/B testing during a campaign.

Stakeholder Acceptance and Project Sign-off: Ensuring that all project deliverables are accepted by stakeholders is a critical component of the Closing phase. This includes formal sign-off on the final product and confirmation that all contractual obligations have been met. In Agile environments, this might mean conducting a final review meeting with stakeholders to demonstrate the completed work and gather feedback.

Project or Phase Formal Closure: Formally closing the project or a project phase involves several administrative tasks, such as releasing project resources, closing out contracts, and updating the organizational asset library with any new templates, processes, or learnings from the project. In Agile, this also means updating the backlog to reflect any remaining work and ensuring that any ongoing obligations are transferred to operational teams.

Ensuring Continuous Improvement: The hallmark of Agile is continuous improvement, not just at the end of the project but embedded throughout the entire lifecycle. The Closing phase should include planning for future projects based on the successes and challenges of the current project. This could involve updating the Agile playbook, refining estimation techniques, or enhancing collaboration tools.

Conclusion: The Closing phase in Agile is not an endpoint but a transition. It ensures that each project contributes to the larger organizational knowledge and that teams are better prepared for future challenges. By systematically reviewing outcomes, capturing lessons learned, and ensuring stakeholder satisfaction, Agile teams can close projects effectively while fostering an environment of continuous improvement and learning.

This detailed approach to the "Closing with Agile" phase aligns with PMBOK's emphasis on formal closing processes while also adhering to Agile's iterative learning and improvement cycles. By integrating these practices, project manager will be equipped with the knowledge to effectively close projects in an Agile environment, ensuring they deliver value and prepare for future success.

Exploring Agile and Hybrid Project Lifecycle Models

Agile Lifecycle Models - Agile lifecycle models such as Scrum, Kanban, and Extreme Programming (XP) offer diverse frameworks for managing projects with an emphasis on flexibility, customer collaboration, and responsiveness to change. Each model supports iterative development, allowing projects to adapt and evolve in response to customer needs and market dynamics.

Scrum:
- **Overview:** Scrum organizes work into sprints, typically lasting 2-4 weeks, with each sprint aiming to deliver a potentially shippable product increment.
- **Key Features:**
  - **Sprint Planning:** Defining what will be delivered in the sprint and how the work will be achieved.

- **Daily Stand-ups:** Short meetings to discuss progress, obstacles, and next steps.

  - **Sprint Review:** A meeting at the end of each sprint to review the work that was completed and not completed.

  - **Retrospective:** Reflecting on the past sprint to identify improvements for the next sprint.

- **Benefits:** Enhances team collaboration and enables quick adaptations to change.

Kanban:

- **Overview:** Kanban focuses on continuous delivery while maximizing workflow efficiency. It uses visual boards to manage work in progress (WIP) limits.

- **Key Features:**

  - **Visual Boards:** Boards that display task progress across different stages.

  - **WIP Limits:** Constraints on the number of tasks in each stage to prevent bottlenecks.

  - **Flow Management:** Continuous observation and optimization of the workflow.

- **Benefits:** Improves task management and efficiency, providing clear visibility into project progress.

Extreme Programming (XP):

- **Overview:** XP emphasizes high-quality software and the ability to adapt to changing customer requirements through rigorous engineering practices.

- **Key Practices:**

  - **Test-Driven Development:** Writing tests before code to ensure requirements are met.

  - **Pair Programming:** Two developers work together at one workstation, enhancing code quality and collaboration.

  - **Continuous Integration:** Regularly integrating and testing code changes to catch and fix errors early.

- **Benefits:** Increases software quality and responsiveness to customer feedback.

Comparative Analysis:

- Scrum is well-suited for projects that benefit from regular feedback and require frequent delivery of functional product increments.

- Kanban is ideal for projects with ongoing or unpredictable workflows, providing the flexibility to adjust priorities on the fly.

- XP focuses on software development projects where quality and responsiveness to changing customer requirements are critical.

Integrating Agile Models with PMBOK Principles: Agile lifecycle models align with PMBOK's emphasis on project delivery, stakeholder engagement, and continuous improvement. While PMBOK provides a broad framework for project management, Agile models offer specific practices that complement these principles, especially in dynamic and complex project environments.

Conclusion: Understanding and selecting the appropriate Agile lifecycle model is crucial for effective project management. By aligning project needs with the strengths of Scrum, Kanban, or XP, project managers can leverage Agile practices to deliver value efficiently, respond to change effectively, and meet customer expectations. This knowledge is essential for PMP candidates, as it prepares them for applying Agile methodologies within a PMBOK-guided project management framework.

Hybrid Lifecycle Models - Hybrid lifecycle models offer a comprehensive framework for project management, blending the methodical nature of traditional project management with the dynamic adaptability of Agile practices. Ideal for projects with a mix of fixed requirements and evolving elements, these models cater to a wide spectrum of industries, from IT to construction, enabling a tailored approach that meets specific project demands while maintaining the flexibility to adapt to unexpected changes.

Key Characteristics:

- **Structured Planning:** Initiates with a robust framework, defining the project's scope, deadlines, and expected outcomes. This phase mirrors the Waterfall approach, providing clear directives and a solid foundation for the entire project lifecycle.

- **Agile Adaptability:** After the initial setup, the project seamlessly transitions into Agile execution phases, utilizing sprints for incremental development and continuous improvement. This approach ensures ongoing adaptability to stakeholder feedback and evolving market conditions.

Detailed Implementation Steps:

1. **Initial Framework Development:** Start with traditional project management techniques to establish a detailed project plan, including risk assessments, budgeting, and resource allocation.

2. **Phase Integration:** Divide the project into smaller, more manageable segments, or phases, each with defined goals and deliverables. This structure allows for regular reassessment and realignment with project objectives.

3. **Agile Execution:** Implement Agile methodologies such as Scrum or Kanban during the execution phase, focusing on task prioritization, team collaboration, and frequent product iterations.

In-depth Benefits:

- **Risk Management:** Combines upfront analysis with ongoing reassessment, enabling proactive issue identification and resolution.

- **Client Satisfaction:** Facilitates a responsive approach to client needs, ensuring product relevance and stakeholder alignment.

- **Team Dynamics:** Encourages a collaborative environment where team members can innovate and address challenges effectively.

Addressing Challenges with Practical Solutions:

- **Cultural and Processual Resistance:** Mitigate through comprehensive training programs and clear communication of hybrid benefits.

- **Integration Complexity:** Simplify by clearly defining transition points between traditional and Agile phases, ensuring smooth workflow progression.

Practical Applications:

- **Software Development:** A software project may start with a Waterfall approach for requirements gathering and architecture design before transitioning to Agile sprints for coding, testing, and deployment, allowing for rapid adaptation to user feedback.

- **Construction Projects:** Initial project planning, permits, and foundational work follow a traditional approach, while interior design and client-specific modifications adopt Agile methodologies, accommodating changes without disrupting the overall timeline.

Comparative Analysis: Hybrid models provide a balanced solution, combining the predictability of Waterfall with the flexibility of Agile, making them suitable for projects with mixed requirements or those transitioning from traditional to modern project management approaches.

Best Practices for Implementation:

- **Clear Communication:** Ensure all stakeholders understand the hybrid approach and their roles within it.

- **Regular Reviews:** Conduct frequent evaluations to adjust strategies and processes, aligning with evolving project needs.

Conclusion: Hybrid lifecycle models represent a versatile and effective approach to managing diverse project requirements. By integrating structured planning with iterative development, these models enable project teams to deliver high-quality outcomes while adapting to changing needs and stakeholder feedback.

Choosing the Right Model - The decision-making process for selecting the right project lifecycle model is crucial and should be based on a deep analysis of the project's unique aspects. It involves understanding not just the technical requirements, but also the team dynamics, stakeholder expectations, and the market environment.

Detailed Criteria for Model Selection:

- **Project Complexity:** Examine if the project involves multiple departments, technologies, or cross-functional teams. Complex projects might benefit from Agile's flexibility, while straightforward projects might be better suited to predictive models.

- **Requirements Stability:** Determine how clear and stable the project requirements are. For projects with fixed requirements, like a bridge construction, a predictive model is suitable. Conversely, for a software development project where user needs might change, an Agile model is preferable.

- **Change Expectancy:** Assess the likelihood of changes during the project. In dynamic sectors like tech, Agile allows for rapid adaptation, whereas, in more regulated industries, a predictive approach might be required.

Examples:

- **Agile Example:** A tech startup developing a new app might use Agile to accommodate rapid market changes and user feedback, employing sprints to iteratively develop features based on user testing.

- **Predictive Example:** A government contractor building a public infrastructure project, with fixed requirements and tight regulatory standards, would likely opt for a predictive model to ensure compliance and predictability.

- **Hybrid Example:** An automotive company launching a new vehicle model might use a hybrid model, employing predictive methods for manufacturing due to safety and compliance, while using Agile for the software development and digital features, allowing for last-minute changes based on user feedback.

Practical Steps for Choosing the Right Model:

- Conduct a stakeholder analysis to understand their needs and expectations.

- Review the market environment and how it might affect project requirements.

- Evaluate your team's expertise and preferences in project management methodologies.

Conclusion: Choosing the correct lifecycle model is a strategic decision that affects not only the project's execution but also its final outcomes. By carefully assessing the project's needs and environment, project managers can select a model that best ensures the project's success.

Implementing Lifecycle Models - Implementing lifecycle models effectively is a comprehensive process that involves several key steps and considerations to ensure they align with both project objectives and organizational culture:

- **Initial Planning:** Start by defining the project's scope, identifying key deliverables, and setting measurable objectives aligned with organizational goals. For example, in a software development project, this could involve determining the software's required features, performance metrics, and deadline for market release.
- **Team and Stakeholder Buy-In:** Ensure all team members understand their roles and the reasons behind choosing a specific lifecycle model. In a construction project, this might involve explaining to stakeholders how a hybrid model can accommodate fixed regulatory milestones while allowing flexibility in design changes due to client feedback.
- **Training and Communication:** Conduct training sessions tailored to different team roles. In an Agile implementation, this could mean Scrum Master training for project leaders and Agile basics for other team members. Establish a regular communication schedule to discuss progress, updates, and address any concerns.
- **Flexibility and Continuous Improvement:** For Agile or hybrid models, set up regular sprint reviews and retrospectives to evaluate what's working and what's not. In a marketing campaign project, for example, review sessions could analyze the effectiveness of different strategies and adjust plans based on consumer feedback.

- **Monitoring and Adjusting Strategies:** Implement a dashboard to track progress against KPIs, such as sprint velocity or feature completion rate. If a tech project falls behind schedule, identify the bottlenecks and reallocate resources or adjust timelines accordingly.
- **Tailoring the Model:** Adjust the lifecycle model based on project feedback and outcomes. For instance, if a product development project starts with a Waterfall approach but needs more flexibility, it might shift to a hybrid model to incorporate more iterative testing phases.

Practical Implementation of Lifecycle Models - Here are some more detailed examples:

Example 1: Developing a New Mobile Application :

1. **Initial Planning:** The project starts with defining the app's core functionalities and target market based on market research and stakeholder input.

2. **Implementation:** The team adopts two-week sprints, focusing initially on creating a minimum viable product (MVP) that includes basic login and navigation features.

3. **Feedback and Adaptation:** After each sprint, user feedback is gathered through beta testing. The feedback leads to new features being prioritized in the backlog, such as enhanced security measures or a more intuitive user interface.

4. **Continuous Improvement:** Regular retrospectives help the team improve their workflow, addressing issues like communication gaps or sprint planning inefficiencies.

Example 2: Launching a New Product Line:

1. **Initial Planning:** The project begins with a predictive approach, setting clear milestones for product design, manufacturing, and launch date.

2. **Agile Integration:** Once initial designs are approved, the project transitions to Agile methodologies for marketing material development and website updates, allowing for iterative improvements based on market feedback.

3. **Stakeholder Collaboration:** Marketing and design teams collaborate closely, using Kanban boards to ensure transparency and timely updates.

4. **Adjustment and Delivery:** After a market analysis reveals a shift in consumer preferences, the project swiftly adapts, revising marketing strategies without affecting the launch timeline.

Example 3: Upgrading an IT Infrastructure:

1. **Initial Planning:** Starts with detailed assessments of current infrastructure, compliance requirements, and end-user needs.

2. **Phased Implementation:** The upgrade is broken down into phases – hardware replacement using predictive models, followed by Agile sprints for software integration and testing.

3. **Feedback Loops:** Regular feedback from IT staff and end-users after each sprint leads to adjustments in the rollout plan, ensuring minimal disruption and improved user satisfaction.

4. **Review and Adaptation:** Post-implementation reviews identify successes and areas for improvement, influencing future upgrades and projects.

Example 4: Product Development in a Tech Company Scenario: A tech company is developing a new mobile application that integrates with wearable technology to monitor health metrics. The project has some well-defined regulatory and privacy requirements but also needs to adapt to user feedback and evolving tech standards.

1. **Lifecycle Selection:** They choose a Hybrid model due to the fixed regulatory requirements and the need for iterative user feedback incorporation.

2. **Initial Planning:** They start with a Waterfall approach for compliance, security protocols, and core functionality based on well-defined health regulations.

3. **Agile Integration:** After setting the regulatory foundation, they switch to Agile sprints for developing user interface features, allowing them to adapt to user feedback from beta testing.

4. **Implementation and Monitoring:** They use Scrum for iterative development, with bi-weekly sprints, daily stand-ups for team coordination, and sprint reviews for stakeholder feedback. They use Kanban boards to track progress and manage tasks.

5. **Review and Adaptation:** Each sprint ends with a retrospective to refine processes and address any issues, ensuring continuous improvement.

Example 5: Infrastructure Project for a Municipal Government Scenario: A city government is upgrading its public transportation system. The project involves constructing new train lines (fixed requirements) and developing an app for ticket purchasing and real-time updates (evolving requirements).

1. **Lifecycle Selection:** A Hybrid model is selected to manage the fixed elements of construction while allowing flexibility for the app development.

2. **Initial Planning:** The construction component follows a predictive lifecycle model, with clear milestones for each construction phase.

3. **Agile Integration:** The app development follows an Agile model, with regular updates based on commuter feedback and technological advancements.

4. **Implementation and Monitoring:** The construction project uses traditional project management tools like Gantt charts for scheduling and progress tracking, while the app development team uses Scrum, with regular sprints and continuous integration for code updates.

5. **Review and Adaptation:** While the construction phases have scheduled reviews after major milestones, the app development includes sprint retrospectives and reviews to adapt to new requirements or feedback.

Conclusion: These examples illustrate how different lifecycle models can be applied to various project scenarios, emphasizing the importance of flexibility, stakeholder engagement, and continuous improvement. By understanding and applying these principles, project managers can navigate complex projects effectively, aligning with both Agile and traditional methodologies to meet and exceed project objectives and stakeholder expectations.

Role of the Project Manager

Responsibilities and Skills of a Project Manager

Core Responsibilities - A project manager's role is multifaceted, demanding a balance between leadership, technical skills, and communication to drive project success. Here's an in-depth look at their core responsibilities:

- **Defining Clear Project Objectives:** A project manager should initiate the project by setting clear, measurable, and achievable objectives. This involves understanding the business case, engaging with key stakeholders to align their expectations, and defining the scope precisely. For instance, if launching a new product, objectives might include market analysis, feature definition, and launch timelines.

- **Planning and Execution:** This includes creating a detailed project plan that outlines the tasks, schedules, resource allocations, and budget. The plan should cover all phases from initiation to closure, incorporating milestones and quality gates. An example would be delineating the phases of a construction project, from design to handover, including key deliverables for each phase.

- **Resource Management:** Involves the strategic allocation and management of resources such as personnel, finances, and materials. This could include negotiating with suppliers for cost-effective materials in a manufacturing project or optimizing team allocation in a software development project to meet sprint goals.

- **Communication:** Establishing a communication plan that details how information will be shared with stakeholders. For example, in a large-scale IT implementation, this might involve regular status reports to executives, daily stand-ups with the project team, and update meetings with end-users.

- **Monitoring Progress:** Regularly tracking the project against its baseline plan using tools like Earned Value Management (EVM) or dashboards. For example, in an IT project, this could involve weekly dashboard reviews to monitor sprint progress, budget expenditure, and scope changes.

- **Adjusting Strategies:** Being prepared to pivot project strategies based on feedback and project status. This could mean reallocating resources in response to a new client requirement or revising the project scope due to unforeseen challenges.

- **Maintaining Quality Standards:** Ensuring the project's outputs meet the required standards and stakeholder expectations. This could involve conducting regular quality reviews and implementing improvements in a software project to ensure that code meets performance criteria.

Essential Skills - The role of a project manager is crucial in navigating the complexities of any project. Success hinges on a combination of technical proficiency, leadership qualities, and interpersonal skills. This section delves into the essential skills required for effective project management, offering insights into how they can be applied to achieve project goals efficiently and effectively.

Leadership and Team Management: Effective leadership goes beyond just delegating tasks; it involves inspiring confidence, setting a vision, and building a sense of community. Project managers should exemplify integrity and empathy, creating an environment where team members feel valued and motivated. For instance, recognizing individual contributions in team meetings can boost morale and productivity, particularly during challenging project phases.

Effective Communication: This encompasses more than just regular updates; it's about ensuring mutual understanding and building trust. Techniques include using clear, concise language, tailoring messages to different audiences, and employing various communication channels to ensure information reaches everyone. Active listening, particularly during stakeholder meetings, ensures all concerns are addressed, fostering a culture of openness.

Problem-solving and Decision-making: Project managers face myriad challenges requiring swift and effective resolution. This involves a systematic approach: clearly defining the problem, gathering relevant information, evaluating options, and implementing solutions. For example, if facing budget overruns, a project manager might need to perform a cost-benefit analysis to decide on areas to cut costs without impacting project quality.

Integration of PMI's Talent Triangle® in Project Management: As a project manager, understanding and developing competencies in alignment with the PMI's Talent Triangle® is essential for both your professional growth and project success. The Talent Triangle® consists of three critical skill sets:

1. **Technical Project Management**: This area focuses on your knowledge of project management principles and practices. It's about applying the right techniques and methodologies to meet your project's specific needs. As you've seen in earlier sections, skills such as defining clear project objectives, planning and execution, and monitoring progress are all integral parts of this component.

2. **Leadership**: Leadership skills enable you to guide, motivate, and ensure the well-being of your project team. Effective leadership involves more than just directing tasks; it's about fostering an environment where team members are empowered and valued. We've discussed various aspects of this, including team management, effective communication, and problem-solving.

3. **Strategic and Business Management**: Understanding the larger business context of your projects is crucial. This skill set involves aligning project goals with the organization's strategic objectives, navigating company politics and cultures, and contributing to the bottom line. While we touch on these in different sections, it's important to view your project through the lens of business impact and strategic alignment.

Incorporating the Talent Triangle® into Your Role: To be a successful project manager in today's diverse and dynamic environment, you should aim to develop skills across all three areas of the Talent Triangle®.

Time Management and Organization: Mastery here involves prioritizing tasks, setting realistic deadlines, and avoiding procrastination. Utilizing project management tools can aid in visualizing schedules and dependencies, helping to keep the project on track. Effective time management also means knowing when to delegate and trusting team members with their tasks.

Risk Management: Identifying and mitigating risks before they become issues is crucial. This starts with a thorough risk assessment, involving team members to leverage their expertise, followed by developing strategies to address identified risks. Regularly reviewing and updating the risk management plan ensures that new risks are promptly addressed.

Adapting to Project Environments - Adapting to various project environments is a critical competency for project managers. This ability ensures project managers can effectively guide their teams, meet stakeholder expectations, and navigate through the complexities of different organizational cultures and project landscapes.

Understanding and Applying Project Management Methodologies: Project managers must be versed in various methodologies like Agile, Waterfall, Scrum, and Lean. Selection should align with the project's goals, team dynamics, and client requirements. For example, use Agile when project requirements are expected to evolve, and Waterfall when the project scope is clear and fixed.

Flexibility in Project Execution: Being flexible involves adjusting project plans, scopes, and methodologies in response to new insights or changes. This could mean shifting from a Waterfall approach to an Agile framework mid-project due to changing customer needs.

Navigating Organizational Cultures and Dynamics: Understanding the culture and dynamics of the organization and adapting management style accordingly is crucial. For instance, a project manager in a startup may adopt a more hands-on, collaborative approach compared to a more structured, hierarchical approach in a large corporation.

Leading Teams Through Change: Effective leadership involves guiding teams through the change process, ensuring they remain motivated and focused. This might include conducting regular team meetings to address concerns, providing training, and ensuring that team members understand how their work aligns with shifting project goals.

Managing Stakeholder Expectations: Maintain open communication with stakeholders to understand their expectations and how they might evolve. This could involve regular status updates and feedback sessions to keep stakeholders informed and engaged.

Case Study: Tech Startup Expansion Project

- **Background:** The project manager, Alex, at a rapidly growing tech startup, is tasked with spearheading the global expansion of their flagship software product. The startup aims to penetrate markets in Europe, Asia, and South America.
- **Challenge:** The team faced unforeseen challenges such as stringent data protection regulations in Europe, language barriers in South America, and significant competition in Asia. Moreover, coordinating tasks across time zones added to the complexity.
- **Action:** Alex strategically segmented the expansion into phases, starting with comprehensive market research to tailor the software features to each region's preferences and legal requirements. They adopted a hybrid Agile-Waterfall methodology, maintaining core development under Waterfall discipline while using Agile sprints for local customization based on real-time feedback. To enhance team cohesion and efficiency across different cultures and

time zones, Alex introduced cloud-based collaboration tools and scheduled overlapping work hours.
- **Outcome:** The targeted approach allowed the software to meet local regulations and user expectations successfully. The product launched sequentially in each market, accommodating feedback from each before moving to the next. This strategy not only ensured compliance and relevance but also built a strong user base and brand recognition in diverse markets.

This case study showcases how adaptability and strategic planning are essential in managing complex, multi-environment projects, providing practical insights for project managers facing similar global challenges.

Stakeholder Engagement - Stakeholder Engagement is a critical component in the landscape of project management, involving the identification and interaction with all parties influenced by the project. This process is fundamental, as it pertains to understanding the varying interests and levels of influence among the project's stakeholders. Effective engagement is crucial for gaining support, ensuring alignment, and fostering an environment of cooperation and mutual respect.

Identification and Analysis: The initial step involves identifying all stakeholders, from team members and customers to suppliers and regulatory bodies. Once identified, the project manager must analyze each stakeholder's influence, interest, and expectations regarding the project. Tools such as the Power/Interest Grid can be instrumental in this phase, helping categorize stakeholders to tailor engagement strategies effectively.

Engagement Strategies: Effective engagement strategies are tailored to the needs and influence levels of different stakeholders. This includes:

- **Regular and clear communication:** Keeping stakeholders informed through updates, meetings, and reports.

- **Inclusive decision-making:** Ensuring stakeholders have a voice in decisions that affect them.

- **Feedback integration:** Actively seeking and incorporating stakeholder feedback into the project's progression.

Practical Application: In practice, a project manager leading an IT system upgrade might engage differently with end-users who require training versus department heads concerned with budget and timelines. Regular workshops might be held for end-users, while executive briefings could be more appropriate for higher-level stakeholders.

Building Trust and Collaboration: Trust is the cornerstone of effective stakeholder engagement. Building trust involves consistent honesty, transparency, and follow-through on commitments. Collaboration is fostered through shared goals and mutual benefits, ensuring all parties feel vested in the project's success.

Monitoring and Adjusting Engagement Approaches: Ongoing monitoring of stakeholder engagement is necessary to adapt strategies as the project evolves. This could involve adjusting communication methods based on stakeholder feedback or re-evaluating stakeholder priorities as the project progresses.

Case Studies for Practical Understanding: Imagine a scenario where a project manager navigates stakeholder engagement in a multinational corporation's expansion project. They must balance the expectations of local government officials, international partners, and the internal team. By employing targeted communication strategies and fostering an inclusive environment, the project manager ensures alignment and compliance across different cultural and regulatory landscapes.

Conclusion: Successful stakeholder engagement is a dynamic and ongoing process that significantly influences project success. By understanding and addressing the diverse needs of stakeholders, project managers can ensure smoother project execution, higher satisfaction rates, and overall project success.

Continuous Learning and Development - In the ever-evolving field of project management, staying updated with the latest industry trends, methodologies, and best practices is not just beneficial; it's essential. Continuous Learning and Development (CLD) ensures that project managers remain at the forefront of their field, adapting to new challenges and leveraging innovative solutions for project success.

Importance of Continuous Learning: Continuous learning helps project managers stay ahead of industry trends, adapt to new methodologies, and implement best practices efficiently. This proactive approach to professional development ensures that project managers can meet the challenges of complex project landscapes and deliver value consistently.

Key Areas for Development:

1. **Industry Knowledge:** Understanding current trends, market conditions, and technological advancements. Regularly reviewing industry publications, attending webinars, and participating in professional forums can keep a project manager well-informed.

2. **Methodological Adaptability:** Staying current with methodologies such as Agile, Waterfall, Lean, and Six Sigma. Familiarity with multiple methodologies allows a project manager to apply the best approach tailored to the project's needs.

3. **Technical Skills:** Enhancing technical skills relevant to the projects managed, such as software tools for project management, data analysis, and team collaboration platforms.

4. **Leadership and Soft Skills:** Developing leadership qualities and soft skills such as communication, negotiation, and conflict resolution to lead diverse teams and manage stakeholder expectations effectively.

5. **Risk Management:** Keeping updated with the latest risk management strategies and learning how to apply them to foresee, mitigate, and manage risks in a project.

Learning Opportunities:

1. **Formal Education:** Pursuing higher education degrees or specialized courses in project management can provide a deep understanding of core principles and practices.

2. **Certifications:** Earning project management certifications, such as the PMP, CAPM, or Agile certifications, validates knowledge and skills, and often leads to increased recognition and career opportunities.

3. **Workshops and Seminars:** Participating in industry workshops and seminars offers practical insights and networking opportunities with peers and mentors.

4. **Online Learning Platforms:** Utilizing online platforms like Coursera, LinkedIn Learning, or PMI's own offerings can provide flexible, self-paced learning options tailored to specific interests or knowledge gaps.

5. **Professional Organizations:** Joining organizations like PMI provides access to a wealth of resources, including publications, case studies, and events that foster professional growth.

Implementing Learning into Practice:

1. **Knowledge Sharing:** Sharing insights and lessons learned with peers and team members enhances collective knowledge and fosters a culture of learning.

2. **Application of New Skills:** Actively applying new methodologies or tools on projects allows for practical understanding and refinement of skills.

3. **Feedback and Reflection:** Seeking feedback from peers, mentors, and stakeholders helps identify areas for improvement and refine approaches based on real-world outcomes.

Case Studies for Practical Understanding:

Case Study 1: Agile Methodology in Software Development

- **Background:** The project manager, Sarah, was tasked with leading a software development project aimed at creating a new customer relationship management (CRM) platform. The initial plan was to follow a traditional Waterfall model, but after initial reviews, it was clear that customer requirements were evolving rapidly.
- **Challenge:** The main challenge was the dynamic nature of the client's needs, requiring a flexible approach to accommodate ongoing changes without derailing the project timeline or budget.
- **Action:** Sarah decided to implement Agile methodologies, specifically Scrum, to better manage the project's fluid requirements. She organized the development team into sprints, focusing on delivering small, incremental updates to the client for feedback. Continuous Integration and Continuous Deployment (CI/CD) practices were introduced to automate the testing and deployment phases, enhancing efficiency and reducing errors. She held daily stand-up meetings to ensure team alignment and used retrospective meetings at the end of each sprint to reflect on what went well and what could be improved. Customer feedback was integrated into the development process, ensuring that the final product closely aligned with customer expectations.
- **Outcome:** The project was a success, with the final CRM platform exceeding client expectations. The Agile approach allowed the team to adapt to changes quickly and efficiently, while CI/CD practices reduced downtime and improved product quality. The project was completed within the allocated time and budget, demonstrating the effectiveness of continuous learning and adaptation.

Case Study 2: Risk Management in Construction

- **Background:** John, a seasoned project manager, was overseeing the construction of a new residential complex. The project was well-planned, but unexpected delays due to weather conditions and supply chain disruptions threatened to push the project over budget and past its deadline.

- **Challenge:** The primary issues were the unforeseen weather conditions that halted construction for weeks and supply chain disruptions that delayed material deliveries. These factors significantly impacted the project timeline and budget.
- **Action:** John implemented comprehensive risk management strategies, including revising the project schedule to account for weather-related delays and diversifying his supply chain to mitigate the risk of future disruptions. He conducted regular risk assessments to identify potential issues and developed contingency plans for each identified risk. He improved communication channels with stakeholders, providing regular updates on project status and the measures being taken to address the challenges. By applying the lessons learned from previous projects, John was able to anticipate potential problems and act proactively.
- **Outcome:** Despite the initial setbacks, the construction project was completed with only a minimal extension of the deadline and slightly over the original budget. John's proactive risk management strategies and effective stakeholder communication minimized the impact of the delays and ensured the project's success. This case study underscores the importance of continuous learning and the application of risk management principles in real-world scenarios.

Challenges and Solutions:

- **Challenge:** Finding time for learning amidst busy project schedules.
  - **Solution:** Setting aside dedicated time each week for professional development and integrating learning into daily routines.
- **Challenge:** Overwhelm with the vast amount of available information.
  - **Solution:** Focusing on specific learning goals and utilizing curated resources to target learning efficiently.
- **Challenge:** Applying theoretical knowledge to practical situations.
  - **Solution:** Engaging in practical projects, simulations, or case study analyses to apply and test new knowledge.

Conclusion: Continuous learning and development are fundamental for a project manager's success and career advancement. By embracing a culture of continuous improvement, project managers can enhance their skills, adapt to changes, and lead projects more effectively, thereby contributing to their professional growth and the success of their organizations.

Leadership and Management Techniques

Leadership Styles - Understanding and applying various leadership styles is critical for project managers to navigate diverse team dynamics and project environments effectively. Leadership styles such as transformational, servant, and authoritative have distinct impacts on team performance, project atmosphere, and overall success. An adept project manager tailors their leadership approach based on the project phase, team composition, and evolving challenges, ensuring efficient guidance through complex projects.

- **Transformational Leadership:** This style is characterized by the ability to inspire and motivate team growth. A transformational leader focuses on pushing team members beyond their comfort zones, encouraging innovation and creativity. For example, in a high-tech project, such a leader might encourage the team to explore cutting-edge technologies to solve existing problems, fostering an environment of learning and self-improvement.

- **Servant Leadership:** Servant leadership emphasizes the needs of the team above all. This leader ensures that team members have the resources, knowledge, and support they need to succeed. In a customer service project, a servant leader might spend significant time understanding team challenges in dealing with customers and then provide tailored training or tools to enhance service quality.
- **Authoritative Leadership:** The authoritative leader provides a clear vision and direction, setting clear objectives and benchmarks. This approach is particularly effective in projects with tight deadlines or those that have veered off course. For instance, in a construction project facing delays, an authoritative project manager might set new, clear milestones and closely monitor progress to get back on track.
- **Intercultural Leadership:** This style is essential in global project settings where team members come from diverse cultural backgrounds. Intercultural leadership emphasizes cultural sensitivity, openness, and adaptability. It involves understanding different cultural norms, communication styles, and work ethics to foster a respectful and productive project environment. For instance, when managing a multicultural team, a project manager needs to tailor communication methods to avoid misunderstandings and ensure all team members feel valued and understood.
- **Digital Leadership:** In today's technology-driven projects, digital leadership is becoming increasingly important. This style focuses on leveraging digital tools and platforms to enhance team collaboration, project tracking, and stakeholder engagement. A digital leader is adept at using project management software, virtual communication tools, and data analytics to streamline project processes and facilitate remote work. For example, a project manager might use a combination of Slack for team communication, Trello for task tracking, and Zoom for virtual meetings to manage a software development project with remote team members.

Adapting Leadership Styles: Effective project managers understand that no single leadership style suits all situations. They adapt their approach based on the unique needs of each project and its team members. For example, a project manager might employ a servant leadership style during the initial stages of team formation to build trust and rapport, switch to transformational leadership to motivate the team during the execution phase, and adopt an authoritative stance to steer the team back on course during times of crisis.

Case Studies for Practical Understanding:

Software Development Project: Agile Methodology Application

Background: In a rapidly evolving tech environment, the project manager, Alex, was assigned to lead a critical software development project aimed at creating an innovative financial analytics platform. The initial strategy was to follow a conventional approach, but it was quickly realized that the dynamic market demands a more adaptable methodology.

Challenge: The project faced numerous challenges, including fluctuating customer requirements, tight deadlines, and a high expectation for product innovation and quality. The traditional approach was proving to be rigid and unable to accommodate the fast-paced changes required by the project.

Action:

1. **Agile Implementation**: Alex decided to pivot to an Agile framework, specifically Scrum, to enhance flexibility and responsiveness. The project was divided into two-week sprints, allowing for rapid iterations and adjustments based on ongoing client feedback.

2. **Continuous Integration/Continuous Deployment (CI/CD)**: Alex integrated CI/CD pipelines to automate build and deployment processes, significantly reducing manual errors and deployment times.

3. **Team Empowerment**: Empowering the development team, Alex encouraged ownership of tasks and fostered an environment of open communication and collaboration, ensuring that team members could contribute their best.

4. **Client Engagement**: Regular sprint reviews with stakeholders were instituted to gather feedback and ensure the product met evolving needs and expectations.

Outcome: The project successfully launched the financial analytics platform ahead of schedule. The Agile approach facilitated quick adaptation to changes, while CI/CD practices minimized downtime and improved quality. The project not only met but exceeded stakeholder expectations, demonstrating the value of flexibility and team collaboration.

Construction Project: Effective Risk Management

Background: The project manager, Jordan, oversaw the construction of a new commercial center. While the project was meticulously planned, unexpected challenges such as supply chain disruptions and unforeseen regulatory changes threatened its timeline and budget.

Challenge: The main hurdles included severe weather conditions delaying construction and supply chain issues leading to material shortages. These external factors risked significant project delays and cost overruns.

Action:

1. **Risk Assessment and Mitigation**: Jordan conducted a comprehensive risk assessment, identifying potential risks and devising mitigation strategies for each identified risk.

2. **Supply Chain Diversification**: To combat material shortages, Jordan diversified suppliers and procured critical materials in advance.

3. **Stakeholder Communication**: Jordan maintained transparent communication with all stakeholders, updating them on risks, mitigation measures, and project status, building trust and managing expectations.

4. **Adaptive Scheduling**: Adjustments to the project timeline were made to accommodate delays without compromising quality, including reallocating resources and adjusting work sequences.

Outcome: Despite initial challenges, the commercial center was completed with minimal delays and slight budget increases. Jordan's proactive risk management and adaptability ensured the project's success, highlighting the importance of preparedness and strategic planning in construction projects.

Software Development Project - Agile Methodology Application:

- **Background**: Project manager Alex leads a software development project aimed at creating an innovative financial analytics platform. Initially planned with a conventional approach, the project pivots to Agile due to dynamic market demands.

- **Actions**:

  1. Transition to Scrum: Implementing two-week sprints for better adaptability.

  2. CI/CD Practices: Automating build and deployment to enhance efficiency.

  3. Team Empowerment: Encouraging ownership and open communication.

  4. Stakeholder Engagement: Regular reviews to align product with user needs.

- **Outcome**: Successful launch of the platform, demonstrating the effectiveness of Agile practices and continuous integration in responding to changing requirements.

Construction Project - Effective Risk Management:

- **Background**: Jordan manages the construction of a new commercial center, facing unexpected challenges like supply chain disruptions and regulatory changes.

- **Actions**:

  1. Comprehensive Risk Assessment: Identifying and strategizing against potential risks.

  2. Diversifying Suppliers: Mitigating material shortage risks.

  3. Transparent Stakeholder Communication: Keeping all parties informed and engaged.

  4. Adaptive Scheduling: Reallocating resources to maintain project timelines.

- **Outcome**: The project is completed with minimal delays, underscoring the value of proactive risk management and adaptive planning.

Challenges and Solutions:

Challenge 1: Integrating Continuous Learning into Busy Schedules

- **Solution**: Implement structured learning sessions into the project timeline and encourage team members to set aside specific times for professional development. Utilize downtime or slow periods for educational workshops or online courses.

Challenge 2: Overcoming Information Overload

- **Solution**: Focus on targeted learning objectives aligned with project needs or personal development goals. Utilize curated educational resources and platforms to streamline learning materials and avoid unnecessary information.

Challenge 3: Translating Theory into Practice

- **Solution**: Engage in simulation exercises, real-world application projects, or shadowing opportunities within the organization. Encourage team members to apply new concepts in controlled environments before full-scale implementation.

Challenge 4: Adapting Leadership Styles to Project Needs:

- **Solution**: Continuously assess team dynamics and project phase to select the most effective leadership approach. For example, starting with servant leadership to build trust, moving to transformational leadership to inspire innovation during peak phases, and adopting authoritative leadership to steer the project back on course during challenges.

Challenge 5: Integrating Contemporary Leadership Approaches:

- **Solution**: Stay informed about the latest trends and technologies influencing project management. Engage in professional development courses focused on digital and intercultural leadership competencies to enhance the ability to manage diverse and distributed teams effectively.

Conclusion: The ability to adapt leadership styles to the needs of the project and the team is a hallmark of effective project management. By understanding the strengths and applications of each leadership style, project managers can guide their teams through the complexities of modern projects, ensuring success and fostering a culture of continuous growth and development.

Team Building - Team building is a cornerstone of successful project management, transcending mere group formation to forge a unit marked by trust, open communication, and mutual respect. Effective team building transforms a collection of individuals into a cohesive unit with a shared vision, enhancing project productivity, morale, and outcomes.

Creating Unity and Trust: Unity and trust form the bedrock of high-functioning teams. Establishing these elements begins with clear, transparent communication of goals and roles, ensuring every team member understands their contribution to the larger mission. Integrative activities, such as problem-solving workshops or team retreats, can cement these relationships, turning disparate individuals into a unified force.

Communication and Collaboration: Frequent and open communication is essential. Structured interactions, like regular team meetings or daily stand-ups, provide forums for transparent dialogue and collective problem-solving. Leveraging collaboration tools ensures continuous alignment and fosters a culture of inclusivity and mutual respect.

Mutual Respect and Inclusivity: Respect and inclusivity ensure all team members feel valued and heard, fostering an environment where diverse ideas can flourish. Techniques to promote this include equitable opportunity for input and leadership, and recognizing the varied backgrounds and skills each member brings to the table.

Detailed Techniques for Effective Team Building:

- **Regular Team Meetings:** Facilitate consistent discussions to review progress, surface issues, and celebrate wins, reinforcing a culture of openness and collective accountability.

- **Team-Building Exercises:** Engage in activities that bolster teamwork and trust, such as collaborative problem-solving challenges or skills-sharing sessions, tailored to the project's context.

- **Clear Role Definitions:** Clarify each person's responsibilities and how they interlock with the broader project goals, enhancing clarity and efficiency.

- **Recognition and Rewards:** Publicly acknowledge achievements, whether through formal rewards or simple acknowledgments, to motivate continued effort and commitment.

Case Studies for Practical Understanding:

- **Software Development Project:** Jordan, overseeing a multicultural software team, faced communication hurdles and siloed operations. By instituting weekly collaborative review sessions and integrating team-building activities relevant to project milestones, Jordan fostered a sense of shared purpose. The result was a series of innovative, user-centered software solutions developed on schedule.

- **Construction Project:** Alex managed a construction team hindered by low morale and segmented operations. Implementing daily cross-disciplinary briefings and pairing experienced workers with novices for specific tasks, Alex cultivated a mentorship culture and operational unity. This approach led to the project overcoming initial setbacks and meeting critical deadlines.

Challenges and Solutions in Team Building:

- **Diverse Personalities and Work Styles:** Address conflicts arising from diverse team dynamics by employing personality assessments and adapting leadership approaches to complement varying styles.

- **Remote Team Dynamics:** Combat the challenges of remote work by utilizing digital tools for collaboration and maintaining regular virtual social interactions to strengthen team bonds.

In conclusion, effective team building is an ongoing process that requires a nuanced understanding of human dynamics and a commitment to fostering a supportive, collaborative environment. By applying these principles and learning from real-life case studies, project managers can lead their teams to achieve remarkable project success.

Effective Communication - Effective communication is a cornerstone skill for project managers, ensuring clarity, alignment, and engagement among all project participants, from team members to stakeholders. This essential skill covers a wide array of activities and practices crucial for the successful navigation and leadership of projects.

Understanding Communication Needs: The first step in effective communication is understanding the diverse needs of the project's audience. This involves assessing the information requirements of all stakeholders, determining the appropriate level of detail, and choosing the optimal frequency of updates. A project manager must be adept at gauging the unique communication styles and preferences of team members and stakeholders to ensure information is received and processed effectively.

Articulating Project Goals and Expectations: Clearly outlining the project's objectives, roles, and expectations is vital. This clarity begins with the project charter and continues through the initiation, planning, execution, monitoring, and closing phases. For instance, when starting a new phase in a software development project, the project manager should reiterate the overarching goals, how each team member's work contributes to these objectives, and any modifications to roles or expectations since the project's inception.

Active Listening and Feedback Integration: Effective communication is not solely about transmitting information but also about listening. Active listening involves giving full attention to the speaker, understanding their message, responding thoughtfully, and remembering the information. This practice helps in uncovering hidden issues, mitigating misunderstandings, and building trust. During stakeholder meetings or team check-ins, a project manager should encourage open dialogue, ask probing questions, and provide constructive feedback.

Utilizing Various Communication Channels: A project manager must adeptly use different communication mediums—emails, meetings, reports, dashboards—to reach and engage the project's audience. For instance, while email may be suitable for quick updates or confirming decisions, complex issues may require face-to-face meetings or video conferences. Additionally, leveraging project management tools that offer dashboards and real-time updates can enhance transparency and keep stakeholders informed.

Tailoring Messages to Different Audiences: Messages should be customized for different groups. Technical details that are crucial for the development team might not be necessary for the marketing department or external stakeholders. For example, when explaining a delay in project timelines, the project manager might discuss specific technical setbacks with the development team while providing a high-level overview to the client, focusing on the impact on delivery dates and next steps.

Navigating Project Challenges Through Communication: Effective communication is particularly crucial when facing project challenges. Whether addressing scope creep, resolving conflicts, or managing stakeholder expectations, a project manager's ability to communicate clearly and persuasively can significantly impact the project's trajectory and outcome. By maintaining open lines of communication, the project manager can facilitate problem-solving, foster collaboration, and ensure that all parties are aligned with the project's revised objectives and plans.

Fostering a Positive Project Environment: Beyond facilitating information exchange, effective communication contributes to a positive project environment. It helps in building and maintaining relationships, encouraging collaboration, and creating a culture of openness and mutual respect. Recognizing individual and team achievements, addressing issues constructively, and promoting inclusivity can bolster team morale and productivity.

In practice, consider a scenario where a project manager is leading a cross-functional team in launching a new product. They would need to communicate technical requirements and progress updates to the development team, market analysis and branding strategies to the marketing department, and overall project status to company executives and external stakeholders. Tailoring each message to suit the audience's interests and knowledge ensures that all parties remain informed, engaged, and aligned with the project goals.

Effective communication underpins every aspect of project management and is instrumental in navigating the complexities of modern projects. It requires continuous refinement and attention to ensure all project participants are engaged, informed, and motivated towards achieving project success.

Decision Making - Decision-making is an indispensable skill for project managers, standing at the heart of project management. This complex process involves a comprehensive analysis of information, careful consideration of various alternatives, and the selection of the most suitable course of action to steer the project towards its strategic goals. Effective decision-making synthesizes intuition, analytical reasoning, and collaborative input from stakeholders, ensuring that every choice advances the project's objectives while mitigating risks and addressing the concerns and needs of all parties involved.

Key Components of Effective Decision-Making:

- **Analytical Thinking:** Involves breaking down complex problems into smaller, manageable parts to understand the underlying issues. This includes leveraging tools like SWOT (Strengths, Weaknesses, Opportunities, Threats) analysis and Root Cause Analysis to gain insights into the project's challenges and opportunities.
- **Intuition:** Sometimes, project managers must rely on their gut feelings, especially when under time constraints or when dealing with incomplete information. This intuition is often built upon years of experience and deep understanding of the project's domain.
- **Stakeholder Consultation:** Engaging with stakeholders to gather diverse perspectives, understand their interests and concerns, and incorporate their feedback into the decision-making process. This can enhance buy-in and support for the project's direction.
- **Information Gathering:** Collecting relevant data and insights to inform the decision. This could involve market research, historical data analysis, or feedback from past projects.
- **Option Evaluation:** Weighing the pros and cons of each alternative, often using techniques like cost-benefit analysis, risk assessment, and scenario planning to predict the outcomes of different choices.

Techniques for Informed Decision-Making:

- **Cost-Benefit Analysis:** Comparing the expected costs and benefits of various options to identify the one that offers the greatest advantage.
- **Risk Assessment:** Evaluating the potential risks associated with each decision and determining the likelihood and impact of adverse events.
- **Consensus-Building:** Facilitating discussions among team members and stakeholders to reach a mutual agreement on the best path forward.
- **Multicriteria Decision Analysis (MCDA):** Using a structured approach to assess and compare the relative importance of different criteria in the decision-making process.

Case Studies for Practical Understanding:

- **Software Development Project:** A project manager faced with choosing between two software development frameworks might conduct a cost-benefit analysis, consult with the development team and stakeholders, and consider the long-term maintenance and scalability before making a decision.
- **Infrastructure Project:** In deciding whether to proceed with construction during adverse weather conditions, a project manager would assess risks, consult with engineers and safety experts, and consider deadlines and costs to make a well-informed decision.

Challenges and Solutions in Decision-Making:

- **Challenge:** Overcoming analysis paralysis due to excessive information or fear of making the wrong decision.

- **Solution:** Setting clear decision-making criteria and deadlines to streamline the process and enhance decisiveness.
- **Challenge:** Managing conflicting stakeholder interests and expectations.
- **Solution:** Engaging in transparent communication and negotiation to find a compromise that aligns with the project's goals.

Conclusion: The ability to make well-considered, timely decisions is crucial for the success of any project. By balancing analytical skills, intuition, stakeholder input, and strategic evaluation of options, project managers can navigate complexities and lead their teams toward achieving project objectives, thereby ensuring the project's overall success and maintaining team confidence and stakeholder satisfaction.

Time Management - Time management is an essential skill for project managers, enabling them to steer complex projects efficiently. It encompasses the strategic allocation of time to tasks, balancing priorities, and ensuring that project milestones are met within stipulated deadlines. This skill set requires not just planning and scheduling but also the foresight to anticipate potential hurdles and the flexibility to adapt as projects evolve.

Core Components of Effective Time Management:

1. **Task Prioritization:**

   - Techniques like the Eisenhower Matrix help categorize tasks into urgent/important matrices, guiding project managers on where to focus their efforts first.

   - The MoSCoW method (Must have, Should have, Could have, Won't have) further aids in identifying tasks critical to project success versus nice-to-haves.

2. **Deadline Setting:**

   - Involves realistic timeline creation, factoring in the scope of work, resource availability, and potential external influences.

   - Balances project needs with client and stakeholder expectations, ensuring commitments are achievable and aligned with project goals.

3. **Schedule Development:**

   - Utilizes tools like Gantt charts for a visual representation of the project timeline, showing task durations, dependencies, and milestones.

   - Techniques such as the Critical Path Method (CPM) and Program Evaluation and Review Technique (PERT) help identify the sequence of crucial and time-sensitive tasks.

4. **Flexibility:**

   - Building in buffers for unforeseen delays ensures the project remains on track despite challenges.

   - Adapting schedules as needed while keeping the overall project objectives in focus.

5. **Resource Allocation:**

- Matches tasks with team members' skills and availability, optimizing individual and collective time utilization.
- Employs resource leveling and smoothing to maintain a steady workflow without overburdening team members.

Strategies for Implementing Effective Time Management:

- **Daily Planning:** Each day should start with a review of priorities and scheduled tasks, aligning daily actions with broader project goals.
- **Time Auditing:** Regularly compare actual time spent on tasks against planned durations to identify discrepancies and areas for improvement.
- **Delegation:** Effective task delegation leverages team strengths and balances workloads, contributing to overall time efficiency.
- **Regular Reviews:** Hold consistent review sessions to assess project progress, reevaluate priorities, and update schedules as necessary.

Challenges and Solutions in Time Management:

- **Overcommitment:** Avoid by setting realistic deadlines, communicating transparently with stakeholders, and prioritizing tasks strategically.
- **Procrastination:** Tackle by breaking tasks into smaller, more manageable segments, establishing mini-deadlines, and incentivizing milestone achievements.
- **Interruptions:** Minimize distractions by setting clear focus times, educating the team on the importance of these periods, and using visual indicators to signal availability.

Case Studies for Practical Understanding:

1. **Software Development Project:**
   - **Scenario:** Managing a complex software development project, broken into two-week sprints with clear objectives and deliverables.
   - **Action:** Implemented time-boxed sprints to ensure focused effort and regular progress evaluations, adapting task priorities based on evolving client feedback and technical discoveries.
   - **Outcome:** Completed on time, with prioritization ensuring critical features were developed first, demonstrating the successful application of Agile methodologies to manage time effectively.

2. **Event Planning Project:**
   - **Scenario:** Orchestrating a large-scale corporate event with numerous stakeholders and fixed event dates.
   - **Action:** Utilized a detailed Gantt chart for scheduling, assigned tasks based on team expertise, and established routine checkpoints for status updates.

- **Outcome:** The event proceeded smoothly, with all key components ready on schedule, illustrating the value of meticulous planning and continuous oversight in time management.

Conclusion: Effective time management enables project managers to align project activities with expected outcomes, ensuring timely completion and overall project success. By mastering these techniques and adapting to project dynamics, managers can lead their teams to deliver exceptional results while maintaining high morale and productivity.

Risk Management Leadership - In the realm of project management, effective risk management leadership is not just a role but a strategic competency that guides teams to proactively identify, assess, and mitigate project risks. This leadership role transcends traditional management by instilling a proactive and risk-aware culture among team members. Here, we delve into the multifaceted aspects of risk management leadership, integrating principles from PMBOK's sixth and seventh editions to equip PMP candidates with the knowledge to navigate project uncertainties successfully.

Cultivating a Risk-Aware Culture: Risk Management Leadership starts with creating an environment where risks are not feared but are identified, communicated, and addressed openly. This involves:

- Educating the team about the importance of risk management and its impact on project success.

- Encouraging open discussions about potential risks in team meetings.

- Rewarding team members who identify and propose solutions to potential risks.

Strategies for Anticipating Potential Issues: Effective risk management leaders employ various strategies to foresee and prepare for potential issues, such as:

- Conducting regular risk assessment meetings to identify new risks and reassess existing ones.

- Utilizing tools like SWOT analysis (Strengths, Weaknesses, Opportunities, Threats) and PESTLE analysis (Political, Economic, Social, Technological, Legal, Environmental) to evaluate external factors impacting the project.

- Implementing a risk early warning system, using project management software or dashboards to monitor risk triggers.

Implementing Risk Response Plans: A key responsibility is developing and executing risk response plans. This includes:

- Prioritizing risks based on their potential impact and likelihood.

- Developing action plans for both negative risks (threats) and positive risks (opportunities).

- Assigning risk owners and setting deadlines for risk response actions.

Ensuring Team Preparedness: Leadership in risk management also means ensuring that the team is ready to handle challenges as they arise. This involves:

- Providing training and resources needed to address identified risks.

- Conducting simulation exercises or scenario planning to prepare the team for different risk outcomes.
- Regularly reviewing and updating risk response strategies based on project progress and changing circumstances.

Fostering Resilience and Confidence: By leading effectively in risk management, leaders foster resilience within their teams, enabling them to handle uncertainties with confidence. This includes:

- Maintaining a positive attitude towards risk and encouraging the team to view challenges as opportunities for growth.
- Sharing lessons learned from past projects to improve future risk response strategies.
- Ensuring transparent communication with all stakeholders about risk status and response measures.

Case Studies for Practical Understanding:

1. **Software Development Project:**
   - **Scenario:** A project manager leads a software development project aimed at launching a new application. Midway through, new data privacy regulations threaten to delay the project.
   - **Action:** The project manager had proactively established a risk management plan that included monitoring regulatory changes. Upon identifying the risk, the team was quickly mobilized to adapt the application features to comply with new regulations, minimizing delays.

2. **Construction Project:**
   - **Scenario:** In a high-rise construction project, the project manager faces the risk of unexpected geological issues that could impede foundation work.
   - **Action:** Through early risk assessments, the project manager had prepared alternative construction methods and sourced multiple suppliers. When the geological issues were encountered, the team was able to switch methods swiftly, avoiding significant project delays.

Challenges and Solutions:

- **Challenge:** Integrating risk management practices into daily project activities can be difficult due to resistance from team members unfamiliar with proactive risk approaches.
- **Solution:** Implement regular risk management training and integrate risk discussions into routine project meetings to foster familiarity and acceptance.

By mastering risk management leadership, project managers can steer their projects through the complexities of today's dynamic project environments, ensuring that risks are managed effectively and project objectives are achieved. This comprehensive approach not only mitigates potential pitfalls but also enhances the project manager's ability to lead teams confidently through uncertain terrains.

Project Management Tools and Techniques

Essential Tools for Project Planning, Execution, Monitoring, and Control

Project Planning Tools - Project planning tools are fundamental components in the project management process, offering a structured approach to organizing, implementing, and monitoring project activities. These tools vary from traditional manual methods to advanced digital solutions, enabling project managers to define scope, schedule tasks, allocate resources, and manage budgets effectively.

Scope of Tools:

1. **Gantt Charts:** Offer visual timelines for project activities, highlighting task durations, dependencies, and critical paths. For instance, a Gantt chart could depict the timeline from the initial design phase to the final delivery in a software development project, enabling the team to track progress against set milestones.

2. **PERT Diagrams:** Focus on task relationships and duration estimation, using optimistic, pessimistic, and most likely time frames to calculate average task durations. A PERT diagram could be used in a construction project to estimate time required for each phase, considering uncertainties.

3. **Resource Allocation Graphs:** These help in visualizing resource utilization over time, ensuring that resources like personnel, equipment, and materials are optimally employed and not overextended.

4. **Budget Management Tools:** Essential for tracking project expenses against the allocated budget, these tools help in forecasting costs, monitoring actual spend, and managing financial resources efficiently.

Integration with Modern Software: Contemporary project management software integrates these tools into a unified platform, enhancing collaboration and communication. Features typically include interactive Gantt charts, real-time updates, cloud-based file sharing, and automated reporting. For example, platforms like Microsoft Project, Asana, or Trello allow project managers to create dynamic project plans, assign tasks, set deadlines, and update stakeholders with real-time progress.

Application in Project Planning:

1. **Defining Project Scope and Objectives:** Utilizing tools like mind maps or WBS (Work Breakdown Structure) software to break down project goals into manageable tasks and deliverables.

2. **Scheduling and Time Management:** Employing Gantt charts and calendars to outline project timelines, set milestones, and identify critical paths.

3. **Resource Planning and Allocation:** Using software features to assign tasks based on team members' skills and availability, ensuring balanced workload distribution.

4. **Budgeting and Cost Estimation:** Leveraging budget management functionalities to estimate costs, track expenses, and control overruns.

5. **Risk Assessment:** Conducting risk analysis using built-in templates and databases to identify potential project risks and develop mitigation strategies.

Case Studies for Practical Understanding:

1. **Software Development Project:**

   - **Background:** A project manager, Sara, was leading a software development team to deliver a new mobile application within six months. Midway, user testing feedback indicated that several features did not meet user expectations.

   - **Action:** Sara quickly convened her team to review the feedback and used an Agile approach to prioritize changes. She implemented continuous integration and continuous deployment (CI/CD) practices to streamline updates and improve product quality.

   - **Outcome:** The application was successfully updated with new features in iterative cycles, leading to improved user satisfaction and on-time project completion.

2. **Construction Project:**

   - **Background:** Tom, a project manager, was overseeing the construction of a new office complex. Unexpected geological issues led to significant delays and budget overruns.

   - **Action:** Tom conducted a risk reassessment, engaged with new geotechnical experts, and revised the project plan to include mitigative actions. He also communicated transparently with stakeholders about the issues and adjustments.

   - **Outcome:** Despite initial setbacks, the project was completed with an extended timeline but within the revised budget, maintaining stakeholder trust and meeting quality standards.

Challenges and Solutions:

1. **Resource Allocation:**

   - **Challenge:** In a marketing project, the team faced resource shortages as key team members were overallocated across multiple projects.

   - **Solution:** The project manager, Lisa, used resource leveling techniques and negotiated with other department heads to reallocate priorities and resources, ensuring her project remained on track without compromising other projects.

2. **Stakeholder Engagement:**

   - **Challenge:** During an IT infrastructure upgrade, stakeholder interests conflicted, leading to disagreements on project priorities.

   - **Solution:** The project manager, Alex, organized a series of workshops with all stakeholders to map out interests and align them with project goals, resulting in a compromise that satisfied all parties and kept the project aligned with business objectives.

Conclusion: Project planning tools are indispensable in navigating the complexities of modern projects. By leveraging these tools, project managers can ensure structured planning, transparent communication, and effective control, ultimately leading to successful project outcomes and alignment with stakeholder expectations.

Execution Tools - Execution tools are crucial in the project management lifecycle for turning strategic plans into tangible results. They encompass a broad spectrum of applications and platforms, each designed to enhance different aspects of project execution:

Task Management Systems: Task management systems are foundational tools that help break down the project scope into manageable actions. They serve as the backbone for:

- **Task Allocation:** Assigning specific tasks to team members based on their skills and workload.

- **Progress Tracking:** Monitoring the status of tasks to ensure they are progressing as planned.

- **Priority Setting:** Identifying high-priority tasks to ensure critical path activities are completed on time.

- **Integration:** Combining with other tools like email and calendar systems for comprehensive task scheduling.

Example: In a complex engineering project, a task management system can distribute detailed tasks, such as design validation and component testing, ensuring that each task is tracked from inception to completion.

Collaboration Platforms: Collaboration platforms address the communication needs of diverse teams, especially in distributed or remote settings. They enhance project execution through:

- **Unified Communication:** Streamlining discussions via chat and video calls to ensure all team members can collaborate effectively.

- **Document Management:** Offering a central repository for project documents, allowing for version control and real-time updates.

- **Accessibility:** Facilitating team access to information and resources anytime, anywhere.

Example: In a global marketing project, a collaboration platform can enable team members from different continents to co-create campaign materials, provide instant feedback, and hold virtual brainstorming sessions.

Agile Project Management Tools: Agile project management tools are tailored for projects that embrace flexibility and iterative development, such as software or product innovation projects. They support:

- **Sprint Planning:** Organizing work into sprints to focus on quick, iterative releases.

- **Backlog Management:** Prioritizing and refining the list of upcoming features or changes.

- **Performance Metrics:** Tracking team velocity and sprint burndown to gauge productivity and pace.

Example: For a mobile application development project, Agile tools can facilitate sprint planning meetings, allow the team to vote on feature priorities, and provide dashboards to monitor sprint progress against goals.

Integrating Execution Tools with Project Goals: Successfully integrating execution tools into project management requires:

- **Goal Alignment:** Ensuring that the use of each tool is directly tied to achieving specific project objectives.

- **Customization and Configuration:** Tailoring tools to fit the project environment and team preferences, enhancing usability and adoption.

- **Training and Support:** Providing comprehensive training sessions and resources to help the team understand and leverage the tools effectively.

Conclusion: The strategic use of execution tools can significantly enhance project efficiency and effectiveness. By carefully selecting and integrating these tools into the project workflow, project managers can ensure that their teams are well-equipped to meet project objectives, adapt to changes, and deliver successful outcomes.

Monitoring Tools - Monitoring tools are indispensable in the realm of project management, offering a comprehensive overview and real-time tracking of a project's progress and performance. These tools are designed to assist project managers in maintaining control over their projects, ensuring they meet the designated milestones, stay within budget, and adhere to the predetermined schedule.

Types of Monitoring Tools:

1. **Dashboards:**

    - Provide a visual summary of a project's key performance indicators (KPIs).

    - Offer real-time data on project metrics such as current vs. planned spend, timeline progress, and resource allocation.

    - Example: A project dashboard might display the percentage completion of tasks, highlighting any areas behind schedule for immediate attention.

2. **Progress Tracking Software:**

    - Allows for detailed tracking of individual tasks and overall project milestones.

    - Facilitates comparison between planned progress and actual progress.

    - Example: Software like Microsoft Project or JIRA can be used to monitor the stages of software development, from inception to testing.

3. **Time Tracking Tools:**

    - Essential for measuring work completion rates and assessing resource utilization.

- Helps in identifying any discrepancies between estimated and actual time spent on tasks.
- Example: Tools such as Toggl or Harvest can provide insights into how project members are allocating their time, revealing potential overwork or inefficiencies.

Integrating Monitoring Tools into Project Management:

- **Setting up the tools:** Begin by selecting tools that integrate well with existing systems and meet the project's specific needs.
- **Training the team:** Ensure all members understand how to use the monitoring tools effectively.
- **Regular reviews:** Schedule consistent check-ins to review data from these tools, allowing for timely adjustments to the project plan.

Benefits of Employing Monitoring Tools:

- **Enhanced visibility:** Stakeholders can see transparent, up-to-date information regarding project status.
- **Improved decision-making:** Real-time data enables more informed and quicker decision-making.
- **Increased accountability:** Team members are more likely to stay on task when they know their progress is being monitored.

Challenges and Solutions:

- **Data overload:** Avoid overwhelming users by customizing dashboards to show only the most relevant information.
- **User resistance:** Overcome resistance through comprehensive training and by demonstrating the value of these tools in easing project tasks.
- **Integration issues:** Select tools that seamlessly integrate with existing software to reduce friction and ensure smooth operation.

Practical Application: Imagine a scenario where a project manager uses a dashboard to identify that a critical path task is lagging. By analyzing time tracking data, they determine the cause is resource overallocation. The project manager can then make informed decisions, such as reallocating resources or adjusting timelines, to mitigate the issue and get the project back on track.

By incorporating monitoring tools effectively, project managers can ensure their projects remain aligned with initial goals, adapting strategies as necessary to address challenges and seize opportunities as they arise, leading to more successful project outcomes.

Control Tools - Control tools play a critical role in steering a project towards its successful completion. They are not just mechanisms for response but proactive measures for ensuring project alignment with its intended goals. These tools help in managing changes, identifying and mitigating risks, and ensuring deliverable quality adheres to predefined standards.

Change Management Systems:

- **Purpose:** Change Management Systems are pivotal in maintaining the project's scope, time, and cost baselines. They ensure every change proposed is thoroughly vetted and approved, preventing scope creep and ensuring project objectives remain aligned.

- **Implementation:** This involves a structured process, starting with a change request logged by any stakeholder or team member. The request is then evaluated for its impact on project objectives, requiring analysis by the project manager and possibly a Change Control Board (CCB). Decisions to approve, reject, or defer the change are documented and communicated to all stakeholders.

- **Example:** In a software development project, if additional features are requested, the change management system would document this request, assess its impact on the current timeline and budget, and ultimately guide the decision on whether these features can be integrated without jeopardizing project success.

Risk Management Software:

- **Purpose:** This software supports proactive project management by identifying, analyzing, and prioritizing project risks. It transforms uncertainties into quantifiable metrics that can be addressed and mitigated.

- **Implementation:** Utilizing risk management software typically starts with risk identification, where potential threats to project success are listed. Each risk is then analyzed to understand its likelihood and impact, usually resulting in a prioritized list of risks that require action.

- **Example:** In a construction project, risk management software could be used to anticipate and strategize for potential delays due to weather conditions or material shortages, assigning probabilities and impacts to each and creating a mitigation plan.

Quality Control Checklists:

- **Purpose:** Checklists are a straightforward yet effective tool for ensuring each deliverable meets established quality criteria before client delivery.

- **Implementation:** Developing a quality control checklist starts with defining the quality standards for the project deliverables. Each item on the checklist represents a standard that the deliverable must meet before it is considered complete.

- **Example:** For a marketing campaign, a checklist might include verification of brand guideline adherence, accuracy of content, and achievement of target audience engagement metrics.

Utilizing Control Tools Effectively: Effective integration of control tools requires:

- Incorporation into the project management plan and routine.

- Continuous monitoring and updating to reflect project evolution.

- Team training on the importance and use of these tools.

Benefits of Control Tools:

- Systematic change management.

- Proactive risk mitigation.

- Assurance of quality standards.

Challenges and Solutions: Implementing control tools can meet resistance or be undermined by complexity:

- To counter resistance, involve the team in the tool selection and clearly demonstrate the value.

- Address complexity by providing comprehensive training and opting for user-friendly software.

Case Studies for Practical Understanding:

- A tech firm could use change management systems to manage updates efficiently, ensuring that each change aligns with the broader project goals and business strategy.

- A non-profit organization could employ risk management software to navigate uncertainties in organizing a large-scale humanitarian event, identifying and mitigating risks related to political instability or natural disasters.

Through diligent application and continuous learning, project managers can leverage these control tools to guide their projects successfully, maintaining alignment with objectives and standards.

Agile Tools and Techniques

Agile Project Management Software - Agile Project Management Software, such as Jira, Trello, and Asana, plays a pivotal role in implementing Agile methodologies like Scrum and Kanban within teams. These platforms are designed to boost collaboration, enhance transparency, and support the flexible nature required in Agile environments, thereby streamlining project workflows and improving team dynamics.

Key Features and Functions:

- **Sprint Planning:** Facilitates the breakdown of complex projects into manageable iterations or 'sprints,' allowing for detailed scheduling and task assignments, which enhance focus and deliverability.

- **Backlog Management:** Empowers teams to create, prioritize, and refine a dynamic list of project tasks, ensuring alignment with overarching project objectives and client needs.

- **Task Tracking and Workflow Visualization:** Offers real-time tracking of task progress against set timelines, utilizing visual boards to depict the workflow and identify potential delays or bottlenecks swiftly.

- **Real-time Collaboration:** Supports instant messaging, document sharing, and update alerts, ensuring all team members stay informed and engaged throughout the project lifecycle.

- **Adaptability and Feedback Integration:** Enables rapid incorporation of stakeholder feedback into the development cycle, allowing teams to adapt to changes without significant setbacks.

Benefits for Agile Project Management:

- **Enhanced Team Collaboration:** Centralizes communication and project information, breaking down silos and fostering a unified team approach.

- **Increased Transparency and Accountability:** Provides all team members with visibility into their tasks and project progress, fostering a sense of ownership and accountability.

- **Improved Flexibility and Responsiveness:** Allows teams to quickly respond to change, ensuring projects stay aligned with client expectations and market trends.

Choosing the Right Agile Software:

- Evaluate compatibility with existing workflows and project complexity.

- Consider integration capabilities with other organizational tools.

- Assess the tool's learning curve against the team's technical proficiency.

Implementing Agile Software:

- Conduct comprehensive training sessions for all users to ensure familiarity with the software's features and functionalities.

- Customize the software's settings to align with specific project workflows and terminologies.

- Regularly review the tool's effectiveness in meeting project needs, adjusting configurations as necessary.

Case Studies for Practical Understanding:

1. **Software Development Project Using Jira:**

   - **Background:** A medium-sized software development team faced challenges with managing multiple product features simultaneously.

   - **Implementation:** The project manager set up Jira to create distinct sprints, enabling focused development and regular review cycles.

   - **Outcome:** The structured approach led to a 30% increase in development speed and significantly improved the product's time-to-market.

2. **Marketing Campaign Managed with Trello:**

   - **Background:** A marketing team struggled with coordinating various campaign elements and deadlines.

   - **Implementation:** Trello boards were used to assign tasks, track progress, and facilitate communication between departments.

   - **Outcome:** Campaign execution became more streamlined, with a noticeable improvement in cross-team collaboration and deadline adherence.

Challenges and Solutions:

- **User Resistance:** Addressed through hands-on workshops demonstrating the software's impact on daily tasks and project outcomes.

- **Integration with Existing Systems:** Solved by selecting platforms with extensive integration options and providing technical support during the transition phase.

Conclusion: Agile Project Management Software is indispensable in modern project environments, marrying the discipline of project management with the flexibility required by Agile practices. When chosen and implemented correctly, it can significantly enhance both project results and team efficiency.

Collaboration and Communication Tools - In the fast-paced environment of Agile project management, collaboration and communication tools like Slack, Microsoft Teams, and Asana have become indispensable. These platforms enable seamless communication and collaboration among team members, breaking down geographical and temporal barriers to ensure a cohesive project execution strategy.

Key Features and Benefits:

1. **Instant Messaging and Channels:** Tools like Slack and Microsoft Teams allow for the creation of project-specific channels. This organizes conversations around different topics or departments, making information retrieval straightforward and keeping team members focused on relevant discussions.

2. **Video Calls and Meetings:** The integration of video calling facilitates real-time discussions, making remote meetings more personal and effective. This feature supports daily stand-ups, sprint reviews, and retrospectives in Agile methodologies, ensuring that all team members, regardless of location, can participate fully.

3. **Document Sharing and Collaboration:** These platforms provide functionalities for sharing documents and collaborating in real-time. Team members can co-edit documents, track changes, and provide instant feedback, streamlining the document review process and accelerating decision-making.

4. **Integration with Other Tools:** The ability to integrate with other project management tools, such as Jira, Trello, or Confluence, allows for a centralized hub of project activities. This integration ensures that tasks, schedules, and updates are synchronized across platforms, providing a comprehensive view of project progress.

5. **Notification and Alert Systems:** Customizable notifications help keep team members informed about relevant updates without overwhelming them with information. This feature is crucial for maintaining awareness of critical tasks and deadlines.

Implementing Communication Tools Effectively:

- **Choosing the Right Platform:** Select a tool that best fits the project needs and team preferences. Consider factors such as ease of use, integration capabilities, and security features.

- **Setting Guidelines and Best Practices:** Establish clear guidelines on how and when to use the communication tools. This might include setting expectations for response times, appropriate use of channels, and meeting etiquettes.

- **Training and Onboarding:** Ensure all team members are comfortable using the selected tools. Provide training sessions and resources to help them navigate and utilize the features effectively.

- **Monitoring and Adjusting Usage:** Regularly review how the team is using the communication tools. Solicit feedback and be prepared to adjust tool settings or usage guidelines to better meet the team's needs.

Case Studies for Practical Understanding:

1. **Global Software Development Project:** In a scenario where a software development team is spread across three continents, the project manager utilizes Microsoft Teams to facilitate communication. Daily stand-ups are conducted via video calls, ensuring all team members are aligned. The team uses shared channels to update progress on tasks, and integrates Microsoft Teams with their project tracking software to streamline workflows.

2. **Marketing Campaign Roll-out:** A project manager leading a marketing campaign uses Slack to coordinate between the creative team, marketing strategists, and external vendors. Specialized channels are created for different aspects of the campaign, such as design, content, and logistics, ensuring relevant discussions are compartmentalized. Slack is integrated with a cloud storage service for easy access to marketing materials and analytics reports.

Challenges and Solutions:

- **Challenge:** Overcoming resistance to new tools or processes.

  - **Solution:** Highlight the benefits, provide comprehensive training, and demonstrate how these tools can simplify tasks and improve project outcomes.

- **Challenge:** Ensuring security and confidentiality.

  - **Solution:** Implement strong security measures, educate the team on best practices, and choose platforms known for their security features.

By embracing collaboration and communication tools, Agile project managers can enhance team coordination, streamline workflows, and lead projects to successful completion. The key is to select the right tools, establish clear usage guidelines, and remain adaptable to changing project needs and team dynamics.

Version Control Systems - Version Control Systems (VCS) such as Git, SVN, and Mercurial are pivotal in contemporary project management, particularly in software development. These systems offer a structured approach to managing changes, whether they pertain to software code or project documentation. By allowing multiple team members to concurrently work on different project segments, VCS ensures that all contributions are synchronized, avoiding overlap or conflicts. This leads to improved team collaboration and maintains a detailed historical record, enhancing both accountability and transparency in project workflows.

Key Features and Benefits:

- **Revision Tracking:** This key feature enables detailed tracking of all changes by each contributor, providing a comprehensive audit trail. This transparency helps in understanding the project's progression and facilitates informed decision-making.

- **Branching and Merging:** These capabilities allow team members to develop features or work on tasks in parallel through separate branches. These branches can be later merged into the main project, streamlining the integration of various contributions without disrupting the project's continuity.

- **Rollback Capabilities:** Should errors or issues arise, VCS offers the ability to revert to previous versions, safeguarding project integrity and enabling continuity without significant setbacks.

Implementing Version Control in Projects:

- **Setup and Configuration:** Choosing the right VCS is critical and depends on the project's specific needs. Initial steps include establishing a central repository, defining clear access rights for team members, and setting up branch management policies.

- **Team Training:** Ensuring all members are well-versed with the chosen VCS is essential. Conduct comprehensive training covering basic operations like commits, as well as advanced features like branching and merging.

- **Integration with Other Tools:** To maximize efficiency, integrate the VCS with continuous integration/continuous deployment (CI/CD) pipelines, project management tools, and other relevant software. This integration streamlines workflows and enhances project coordination.

Best Practices:

- Ensure commit messages are concise yet descriptive to communicate the changes effectively.

- Regularly sync changes with the central repository to maintain team alignment.

- Adopt code review practices and utilize pull or merge requests to uphold code quality and document coherence.

Challenges and Solutions:

Challenge 1: Team Misalignment:

- **Solution**: Establish clear roles and responsibilities, conduct team-building activities, and maintain regular communication to ensure all members are aligned with the project's objectives and progress.

Challenge 2: Adapting to Change:

- **Solution**: Implement an Agile approach, allowing for flexibility and iterative development. Encourage open feedback channels with stakeholders and the project team to swiftly identify and address changes.

Challenge 3: Resource Constraints:

- **Solution**: Perform a detailed resource analysis, prioritize tasks based on available resources, and negotiate for additional resources or adjust project scope as necessary.

Case Studies for Practical Understanding:

1. Software Development Project Case Study:

Background: The project manager, Sarah, was tasked with leading the development of a new financial software application designed to help small businesses manage their finances more effectively.

Challenge: The project faced multiple challenges, including shifting regulatory requirements, diverse user needs, and tight deadlines. Additionally, the development team was newly formed and had varying levels of experience.

Actions:

- Sarah initiated regular team-building activities to foster trust and improve communication among team members.

- She organized weekly meetings focused on transparency and open discussion to ensure all team members were aligned with the project goals and progress.

- Implementing Agile methodology, Sarah encouraged iterative development and frequent feedback from potential users, allowing the team to quickly adapt to changing requirements and incorporate user feedback into the development process.

- She also established a mentorship program within the team to pair less experienced developers with senior ones, enhancing skills transfer and cohesion.

Outcome: Despite initial setbacks, the team successfully developed and launched the software on time. The application received positive feedback from users for its user-friendly interface and functionality, and the team's morale was significantly boosted by the project's success.

2. Construction Project Case Study:

Background: David, a project manager with extensive experience in residential construction, was overseeing the development of a new high-rise apartment complex.

Challenge: The project encountered unexpected delays due to severe weather conditions and supply chain disruptions, threatening to push the project over budget and past its deadline.

Actions:

- David conducted a comprehensive risk assessment to identify potential further delays and developed a contingency plan.

- He re-sequenced construction activities to allow work to continue in other areas unaffected by the weather.

- David negotiated with suppliers for faster delivery times and sought alternative materials that met the project's quality standards but were more readily available.

- He organized weekly update meetings with stakeholders to keep them informed of the challenges and the measures taken to address them, maintaining transparency and managing expectations.

Outcome: The apartment complex was completed with a slight delay but remained within the budget. The proactive communication strategy maintained stakeholder trust, and the project's success established the construction company as a reliable and resilient business.

Conclusion: The integration of Version Control Systems into project management is indispensable for maintaining high levels of collaboration, efficiency, and adaptability. By incorporating VCS into standard practices, project teams can significantly improve alignment and productivity, effectively meeting the challenges of dynamic project requirements and ensuring successful project outcomes in complex environments.

Continuous Integration/Continuous Deployment (CI/CD) Tools - Introduction to CI/CD: Continuous Integration (CI) and Continuous Deployment (CD) form the backbone of modern software development practices, especially within Agile frameworks. These practices aim to automate and streamline the phases of integration, testing, and deployment, thereby enhancing development efficiency and reducing the risk of errors in production.

Explanation and Benefits:

- **CI (Continuous Integration):** This practice involves merging all developers' working copies to a shared mainline multiple times a day. The key benefit here is the significant reduction in integration challenges, as frequent integrations prevent the divergence and complications of different code branches. Tools like Jenkins, Travis CI, and CircleCI are often used to automate these integrations, providing instant feedback on code integrity and quality.

- **CD (Continuous Deployment):** CD takes automation a step further by automatically deploying all code changes to a testing or production environment after the build stage. This means the software is always in a deployable state, facilitating rapid iterations and continuous improvement. It supports Agile's emphasis on fast delivery and helps in quickly addressing user needs and market changes.

Integration with Agile Principles: CI/CD dovetails with Agile methodologies by promoting adaptive planning, evolutionary development, and early delivery. These practices enhance the Agile principle of continual improvement and rapid adaptation to change through fast feedback loops. This allows project teams to quickly identify and rectify issues, ensuring higher product quality and customer satisfaction.

Practical Application: A practical example of CI/CD implementation could involve setting up a Jenkins pipeline for a web application project. This setup would automate code pulls from version control, run unit and integration tests, and, if these are successful, deploy to a staging environment for further acceptance testing before final deployment.

Challenges and Solutions:

- **Challenge:** Diverse team with varying communication styles leading to misunderstandings.

- **Solution:** Implementing communication training sessions and establishing clear channels and norms for team communication.

- **Challenge:** Resistance to teamwork due to competitive or siloed working environments.

- **Solution:** Creating opportunities for cross-functional collaboration, recognizing team achievements, and promoting a culture of unity and shared goals.

Case Studies for Practical Understanding:

1. **Software Development Team Integration**:
   - **Background**: A project manager, Lisa, faced challenges integrating new members into an existing software development team, causing delays and communication breakdowns.
   - **Action**: Lisa organized a series of team-building retreats focused on collaboration and communication exercises. She implemented daily stand-up meetings to encourage open dialogue and set up a mentorship program pairing new members with experienced team members.
   - **Outcome**: The team's productivity and morale improved significantly, demonstrated by a 30% reduction in project delays and a noticeable improvement in team synergy.

2. **Construction Project Team Coordination**:
   - **Background**: Mark, a project manager, was overseeing a large construction project when unexpected conflicts arose between the design and construction teams, leading to project standstills.
   - **Action**: He initiated conflict resolution workshops and regular coordination meetings to foster understanding and respect among team members. Mark also introduced an integrated project delivery approach, encouraging joint problem-solving and decision-making.
   - **Outcome**: The project saw a decrease in conflicts, with a smoother workflow and on-time project delivery, enhancing stakeholder satisfaction.

Alignment with PMBOK Guidelines: Integrating CI/CD aligns with several PMBOK process areas, including Quality Management by ensuring that products meet quality standards continuously; Risk Management by identifying and addressing risks early in the process; and Stakeholder Engagement by providing stakeholders with up-to-date information on project progress and product quality.

Conclusion: CI/CD practices are integral to enhancing efficiency, quality, and adaptability in project management, particularly within Agile environments. By automating integration and deployment processes, project managers can ensure that their projects remain responsive to user needs and market changes, significantly improving project outcomes and team productivity.

Agile Metrics and Reporting Tools - Agile metrics and reporting tools are indispensable in an Agile project management environment, serving as the compass that guides the project's direction and pace. These tools and metrics provide a quantitative basis to assess the performance and progress of Agile projects, enabling project managers and teams to maintain control over the project's trajectory and make data-driven decisions.

Understanding Agile Metrics: Agile metrics like velocity, sprint burndown rates, and feature completion rates offer invaluable insights into team performance and project progress. These metrics facilitate early identification of issues, enabling timely interventions to keep the project on course.

- **Velocity:** This metric tracks the amount of work a team completes in each sprint, providing a reliable basis for future sprint planning. For example, if a team consistently completes 30 story points per sprint, the project manager can forecast future sprints more accurately.

- **Sprint Burndown Rates:** These rates show the remaining workload in a sprint. A chart displaying a day-by-day reduction helps teams gauge if they are on schedule. If the burndown chart deviates significantly from the expected path, it signals that the team may not complete the sprint on time, prompting immediate action.

- **Feature Completion Rates:** This metric measures the completion rate of features against the total planned features, offering insights into how effectively the project is delivering value to stakeholders.

Implementing Reporting Tools: Agile reporting tools bring metrics to life through visualizations, enhancing understanding and communication among team members and stakeholders:

- **Dashboards:** They provide a snapshot of the project's status, enabling stakeholders to quickly grasp the project's health and progress without delving into the minutiae.

- **Burn Charts:** These charts, both sprint and project burn charts, offer visual representations of remaining work against time. They are crucial for assessing whether the project is on track to meet deadlines.

- **Cumulative Flow Diagrams:** These diagrams show the breakdown of work in various stages, highlighting bottlenecks in processes and workflows, thereby facilitating targeted improvements.

Effective Use of Metrics and Tools: For Agile metrics and tools to be genuinely beneficial, project managers should:

- Choose metrics that reflect the project's core objectives and stakeholder values.
- Conduct regular reviews with the team and stakeholders to maintain alignment and transparency.
- Utilize data from these tools to stimulate discussion during retrospectives, pinpointing areas for enhancement.
- Adjust tactics based on insights gleaned from these metrics, aligning more closely with project goals and deadlines.

Case Studies for Practical Understanding:

1. Software Development Project:

- **Background:** A project manager, Sophia, at a tech startup is tasked with leading the development of a new mobile application aimed at improving user engagement.
- **Challenge:** The project faced significant shifts in market demands and user preferences, necessitating frequent updates to the application's features.
- **Action:** Sophia implemented Agile methodologies, organizing work into two-week sprints, allowing the team to adapt quickly to feedback from beta testing. She also introduced continuous integration and deployment (CI/CD) practices to streamline updates and ensure quality.
- **Outcome:** The application was developed with adaptable features that could be updated in response to user feedback, leading to a 40% increase in user engagement.

2. Construction Project:

- **Background:** Project manager Mike oversees the construction of a new commercial building.

- **Challenge:** The project encountered unexpected geological issues leading to delays, and budget overruns.
- **Action:** Mike employed a thorough risk management strategy, which included revising the project schedule and budget, negotiating with suppliers for faster delivery times, and reallocating resources to critical areas.
- **Outcome:** Despite initial setbacks, the building was completed within a revised timeline and budget, maintaining quality standards and stakeholder satisfaction.

Challenges and Solutions:

Team Communication in Remote Projects:

- **Challenge:** A project team spread across different time zones struggled with communication and collaboration.
- **Solution:** The project manager introduced a set of standardized communication tools and scheduled regular cross-time-zone meetings, ensuring all team members were updated and engaged.

Stakeholder Engagement in Complex Projects:

Challenge: In a complex infrastructure project, stakeholders had conflicting interests and requirements.

Solution: The project manager organized a series of stakeholder engagement workshops to identify common goals, prioritize requirements, and develop a shared project vision, leading to aligned expectations and smoother project execution.

PMP Exam Preparation

Detailed Coverage of the Examination Content Outline

Introduction to the Content Outline - The PMP Examination Content Outline is an essential document designed to provide candidates with a detailed framework of the Project Management Professional (PMP) exam. It delineates the exam's structure, including the domains of project management it covers, specific tasks a project manager is expected to perform, and the requisite knowledge and skills necessary for effective project management. This outline is instrumental for candidates preparing for the PMP exam, offering them a clear roadmap of the content areas on which to focus their study efforts.

Domains Covered:

- **Project Initiating:** Tasks involved in defining a new project or a new phase of an existing project by obtaining authorization to start the project or phase.

- **Project Planning:** The processes required to establish the scope of the project, refine the objectives, and define the course of action required to attain the objectives that the project was undertaken to achieve.

- **Project Executing:** Involves leading and performing the work defined in the project management plan and implementing approved changes to achieve the project's objectives.

- **Project Monitoring and Controlling:** The tracking, reviewing, and regulating of the progress and performance of the project; identifying any areas in which changes to the plan are required; and initiating the corresponding changes.

- **Project Closing:** Finalizing all project activities across all the Project Management Process Groups to formally complete the project or phase.

Tasks and Knowledge Areas: Each domain encompasses specific tasks that a project manager is expected to competently perform. These tasks are supported by defined knowledge and skills areas, such as risk management, stakeholder engagement, communication, resource management, and more. Understanding these areas is vital for applying best practices and methodologies in project management, from initiating and planning through executing, monitoring, controlling, and closing the project.

Skills Required: The outline emphasizes the importance of both hard and soft skills in project management. Hard skills include project scope management, schedule development, and budget planning, while soft skills highlight leadership, communication, and negotiation. The integration of these skills enables the project manager to navigate complex project environments, manage stakeholder expectations, and lead projects to successful completion.

Preparation Strategies: To effectively prepare for the exam, candidates should:

- Review each domain and its associated tasks to understand the scope of the exam fully.
- Identify personal strengths and weaknesses within these areas to tailor study efforts.
- Engage with various study materials, including PMBOK, practice exams, and other PMP preparation resources.

- Participate in study groups or training sessions to enhance understanding and application of project management principles.Conclusion: The PMP Examination Content Outline is more than just an exam guide; it is a comprehensive overview of the competencies and skills necessary for effective project management. By aligning study and preparation efforts with the domains and tasks detailed in the outline, candidates can ensure they are well-prepared for the PMP exam and their future roles as project management professionals.

Practical Application and Case Studies: Applying real-world scenarios and case studies related to the content outline can significantly enhance preparation. For instance, analyzing a case study that illustrates risk management in action can provide deeper insights into theoretical concepts, making the study more applicable and retaining knowledge.

Challenges and Solutions: Candidates may face challenges such as understanding complex project management terminologies or applying theoretical concepts to practical scenarios. Solutions include seeking clarification from experienced professionals, using practical examples to ground abstract concepts, and regular testing of knowledge through quizzes and practice exams.

Conclusion: The PMP Examination Content Outline is more than just a syllabus; it is a comprehensive guide that structures a candidate's preparation journey. By deeply understanding and internalizing this outline, candidates can ensure they cover all necessary topics and domains, thereby significantly increasing their chances of success on the exam. This in-depth approach to preparation, combined with practical application and continuous learning, will equip candidates with the skills and knowledge required to excel as project management professionals.

Domain-specific Strategies - Successfully preparing for the PMP exam requires a deep understanding of the distinct challenges and subject matter within each domain: People, Process, and Business Environment. A focused study plan that addresses the unique aspects of these domains ensures a holistic grasp of project management principles and practices.

People Domain:

1. **Key Tasks and Knowledge Areas:** Prioritize learning how to lead project teams effectively, manage conflicts, engage stakeholders, and build cohesive teams. Develop skills in emotional intelligence, motivation techniques, and effective communication.

2. **Study Approaches:**
   - Engage in group studies or discussions to tackle leadership concepts and team dynamics.
   - Participate in role-playing exercises that simulate real-world conflict resolution and stakeholder management scenarios.
   - Dive into case studies that highlight effective team building and leadership strategies.

3. **Real-world Applications:**
   - Reflect on personal experiences where leadership made a significant impact on project outcomes.
   - Consider how different approaches to team building and stakeholder engagement could have altered the course of past projects.

Process Domain:

1. **Key Tasks and Knowledge Areas:** Concentrate on mastering the phases of project management from initiation to closing. Focus on learning various methodologies, improving time management skills, and enhancing cost control measures.

2. **Study Approaches:**

   - Utilize diagrams such as flowcharts and process maps to visualize project management processes.

   - Practice identifying and applying correct processes through scenario-based questions.

   - Create checklists based on PMBOK guidelines to ensure all steps are covered.

3. **Real-world Applications:**

   - Analyze previous projects to identify which phases and processes were used and how they could have been applied differently.

   - Map out a past project, noting where each PMBOK process was or could have been implemented.

Business Environment Domain:

1. **Key Tasks and Knowledge Areas:** Grasp how projects influence and are influenced by broader business contexts. Study topics such as compliance, organizational change, strategic alignment, and market condition analysis.

2. **Study Approaches:**

   - Explore case studies that connect project outcomes with business success.

   - Use business strategy frameworks to understand the alignment between projects and organizational objectives.

   - Examine principles of corporate governance and their impact on project decisions.

3. **Real-world Applications:**

   - Evaluate the business impact of past projects, considering factors like return on investment and market expansion.

   - Hypothesize how different decisions could have better aligned a project with its business environment.

Enhanced Study Techniques:

- Integrate various study materials with interactive learning experiences such as workshops or webinars.

- Regularly use exam simulators and practice questions to become comfortable with the PMP exam format.

- Join study groups or find a mentor to discuss topics and clarify concepts.

Challenges and Solutions:

- Tackle common study challenges by creating a structured study plan, breaking down information into manageable segments, and applying theoretical knowledge to practical scenarios.

- Use prioritization techniques to focus on high-value study topics and use real-world applications to deepen understanding.

Conclusion: By delving into the PMP domains and tailoring your study approach to the specific requirements of each, you enhance not only your readiness for the exam but also your competency in managing real-world projects. This comprehensive preparation strategy will equip you with the necessary skills and knowledge to succeed as a project manager.

Study Techniques for Each Domain -

1. People Domain: Understanding the People domain is crucial as it focuses on leadership, team dynamics, and human resource aspects of project management.

- **Flashcards:** Create flashcards covering key terms and theories related to leadership styles, conflict resolution, team motivation, and communication. This technique aids in memorization and quick recall.
- **Group Discussions:** Engage in discussions with peers or study groups to delve into topics like emotional intelligence, team building, and stakeholder management. Real-life examples can be shared and analyzed to deepen understanding.
- **Role-Playing Exercises:** Simulate real-world scenarios where different leadership approaches and team dynamics are explored. This hands-on approach helps in understanding the practical application of theories.
- **Mentorship and Coaching Sessions:** Pair up with a mentor or coach to receive feedback on leadership approaches and team management strategies.

2. Process Domain: The Process domain encompasses the technical aspects of project management, including lifecycle phases and process groups.

- **Process Flowcharts:** Develop detailed flowcharts for each process group and knowledge area. Visualizing processes helps in understanding the sequence and interdependencies of different tasks.
- **Scenario-Based Exercises:** Work through real-life or hypothetical project scenarios to apply process knowledge. These exercises should cover planning, execution, monitoring, controlling, and closing.
- **Templates and Checklists:** Utilize project management templates and checklists to familiarize yourself with documents used throughout the project lifecycle.
- **Time-Management Techniques:** Practice using tools and techniques such as Gantt charts, critical path method (CPM), and Program Evaluation and Review Technique (PERT) to enhance proficiency in project scheduling and time management.

3. Business Environment Domain: This domain focuses on aligning project management practices with organizational strategy and understanding the business context.

- **Case Studies:** Analyze comprehensive case studies that showcase the integration of project management within various business environments. Focus on strategic alignment, compliance, and value delivery aspects.
- **Current Business Trends:** Stay updated with the latest business trends by reading industry reports, attending webinars, and participating in relevant forums. Understanding market forces and organizational strategies will contextualize project management practices.
- **SWOT Analysis:** Conduct SWOT analyses on real or hypothetical projects to understand external and internal factors affecting projects in different business environments.
- **Benefit Realization Plan:** Learn how to develop and assess a benefit realization plan, ensuring that the project delivers the intended business value.

Integrating Study Methods for Comprehensive Preparation: By incorporating diverse study methods tailored to each domain, candidates can ensure comprehensive preparation. This approach addresses the diverse nature of the PMP exam content areas, equipping candidates with the knowledge, skills, and perspective needed to succeed in the exam and in their project management careers.

Utilize a mix of reading, visual aids, practical exercises, and interactive discussions to cover the extensive material effectively. Regularly review and adapt your study plan based on progress and areas needing improvement. Collaboration with peers, participation in study groups, and seeking feedback from experienced professionals can enhance understanding and retention of project management principles.

Understanding the Exam Format - Navigating through the PMP exam requires an in-depth understanding of its comprehensive format. The exam is strategically crafted to evaluate your expertise and application skills in project management across multiple spectrums. Let's dissect the format and delve into effective preparation strategies.

Question Types:

1. **Multiple-Choice Questions (MCQs):**

    - **Nature:** Each MCQ consists of a problem or scenario followed by four potential answers, out of which only one is correct. They range from simple knowledge checks to complex situational analyses.

    - **Preparation Tips:** Sharpen your skills by focusing on critical thinking and scenario analysis. Break down each question, understand its context, and apply elimination strategies to weed out incorrect answers. Practicing with a variety of MCQs enhances familiarity and aids in understanding the examiners' questioning patterns.

2. **Matching Questions:**

    - **Nature:** These questions require you to match items from two columns based on their relationships or associations. They test your understanding of concepts and their interrelations within project management frameworks.

    - **Preparation Tips:** Grasp the core concepts of project management and their practical interconnections. Use diagrams and tables to visualize relationships between different project management elements, which can aid in quicker recall during the exam.

3. **Multiple Responses:**
   - **Nature:** Extending beyond MCQs, these questions have multiple correct answers. They challenge your comprehension and the ability to identify all appropriate options.
   - **Preparation Tips:** Develop a nuanced understanding of project management scenarios where multiple elements can be correct. Practice with questions that have nuanced distinctions to improve judgment and decision-making skills in complex situations.

4. **Fill-in-the-Blank:**
   - **Nature:** These direct queries require you to provide specific terms or numerical values, testing your direct recall and understanding of project management terminologies or formulas.
   - **Preparation Tips:** Regularly review and memorize key terminologies, acronyms, and formulas. Employ flashcards or mnemonic devices to enhance memory recall and accuracy for these types of questions.

Comprehensive Domain Insights:

I. People (42% of the exam):

- Dive deep into leadership principles, team dynamics, and conflict resolution techniques. Understanding motivational theories, communication styles, and cultural sensitivity can vastly improve your handling of this domain.
- Strategies: Role-play various leadership scenarios and reflect on team-building practices. Engaging in case studies focusing on ethical dilemmas and stakeholder management can also provide practical insights.

II. Process (50% of the exam):

- Focus on the life cycle of project management from initiation to closing. Understand various methodologies, integration techniques, and how to manage resources effectively throughout the project phases.
- Strategies: Develop a thorough understanding of each process group and knowledge area. Create flowcharts to understand the sequence and dependencies of processes. Utilize simulation exercises to apply these concepts in controlled environments.

III. Business Environment (8% of the exam):

- Concentrate on aligning project goals with organizational strategy and understanding the impact of external factors on project success.
- Strategies: Study the effects of market conditions, legal regulations, and environmental considerations on project outcomes. Engage with real-world business cases to see how strategic alignment and compliance are achieved in practice.

Targeted Exam Preparation Strategies:

1. **Mastering Question Formats:** Tailor your study sessions to include diverse question types. Create or use existing question banks that mimic the PMP exam's complexity and variety.

2. **Effective Time Management:** Develop the skill to gauge the time needed per question. Practice full-length, timed exams to build endurance and speed, ensuring that every question gets adequate attention without compromising overall performance.

3. **Practice Exams and Question Banks:** Utilize these resources to identify weak areas and track progress. Simulate the exam environment as closely as possible, using timed sessions and avoiding distractions.

4. **Domain-Specific Review:** Allocate study time based on the weight of each domain. Create a study plan that covers all areas but prioritizes domains with higher question percentages.

5. **PMBOK® Guide Mastery:** Dive into the PMBOK® Guide, focusing on understanding rather than memorization. Relate its principles to real-life project scenarios to strengthen practical understanding.

6. **Real-World Application:** Integrate theoretical knowledge with practical applications. Discuss scenarios with peers or mentors to gain different perspectives and solutions.

7. **Active Engagement:** Participate in study groups and discussions. Teaching concepts to others or debating different approaches can reinforce your own understanding and uncover gaps in knowledge.

8. **Agile and Hybrid Methodologies:** With the growing trend towards Agile and hybrid approaches in project management, ensure you are proficient in these areas. Familiarize yourself with the nuances and applications of Agile principles and how they compare to traditional project management practices.

Conclusion: Achieving PMP certification is a testament to your dedication and mastery in the field of project management. Understanding the exam format is not just about navigating the questions but also aligning your preparation to meet the nuanced demands of each domain. By delving deep into the types of questions and meticulously reviewing the core domains, you are setting a solid foundation for your success.

Approach your PMP exam preparation as you would a complex project: with strategy, adaptability, and an unwavering focus on the goal. Remember, the PMP exam is not only testing your knowledge but also your ability to apply this knowledge in varied and challenging scenarios. Utilize every resource at your disposal, from the PMBOK® Guide to real-world applications and active learning communities. By embracing a holistic and disciplined approach to your study, you enhance not just your chances of passing the exam but also your readiness to tackle real-world project management challenges.

In summary, transform your preparation into an active and engaging journey. Reflect on each concept, understand its application, and continuously test your knowledge against the myriad question formats. With diligence, understanding, and strategic preparation, you are well on your way to achieving PMP certification and advancing your career in project management. Embrace this challenge with confidence and perseverance, and the rewards will be substantial and fulfilling.

Tips for Exam Day - The day of the PMP exam is the culmination of your rigorous preparation and hard work. It's essential to approach this day with a clear strategy and mindset to optimize your performance. Here's a detailed breakdown of strategies to help you navigate exam day efficiently and confidently.

Before the Exam Day:

1. **Rest and Relaxation:** A well-rested mind is critical for optimal performance. Ensure you get 7-9 hours of sleep prior to the exam day. Avoid last-minute cramming as it can lead to mental exhaustion and negatively impact your recall and decision-making abilities. Engage in relaxing activities instead, such as meditation or a light walk, to calm your nerves.

2. **Preparation and Packing:** Compile all necessary items the night before. This includes your official identification, exam confirmation, and any allowed materials as specified by PMI. Check the latest PMI exam policies to ensure you're not carrying prohibited items. Organize your materials in a clear and accessible manner to reduce stress on the morning of the exam.

3. **Know Your Venue:** Familiarize yourself with the location, parking facilities, and the route to the testing center. If possible, visit the center beforehand to understand how much time you'll need to get there. This helps mitigate any potential travel-related stress on the day of the exam.

On the Exam Day:

1. **Arrival at the Testing Center:** Plan to arrive at least 30 minutes early. Early arrival allows for a calm check-in process, gives you time to familiarize yourself with the environment, and helps mitigate any unforeseen circumstances like traffic or parking issues.

2. **Understanding Exam Structure:** Knowing the structure of the PMP exam – including the types and number of questions and the total duration – is crucial. This knowledge allows you to allocate your time effectively, ensuring you can answer all questions without rushing and have ample time for review.

3. **Identification and PMI's Exam Policies:** Double-check that you have the proper identification required by PMI. Be thoroughly familiar with the exam policies, particularly those concerning breaks and prohibited items, to avoid any exam-day surprises or penalties.

During the Exam:

1. **Reading Questions Carefully:** Pay close attention to each question, particularly situational ones that assess your ability to apply theoretical knowledge in practical scenarios. Understanding the context and specifics of each question is essential for choosing the correct answer.

2. **Answering Strategies:**

   - **Elimination Technique:** For multiple-choice questions, systematically eliminate incorrect answers to narrow your choices and increase your chances of selecting the right answer.

   - **Mark and Review:** Use the exam software's mark and review feature to flag questions you are unsure about. This allows you to focus first on questions you can answer confidently and return to the more challenging ones later.

3. **Pacing Yourself:** Develop a pacing strategy based on the total number of questions and the exam duration. Break the exam into segments, setting mini-goals for each segment to maintain a steady pace and ensure you cover all questions within the allotted time.

4. **Taking Breaks:** Utilize permitted breaks wisely to recharge mentally and physically. Even short breaks can help alleviate stress, refresh your mind, and maintain focus. Practice time

management during these breaks to ensure you return to the exam refreshed yet mindful of the remaining time.

5. **Maintaining Calmness and Focus:**

   - **Breathing Exercises:** Implement deep breathing techniques to manage stress and maintain composure during the exam.

   - **Positive Reinforcement:** Regularly remind yourself of your preparation and the effort you've invested. Self-confidence can significantly influence your exam performance.

6. **Physical Comfort:** Dress in layers to adapt to varying room temperatures. Ensure your physical comfort to prevent any distractions that could detract from your focus during the exam.

7. **Managing Stress:** Recognize when you're feeling overwhelmed and have strategies ready to manage stress effectively. This could include taking a moment to close your eyes and breathe deeply, practicing positive visualization, or quietly stretching.

After the Exam:

1. **Post-Exam Review:** Regardless of your immediate perception of how the exam went, take time to decompress and reflect on the experience. Recognize the extensive effort you've invested in your PMP journey.

2. **Reflecting on the Experience:** Write down your thoughts and any areas you found challenging immediately after the exam. This reflection can be invaluable for future reference or in the unlikely event you need to retake the exam.

3. **Continuing the Learning Journey:** Irrespective of the outcome, view the PMP exam as a valuable learning experience. Use this opportunity to identify areas for professional growth and continue your learning journey in project management.

Conclusion: The PMP exam day is not just a test of your knowledge but also a test of your preparation, strategy, and mental fortitude. By implementing these detailed strategies, you ensure that you are well-prepared not just academically, but also mentally and physically for the exam's challenges. Remember, this certification reflects your commitment and expertise in project management. Approach the day with confidence, knowing you have prepared thoroughly.

By adopting a comprehensive approach—balancing mental preparation with strategic planning and physical readiness—you position yourself for success. The journey to achieving PMP certification is rigorous, but it's also immensely rewarding. This detailed preparation not only sets you up for success on exam day but also enriches your overall understanding and application of project management principles.

In conclusion, let the day of the exam be a reflection of your dedication and hard work. Follow these detailed tips to manage your time, maintain focus, and apply your knowledge effectively. With the right preparation and mindset, you'll navigate the exam confidently and step into your next phase of professional growth as a certified Project Management Professional. Good luck, and remember, every step you've taken in preparation has led you to this moment. Embrace it with confidence and clarity, ready to demonstrate your mastery of project management.

Tips and Strategies for Exam Preparation

Understanding the Exam Content - Navigating through the PMP exam demands a profound comprehension of the content outlined by the PMI. The key to success lies not only in understanding theoretical concepts but in aligning your study strategy with the practical demands of project management roles as delineated in the PMI's Examination Content Outline.

1. Comprehensive Review of the PMI's Examination Content Outline:

- **Purpose and Utility:** The Examination Content Outline is not just a document; it's your foundational guide to the PMP exam. It delineates not only the exam structure but also the pivotal domains of project management, reflecting real-world demands and expectations.

- **Structural Breakdown:** The outline categorizes project management into three main domains: People, Process, and Business Environment. Each domain encompasses tasks and knowledge areas crucial for effective project management, shaping the scope and focus of your preparation.

2. Analytical Breakdown of the Examination Content:

- **People Domain (42%):** Delve deep into the elements of team management and leadership. Explore conflict resolution techniques, motivation strategies, and communication methodologies that foster effective team dynamics. This domain assesses your ability to navigate interpersonal and group interactions positively.

- **Process Domain (50%):** This domain is the bedrock of the exam, requiring a comprehensive understanding of project lifecycle and methodologies. Familiarize yourself with initiation, planning, executing, monitoring, controlling, and closing phases, underpinning each with PMBOK® Guide standards.

- **Business Environment Domain (8%):** Understand the broader context in which projects operate. Study how projects align with organizational goals, adhere to compliance standards, and respond to external business factors.

3. Identifying Study Priorities and Formulating a Plan:

- **Self-assessment:** Conduct a thorough self-assessment to identify your strengths and areas for improvement. Utilize tools such as SWOT analysis to pinpoint these areas effectively.

- **Time Allocation:** Develop a strategic study plan, dedicating more time to domains where you're less confident, while maintaining a comprehensive approach that covers all areas.

4. Familiarization with Question Distribution:

- Realize the significance of domain weightings in the PMP exam. This understanding allows for an optimized study approach, ensuring you allocate your efforts effectively according to the prominence of each domain in the exam.

5. Deep Dive into Each Domain:

- **People:** Beyond theoretical understanding, engage in real-life applications of leadership and team management skills. Seek feedback on your leadership style, participate in conflict resolution workshops, and practice active listening and clear communication.

- **Process:** Utilize visual aids like flowcharts and process maps to visualize project management processes in a real-world context. Engage in simulation exercises and use project management software to get hands-on experience.

- **Business Environment**: Connect your project management practice with business outcomes. Study market trends, understand organizational strategy, and learn how to conduct compliance checks and business impact analyses.

6. Leveraging Study Materials and Community Resources:

- Combine the insights from the PMBOK® Guide with a variety of study materials. Engage in community forums, join study groups, and attend webinars to gain diverse perspectives and insights.

7. Real-World Application through Case Studies:

- Implement what you've learned by analyzing real-world case studies. This helps bridge the gap between theory and practice, offering deeper insights into the practical application of project management principles.

8. Overcoming Challenges Through Resources and Community:

- Confront common challenges by leveraging community wisdom and targeted resources. Don't hesitate to reach out to mentors or peers when faced with difficult concepts or scenarios.

9. Commitment to Continuous Review and Adaptation:

- Establish a routine for regular review sessions, adapting your study plan based on evolving understanding and exam readiness. Utilize practice tests to gauge progress and fine-tune your approach accordingly.

10. Active Engagement for Deeper Understanding:

- Deepen your understanding through active participation in study groups and discussions. Teach others or explain your reasoning, as articulating your thoughts can solidify your knowledge and uncover any lingering misunderstandings.

Conclusion: Mastering the PMP exam content goes beyond mere memorization; it requires a strategic, comprehensive approach aligned with the demands of modern project management. By dissecting the PMI's Examination Content Outline, prioritizing your studies based on personal proficiency and exam weightage, and applying theoretical knowledge in practical scenarios, you prepare yourself not just for the PMP exam but for a successful career in project management. Embrace this journey with dedication, utilizing every resource at your disposal, and remember that the path to certification is also a path to becoming a more effective, versatile project manager.

Study Plan Development - Creating a structured and personalized study plan is fundamental for your success on the PMP exam. This comprehensive guide aims to help you develop a study plan that not only fits your learning style and schedule but also covers all necessary topics systematically and efficiently.

Initial Assessment and Time Allocation:

- **Self-Evaluation**: Begin with a self-assessment to understand your strengths and weaknesses across the PMP exam domains: People, Process, and Business Environment. Use online quizzes or the feedback from past projects to gauge your proficiency in each area.

- **Time Management**: Allocate study time based on your assessment. Heavier weights should be given to areas where your knowledge is weaker, and to domains that have a larger percentage of exam questions, like the Process domain. For instance, if you are less experienced in Process, allocate more study hours to this domain.

- **Study Schedule Creation**: Design a study schedule that breaks down your available time before the exam into manageable study sessions. Consider your personal and professional commitments and identify consistent, uninterrupted times each day dedicated to study.

Integrating Learning Styles:

- **Identify Your Learning Style**: Are you a visual, auditory, or kinesthetic learner? Identify your style and tailor your study materials accordingly. Visual learners might use diagrams and mind maps, auditory learners could benefit from podcasts or discussions, while kinesthetic learners should seek hands-on activities or apply concepts through practical project management tools.

- **Customize Study Methods**: Based on your learning style, select study methods that enhance your comprehension and retention. Use a mix of textbooks, video tutorials, practice questions, and group study sessions to cater to a variety of learning preferences.

Utilization of Practice Exams:

- **Baseline Testing**: Start with a practice exam to establish your baseline performance. This initial score will help you identify areas for improvement and tailor your study plan effectively.

- **Regular Practice**: Schedule regular practice exams throughout your preparation period. These should increase in frequency as you get closer to the exam date. After each practice exam, spend ample time reviewing your answers, especially the incorrect ones, to understand your mistakes and learn from them.

- **Time Management Practice**: Use these exams to improve your time management skills. Aim to answer questions more quickly and accurately over time, ensuring you can complete the exam within the allotted period.

Incorporating Breaks and Revision:

- **Scheduled Breaks**: Integrate short, frequent breaks into your study sessions to avoid burnout and enhance retention. Techniques like the Pomodoro Technique (25 minutes of focused study followed by a 5-minute break) can be highly effective.

- **Revision Sessions**: Allocate regular time slots each week for revising previously studied material. This helps solidify your understanding and ensures that earlier topics remain fresh in your mind.

Setting Realistic Goals:

- **SMART Goals**: Set Specific, Measurable, Achievable, Relevant, and Time-bound goals within your study plan. Examples could include mastering a specific number of process groups each week or completing a set number of practice questions each day.

- **Progress Tracking**: Keep track of your progress against these goals. Use tools such as checklists, apps, or journals to visualize your advancements and adjust your plan as needed.

- **Adaptability**: Be prepared to adjust your goals and study plan based on your progress and any life events that may arise. Flexibility is key to avoiding frustration and ensuring continuous progress.

Final Considerations:

- **Study Environment**: Create a conducive study environment that is quiet, comfortable, and free from distractions. Having a dedicated study space can improve focus and efficiency.

- **Peer Support**: Engage with a study group or find a study partner. Discussing topics and explaining concepts to others can deepen your understanding and uncover areas that require further study.

- **Health and Wellness**: Remember to maintain a balanced diet, exercise regularly, and get adequate sleep. Physical well-being significantly impacts mental performance and overall exam readiness.

- **Mental Preparation**: Develop a routine to manage stress and maintain a positive mindset. Techniques like meditation, deep breathing, or visualization can enhance focus and reduce anxiety leading up to the exam.

- **Review and Adjustment**: Regularly review your study plan to ensure it remains aligned with your learning needs and exam preparation goals. Don't hesitate to make adjustments in response to your evolving understanding or changes in your schedule.

By following these detailed steps, you can develop a personalized and effective study plan for the PMP exam. Remember, the key to success is not just hard work but also smart planning and consistent effort aligned with your personal learning style and life circumstances. Stay committed, stay flexible, and approach your PMP exam preparation with confidence and clarity.

Resource Selection - Embarking on the journey to achieve PMP certification demands not only dedication and hard work but also the right set of resources. The materials you choose will lay the foundation for your study regime and ultimately influence your success on the exam. Here, we will dive deeply into how to choose the best resources tailored to your learning style, ensuring they complement your study plan and enhance your exam readiness.

Primary Study Material: PMBOK Guide

- **Latest Edition**: Always opt for the most current edition of the PMBOK Guide. The PMP exam is directly aligned with the principles and knowledge areas outlined in this guide, making it your indispensable resource.

- **Thorough Review**: Don't just skim through the PMBOK Guide. Dedicate time to understanding each section and its application in real-world project management. Utilize additional notes or companion guides if necessary to clarify complex concepts.

- **Active Engagement**: As you read the PMBOK Guide, actively take notes, highlight key points, and summarize each chapter to reinforce retention and understanding.

Supplemental Resources: PMP Exam Prep Books

In your journey to PMP certification, having access to the right supplemental resources is crucial. While the PMBOK Guide is your foundational text, this PMP Exam Prep Book, the one you are currently reading, has been meticulously designed to serve as your primary supplemental resource. Here's why this manual stands out and how you can maximize its benefits during your study:

- **Tailored Content:** This manual has been developed with the latest PMP exam specifications and the PMBOK Guide's most recent edition in mind. Each chapter is aligned with the exam's domains and tasks, ensuring you receive up-to-date and relevant information.

- **In-Depth Coverage:** Unlike other materials that may only skim the surface, our book delves deeply into each topic covered on the PMP exam. We provide comprehensive explanations, real-world examples, and case studies that help bridge the gap between theoretical knowledge and practical application.

- **Practice Questions and Exams:** Embedded throughout this manual are numerous practice questions and mock exams designed to reflect the format and difficulty of the actual PMP exam. These resources allow you to assess your understanding, improve time management, and build exam confidence. After each set of questions, detailed explanations are provided to enhance learning and clarify any misconceptions.

- **Strategies and Tips:** Beyond just covering the exam content, this book is filled with proven strategies, study tips, and psychological tactics to help you approach the exam with confidence and efficiency. From tackling tricky questions to managing exam-day stress, these insights can significantly impact your preparation and performance.

- **Continuous Learning:** This manual is not just for passing the PMP exam; it's a resource for lifelong learning in project management. The concepts, tools, and techniques discussed herein are applicable beyond the exam and can be valuable in your professional career.

Structured Learning: PMP Preparation Courses

- **Accreditation and Instructor Experience**: Verify that the course is accredited by PMI and that instructors are PMP-certified with significant real-world project management experience.

- **Course Structure**: Choose a course that covers all exam content areas comprehensively, offering a structured approach to learning. Assess the course's format (live, on-demand, in-person, online) and choose what best fits your schedule and learning preferences.

- **Additional Benefits**: Look for courses that provide extra resources, such as study guides, flashcards, or access to a question bank. Check if they offer forums or groups for student interaction.

Collaborative Learning: Online Forums and Study Groups

- **Active Participation**: Engage actively in online forums and study groups. These platforms allow you to ask questions, share insights, and learn from the experiences of others who are also preparing for the exam.

- **Selection of Platforms**: Choose forums and groups with a positive, supportive atmosphere and a track record of helping candidates succeed. Platforms like Reddit, LinkedIn groups, or dedicated PMP community sites are popular choices.

- **Regular Engagement**: Dedicate a portion of your study time each week to participate in these communities. Sharing knowledge and solving others' queries can significantly enhance your own understanding.

Tailoring Resources to Your Learning Style:

- **Visual Learners**: If you're a visual learner, look for resources that include charts, graphs, and videos. Supplement your study with mind maps and infographics that illustrate project management processes and knowledge areas.

- **Auditory Learners**: Auditory learners should seek out podcasts, webinars, and online courses that provide audio explanations of PMP concepts. Participating in study group discussions can also be beneficial.

- **Kinesthetic Learners**: If you learn best by doing, focus on resources that offer interactive elements like quizzes, flashcards, or project simulation tools. Applying theoretical knowledge through practical exercises or real-world project management software can be particularly effective.

Resource Quality and Up-to-dateness:

- **Currency**: Ensure all resources are current and reflect the latest PMP exam format and PMBOK Guide edition. Outdated materials can lead to studying irrelevant or incorrect information.

- **Quality over Quantity**: It's better to have a few high-quality resources than a plethora of subpar materials. Quality resources are more likely to provide accurate, comprehensive information and effective study strategies.

- **Reviews and Recommendations**: Before investing in any resource, read reviews from other PMP candidates or certified professionals. Personal recommendations can guide you to the best materials.

Integration with Your Study Plan:

Remember, these resources should complement your study plan, not overwhelm it. Integrate them systematically into your schedule, allowing ample time for review and practice. Rotate between different types of materials to cover all learning styles and keep the study process engaging.

By selecting and effectively utilizing the right mix of resources, you significantly enhance your understanding and readiness for the PMP exam. While this manual serves as a guide, your personal selection of study materials, aligned with your unique learning preferences and study habits, will play a crucial role in your preparation and eventual success on the PMP exam. Remember, the path to PMP certification is a marathon, not a sprint; choose your resources wisely, plan your study schedule carefully, and commit to consistent, focused preparation.

Practice Exams and Question Analysis - Engaging with practice exams is a cornerstone of effective PMP exam preparation. These exams serve not merely as test runs but as critical tools for deepening your understanding of the PMBOK's principles and the PMP exam's structure. Regularly taking timed practice exams helps simulate the actual test environment, providing an invaluable opportunity to adapt to the exam's format and the variety of question styles you will encounter.

Benefits of Regular Practice:

- **Familiarization with Exam Format:** Understanding the layout, time constraints, and question formats of the PMP exam reduces surprises on the exam day, allowing you to focus on content rather than logistics.

- **Time Management Skills:** Practice exams are an effective way to enhance your time management, teaching you how to allocate your minutes wisely across different question types and sections.

- **Identification of Weak Areas:** These exams highlight your strengths and pinpoint areas needing improvement, guiding your study focus and revealing topics that require additional review.

- **Confidence Building:** Each completed practice exam builds your confidence and reduces test anxiety by familiarizing you with the exam process and type of questions asked.

Incorporating Practice Exams into Your Study Plan:

- **Frequency and Timing:** Begin with weekly practice exams and increase frequency as your exam date approaches. Initially, focus on understanding question formats; closer to the exam, use these as full simulation tests.

- **Realistic Conditions:** Mimic exam conditions as closely as possible—find a quiet space, time yourself strictly, and take only the breaks allowed during the actual exam.

- **Selection Criteria:** Choose practice exams that are up-to-date with the latest PMBOK editions and PMP exam formats. Prioritize quality and relevance over quantity.

Deep Dive: Analyzing Exam Questions and Answers:

- **Post-Exam Review:** Dedicate ample time after each practice exam to thoroughly review all answers. Understand why each answer is correct or incorrect, referencing the PMBOK Guide or other study materials to clarify any misunderstandings.

- **Rationale Analysis:** For each question, especially those answered incorrectly, dissect the reasoning behind each choice. This helps in understanding the PMBOK Guide's application in different scenarios and deepens your project management knowledge.

- **Pattern Recognition:** Identify recurring themes or concepts that you frequently struggle with. This insight allows for targeted study and reinforces learning in areas of weakness.

Feedback Loop and Continuous Improvement:

- **Tracking Mistakes:** Maintain a log of errors and misunderstandings from your practice exams. Use this log to focus your studies and review specific topics or PMBOK Guide sections.

- **Adjusting Study Plans:** Use insights gained from practice exams to adapt your study plan. Allocate additional time to weak areas and revise strategies that aren't yielding expected improvements.

- **Seeking Clarification:** For confusing or repeatedly missed concepts, seek clarification through study groups, forums, or mentors. External perspectives can provide new insights and aid understanding.

Maximizing the Impact of Practice Exams:

- **Diverse Sources:** Utilize practice exams from multiple sources to experience a variety of question types and wording. This diversification helps prepare you for the unpredictability of the actual exam.

- **Balanced Approach:** While focusing heavily on practice exams as the exam date nears, ensure this does not completely replace other forms of study. Continue to engage with the PMBOK Guide, supplementary materials, and other resources.

- **Reflection and Mindfulness:** Reflect on each practice exam's outcome with a constructive mindset. Understand that mistakes are opportunities for learning, not setbacks. Maintain a positive attitude and approach each new practice exam as a step closer to your certification goal.

Conclusion: By integrating practice exams into your preparation strategy, you bridge the gap between theoretical knowledge and practical application. This approach not only prepares you for the structure and demands of the PMP exam but also deepens your understanding of project management principles in a tangible, applicable manner. Remember, the goal of these exams is not just to pass but to prepare you for real-world project management challenges. Continuously refine your approach based on practice exam outcomes, and approach your PMP journey with the confidence and knowledge needed to succeed.

Group Study and Discussion Forums - Participating in group study sessions and engaging in active discussions within forums is a pivotal strategy in preparing for the PMP exam. This approach not only diversifies your understanding but also provides a supportive environment conducive to deeper learning. Here's how to make the most out of these collaborative platforms.

1. **The Power of Group Study**

Formation and Functioning:

- **Creating the Right Group:** Form a study group with fellow PMP aspirants. This could be with colleagues, through local PMI chapter meetings, or via online community boards. Aim for a diverse mix, bringing together individuals with different strengths and backgrounds.

- **Structure and Schedule:** Establish a regular schedule and stick to it. Consistency is key. Decide whether you'll meet weekly, bi-weekly, or at another frequency. Each session should have a clear agenda – perhaps a chapter from the PMBOK Guide or a specific domain from the exam content outline.

- **Roles and Responsibilities**: Rotate the role of the leader for each session to ensure active participation. The leader can guide the discussion, keep time, and ensure the session stays on topic.

2. **Engagement and Efficiency**:

- **Focused Discussions**: Each meeting should focus on discussing complex topics, clarifying doubts, and sharing insights. Utilize different perspectives to explore multifaceted project management scenarios.

- **Active Participation**: Encourage all members to contribute, ensuring a collaborative learning environment. Everyone should come prepared with questions or topics they need clarity on.

- **Utilization of Resources**: Bring diverse resources into your sessions. This could include sections from the PMBOK Guide, practice questions, or real-world case studies. Relate these materials back to exam content and real-life project management practices.

3. **Leveraging Discussion Forums**:

Selection and Engagement:

- **Choosing the Right Forums**: Opt for active, well-moderated forums frequented by PMP aspirants and certified professionals. The Project Management Institute's official forums, LinkedIn groups, or dedicated PMP preparation websites are excellent places to start.

- **Active Involvement**: Don't be a passive observer. Post your queries, share your study tips, and respond to others' questions. The more you engage, the more you benefit.

- **Information Verification**: Cross-check any advice or information received with credible sources like the PMBOK Guide or official PMI materials. Remember, while forums are invaluable for insights, they can sometimes contain misinformation.

Experiences and Insights:

- **Learning from Others' Experiences**: Pay special attention to contributions from individuals who have recently passed the PMP exam. Their tips, strategies, and study habits can provide crucial insights.

- **Sharing Successes and Setbacks**: Share your own experiences, including both successes and challenges. This not only helps others but can provide you with different perspectives and solutions.

- **Resource Exchange**: Utilize forums for exchanging study materials, such as templates, checklists, or flashcards. However, ensure that any shared resources comply with copyright and PMI's code of ethics.

4. **Best Practices for Collaborative Learning**:

Respect and Constructive Feedback:

- **Maintaining Respect**: Uphold a respectful tone in all discussions, whether in-person or online. Valuing diverse opinions fosters an inclusive and productive learning environment.

- **Constructive Criticism**: Provide and welcome constructive feedback. Aim to make criticisms specific and actionable, rather than general or disparaging.

Balancing Group and Individual Study:

- **Integration with Personal Study**: Use insights from group sessions and forums to inform your individual study. However, ensure these collaborative activities complement rather than replace your personal study time.

- **Reflective Practice**: After each group session or forum discussion, reflect on what you've learned. Apply these insights to your personal study notes and practice questions.

Conclusion: Engaging in group study and discussion forums should be an integral part of your PMP exam preparation strategy. These platforms provide opportunities to clarify doubts, understand different viewpoints, and solidify your own understanding of complex project management principles. By actively participating, respecting diverse perspectives, and integrating collaborative learning with personal study, you create a well-rounded preparation approach that not only aids in passing the PMP exam but also enriches your professional skills.

Remember, the journey to PMP certification is challenging but not solitary. Leverage the collective knowledge and support of your peers, and contribute your own insights to the community. This collaborative spirit not only aids in exam preparation but also reflects the essence of effective project management.

Time Management - Effective time management is a cornerstone of successful PMP exam preparation. It requires a strategic approach, blending structured planning with flexibility, to ensure comprehensive coverage of all exam topics while balancing personal and professional commitments. Below, we delve into how to construct and adhere to a realistic study schedule, drawing on principles from both the PMBOK Guide 6th and 7th editions.

Developing a Realistic Study Schedule:

- **Assessment and Planning**: Begin by assessing the volume of material to be covered and estimate a realistic timeframe for your preparation, considering your current knowledge level and learning pace. Reference the structure and content areas detailed in the PMBOK Guide to ensure your plan is comprehensive.

- **Scheduling**: Divide your study material into manageable sections, assigning them to specific weeks or months leading up to the exam. Utilize tools like digital calendars or project management apps to create your schedule, making sure to include all key topics outlined in the PMBOK Guide.

- **Time Allocation**: Allocate study time based on the complexity of topics and your familiarity with them. Topics that are more challenging or unfamiliar should get more time. Balance your study sessions to cover both the People, Process, and Business Environment domains, aligning with their respective weights on the exam.

Optimizing Study Sessions:

- **Identifying Productive Times**: Determine the times of day when you are most alert and focused. Schedule your most challenging study sessions during these periods to maximize efficiency.

- **Goal Setting**: For each study session, set clear, specific, and achievable goals. This could be understanding a particular process group, mastering a set of practice questions, or revisiting challenging concepts from the PMBOK Guide.

- **Consistency and Routine**: Establish a regular study routine to build momentum and create a habit. Whether it's early mornings, late evenings, or weekends, find times that work for you and stick to them.

Incorporating Breaks and Self-Care:

- **Importance of Breaks**: Schedule short breaks (5-10 minutes) during your study sessions to prevent burnout and enhance retention. For longer study periods, consider incorporating longer breaks (30 minutes to an hour) to recharge completely.

- **Activities During Breaks**: Use your breaks wisely—step away from your study space, stretch, go for a walk, or engage in a relaxing activity to clear your mind.

- **Health and Wellness**: Maintain a balanced lifestyle with proper nutrition, exercise, and adequate sleep. A healthy body supports a sharp mind, which is crucial for effective studying and retention.

Review and Practice Exams:

- **Regular Reviews**: Set aside time each week to review previously covered material. This reinforces learning and helps identify areas that might require further study.

- **Practice Exams**: Begin incorporating practice exams into your routine as you get closer to your exam date. Start with shorter quizzes focused on specific topics, gradually moving to full-length practice exams to simulate the actual test conditions.

- **Analysis and Adjustment**: After each practice exam, thoroughly review your answers, especially the incorrect ones. Analyze why you missed questions and revisit the relevant sections of the PMBOK Guide or your study materials to deepen your understanding.

Balancing Commitments:

- **Professional Commitments**: Communicate with your employer, if possible, about your exam preparation. Many organizations support employee certification efforts. Look for ways to integrate study into your professional life, such as applying PMBOK principles to current projects.

- **Personal Commitments**: Inform family and friends of your study goals and schedule. Seek their support to minimize interruptions and understand your availability. Incorporate study breaks to spend time with loved ones and rejuvenate.

Time Management Tools and Techniques:

- **Digital Tools**: Leverage digital tools like calendar apps, time tracking apps, and project management software to schedule and track your study sessions, set reminders, and monitor your progress.

- **Pomodoro Technique**: Consider using the Pomodoro Technique or similar time management methods to enhance focus and productivity during study sessions.

- **Adjustments and Flexibility**: Regularly review and adjust your study plan based on your progress and personal circumstances. Be flexible and adapt your plan as needed to ensure it remains effective and manageable.

Conclusion: Effective time management for PMP exam preparation is about more than just scheduling—it's about making intentional, strategic choices that align with your goals, learning style, and life commitments. By creating a tailored, realistic study plan, setting achievable goals, and incorporating regular reviews and practice exams, you can ensure comprehensive coverage of all exam topics. Remember, the journey to PMP certification is a marathon, not a sprint. Pace yourself, stay disciplined, and remain adaptable to navigate this journey successfully.

Exam-Day Strategies - Approaching the PMP exam requires more than just a thorough understanding of project management principles; it demands a strategic, composed, and well-planned approach on the day of the test. This comprehensive guide is designed to navigate you through the exam day, ensuring you are fully prepared, mentally and physically, to tackle the exam with confidence.

Preparation for Exam Day:

1. **The Night Before**:

   - **Review Essentials**: Check the PMI's exam-day instructions and prepare a checklist. Ensure your ID and confirmation letter are ready.

   - **Pack Your Bag**: Gather all necessary materials, including your ID, confirmation letter, and allowable items as per PMI guidelines.

   - **Relax and Rest**: Avoid last-minute cramming. Relax with light review notes if needed, then ensure you get a good night's sleep.

2. **Morning Rituals**:

   - **Healthy Breakfast**: Eat a balanced meal to fuel your brain for the hours ahead.

   - **Mindset and Visualization**: Engage in a brief meditation or visualization session. Picture yourself successfully navigating the exam.

Arrival at the Test Center:

- **Timing**: Arrive at the test center at least 30 minutes early. Account for traffic and potential delays to avoid unnecessary stress.

- **Pre-Exam Setup**: Complete all necessary check-in procedures. Use this time to acclimatize to the testing environment, take deep breaths, and center yourself.

During the Exam:

1. **Time Management**:
   - **Initial Planning**: Allocate a set time to read through instructions and plan your approach. Divide your time effectively among the questions.
   - **Pacing**: Keep an eye on the clock but don't obsess. Aim to spend just enough time on each question without rushing.

2. **Question Strategies**:
   - **Reading Carefully**: Read each question thoroughly, paying special attention to scenario-based ones. Note key information and requirements.
   - **Process of Elimination**: Use this technique to narrow down choices in multiple-choice questions. Dismiss obvious wrong answers first to improve your odds of selecting the correct one.
   - **Focus and Move On**: Answer each question to the best of your ability, then move on. Avoid dwelling on uncertainty; flag if review is needed and time allows.

3. **Maintaining Calm and Focus**:
   - **Breathing Techniques**: Practice deep breathing exercises if you feel anxious or overwhelmed. This can help reset your focus and reduce stress.
   - **Positive Reinforcement**: Remind yourself of your preparation and knowledge. Maintain a positive attitude throughout the exam.

4. **Breaks and Physical Well-being**:
   - **Utilizing Breaks**: If breaks are allowed, use them wisely. Step away from your desk, stretch, hydrate, and clear your mind.
   - **Physical Comfort**: Ensure you are dressed comfortably for the exam duration. Consider layers to adapt to varying room temperatures.

Post-Question Strategy:
- **Review**: If time permits, review flagged questions. Ensure that every question has been answered, as there is no penalty for incorrect responses – unanswered questions are missed opportunities.
- **Final Check**: Before submitting, do a quick scan to ensure that all questions have been addressed and that you have not missed sections due to oversight.

Post-Exam Reflection:
- **Immediate Reflection**: After the exam, take a moment to reflect on the experience. Consider what went well and what could have been improved.
- **Relax and Detach**: Regardless of your immediate feelings about how the exam went, take time to relax and decompress. Avoid post-exam analysis until results are received.

Conclusion:

Effective exam-day strategies extend beyond the mastery of content; they encompass the management of time, emotions, and physical well-being. By following these strategies, you can approach the PMP exam not just as a test of your project management knowledge, but as an opportunity to apply the principles of time, resource, and self-management—core aspects of what the PMP certification stands for. Remember, your performance on the exam is not just a reflection of your ability to memorize and regurgitate information, but your capability to think critically, manage resources, and stay composed under pressure—key traits of a successful project manager.

By entering the exam with a clear, well-practiced strategy, you maximize your ability to perform to the best of your abilities, significantly enhancing your likelihood of success.

Advanced Strategies for Tackling PMP Exam Questions

Question Analysis Techniques - Successful navigation of the PMP exam hinges on a nuanced understanding and application of question analysis techniques. This comprehensive approach isn't just about skimming through; it involves a deep dive into the essence of each question, dissecting its components, and aligning your responses with the robust framework provided by the PMBOK Guide's latest editions.

Understanding Question Requirements:

- **Initial Assessment**: Begin with a thorough read to grasp the question's scenario and requirements. Avoid rushing—misinterpreting the question is a common pitfall.

- **Keyword Focus**: Identify critical keywords or phrases. Words like "initial," "best," "next," or "most effective" signal the nature of the response needed. Terms related to project management concepts should resonate with PMBOK Guide terminologies.

- **Contextual Clues**: Each question is set within a specific context or situation which often hints at the applicable PMBOK area. Deciphering this context is crucial in applying the correct principle or process.

Dissecting the Scenario:

- **Relevant Information Extraction**: Distinguish essential details from the fluff. This skill becomes vital in scenario-based questions where not all provided information impacts the correct answer.

- **Application of PMBOK Principles**: Relate the scenario to specific principles, processes, or knowledge areas outlined in the PMBOK Guide. Is the question about risk management strategies, stakeholder engagement, or scope definition? Understanding this connection is key.

- **Answer Options Analysis**: Scrutinize each option in relation to the question's context and requirements. Eliminate options that are clearly out of scope or misaligned with PMBOK principles.

Strategic Approach to Answers:

- **Elimination Technique**: Systematically exclude incorrect or less relevant answers. This increases your probability of selecting the correct option from the remaining ones.

- **Optimal Choice Determination**: When faced with seemingly correct options, choose the one that best aligns with the PMBOK Guide's best practices and the specifics of the question's scenario.

- **Avoidance of Common Traps**: Beware of options that seem familiar or reflect "common sense" practices but don't align with PMBOK standards. Also, be cautious with absolutes like "always" or "never," which are rare in the flexible world of project management.

Enhancing Practice with Real-World Application:

- **Consistent Practice**: Engage regularly with practice questions. Use them not only to test your knowledge but to refine your question analysis technique.

- **In-depth Review**: After answering, review not just what the correct answer was, but why it was correct and why others were not. This reflection enhances understanding and retention.

- **Feedback Incorporation**: Learn from mistakes by revisiting concepts or sections in the PMBOK Guide related to frequently missed questions. Adjust your study approach based on these insights.

Practical Tips for Mastery:

- **Study Group Discussions**: Leverage study groups to discuss and dissect practice questions. Hearing different perspectives can deepen understanding and uncover nuances in question interpretation.

- **Timed Practice Sessions**: Simulate exam conditions to improve not just your knowledge but also your time management and stress handling. Time pressure can significantly impact question analysis.

- **Regular PMBOK Consultation**: Make the PMBOK Guide your cornerstone; regularly cross-reference it during your study sessions, particularly when reviewing practice questions.

- **Mindful Reflection**: After each study or practice session, take a moment to reflect on what was learned and how it applies to PMBOK principles and real-world project management scenarios.

- **Continuous Learning**: Keep abreast of updates to the PMBOK Guide and incorporate these changes into your study and question analysis strategies.

Conclusion: Mastering question analysis techniques for the PMP exam is an iterative process that blends understanding PMBOK principles, practicing consistently, and learning from each question encountered. By adopting a meticulous approach to reading, dissecting, and understanding each question, you refine your ability to apply theoretical knowledge in practical scenarios, enhancing your decision-making skills under exam conditions.

Remember, the PMP exam is less about rote memorization and more about applying principles effectively in varied situations. Hence, your focus should be on understanding concepts deeply and practicing their application through numerous well-analyzed questions. This holistic approach not only prepares you for the PMP exam but also lays a strong foundation for your future as a project management professional.

Time Management for Question Types - The PMP exam is a rigorous assessment that not only tests your project management knowledge but also your ability to manage time effectively. The variety of question types presented can vary significantly in complexity and required time to answer. Mastering how to navigate these differences is crucial for maximizing your exam performance. Here's an in-depth approach to managing your time effectively across different question types:

Understanding Question Types and Time Allocation:

1. **Question Type Recognition**: Familiarize yourself with the common types of questions on the PMP exam—situational, formula-based, knowledge-based, and interpretative. Each type requires different strategies and time allocations.

2. **Initial Assessment and Strategy**:

   - **Situational Questions**: Typically the most time-consuming due to their complexity and length. Allocate more time to these, but not at the expense of other simpler questions.

   - **Formula-Based Questions**: If you're well-practiced, these can be quick. However, ensure you double-check calculations to avoid simple errors.

   - **Knowledge-Based Questions**: These should be quicker to answer, as they often require recall of specific PMBOK Guide content.

   - **Interpretative Questions**: These require understanding and applying concepts to specific scenarios and can vary in the time required based on complexity.

3. **Allocating Time**: While the average time per question is about one minute, situational questions may need up to two minutes, whereas knowledge-based questions might be answered in less than a minute. Adjust your pacing accordingly.

Strategic Approach During the Exam:

1. **Initial Skim and Time Plan**: Begin by quickly skimming through the section to gauge the mix of question types. Formulate a time allocation plan based on your initial assessment.

2. **Tackling Questions Strategically**:

   - **Answer Immediately**: Questions within your strong areas or those that are straightforward should be answered immediately to secure easy marks and build confidence.

   - **Skip for Review**: Questions that seem time-consuming or slightly unclear should be marked for later review. This prevents getting bogged down early on.

   - **Mark for Educated Guessing**: If after a brief analysis you're unsure, mark these for potential educated guesses. Spend your time more wisely on questions you can solve.

3. **Time Checkpoints**: Set mental or physical (if allowed) checkpoints to ensure you're on pace, such as checking the clock after every 20 questions to ensure you're not falling behind.

Effective Review and Guessing Strategies:

- **Review Phase**: Return to skipped questions with any remaining time, starting with those you felt were manageable. Use elimination techniques to increase your odds even if guessing.

- **Educated Guessing**: When necessary, apply educated guessing to questions marked earlier. Utilize knowledge of PMBOK Guide principles and elimination strategies to improve your chances.

- **Final Sweep**: Ensure all questions have been answered. With no penalty for wrong answers, it's better to guess than to leave anything blank.

Practical Tips for Maximizing Exam Efficiency:

- **Practice with Timed Quizzes**: Regularly practice with timed quizzes to build your ability to gauge question complexity quickly and adjust your pace accordingly.

- **Develop Mental Stamina**: Build your concentration and stamina through longer study sessions and practice exams to better handle the mental demands of the actual exam.

- **Study PMBOK Guide Thoroughly**: Deep familiarity with the PMBOK Guide content can significantly reduce the time needed for knowledge-based and interpretative questions.

- **Simulate Exam Conditions**: Regularly practice under conditions similar to the exam to improve your time management and comfort under pressure.

- **Mindful Breaks**: Learn to recognize when a brief mental break can help reset your focus, even during the exam if allowed, to maintain peak performance throughout.

Conclusion: Effective time management during the PMP exam is as critical as the knowledge you bring into the testing center. By understanding the types of questions you'll encounter and developing a strategic approach to time allocation and question analysis, you enhance your ability to perform under pressure and increase your chances of success.

Remember, the goal is not only to answer all the questions but to answer them accurately within the limited time. Through practice, self-awareness, and strategic planning, you can optimize your exam performance, turning time management from a potential obstacle into a valuable asset in achieving your PMP certification.

Elimination Methods - In the quest to conquer the PMP exam, mastering elimination methods is a critical strategy. This approach, particularly effective for multiple-choice questions, involves discerning and dismissing less accurate answers to enhance the likelihood of selecting the correct option. Let's dive deep into how to leverage elimination methods, integrating insights from both the sixth and seventh editions of the PMBOK Guide.

The Foundation of Elimination Methods

- **Understanding Question Types**: Begin with recognizing the diverse question formats presented in the PMP exam. From situational puzzles that test your application of PMBOK principles to knowledge-based queries seeking direct information from the guide, each question type demands a tailored approach to elimination.

- **Initial Scan for Keywords**: Identifying keywords or phrases in the question can provide crucial hints towards the correct answer. Words like "first," "next," "best," or "most effective" signal the need for a prioritization based on PMBOK guidelines.

- **Contextual Clues**: Every question is set within a specific scenario, implicitly testing your knowledge of a particular process, knowledge area, or project management concept. Grasping this context is vital for effective elimination.

Strategic Elimination Techniques

- **Discarding Outliers**: Some options may blatantly conflict with PMBOK principles or the given scenario's logical flow. These should be the first to be eliminated.

- **Identifying Absolutes**: Answers framed in absolutes (e.g., "always," "never") are often misleading, given the situational nature of project management. Be skeptical of these options unless the question's context unequivocally supports them.

- **Comparing Similar Options**: When options appear closely related, delve deeper into their nuances. Often, the correct answer lies in a subtle distinction or a more comprehensive alignment with PMBOK standards.

- **Utilizing Project Management Principles**: Apply your understanding of project management principles directly. If an option contradicts fundamental concepts like the project life cycle stages, risk management processes, or stakeholder engagement techniques discussed in the PMBOK, it's likely incorrect.

Practical Application and Continuous Practice

- **Practice with Purpose**: Engage with practice questions not just to find the right answer but to hone your elimination skills. Reflect on why each incorrect option was plausible and why it was ultimately unsuitable.

- **Learn from Mistakes**: Each incorrect answer on a practice test offers a learning opportunity. Revisit the relevant PMBOK sections to reinforce your understanding and improve your future elimination strategy.

- **Time Management Integration**: Effective elimination contributes to better time management. Develop a sense for when to move on from a question after narrowing down the options, balancing thoroughness with the need to address all questions within the exam's time constraints.

- **Feedback Loops**: Incorporate feedback from practice sessions to refine your approach. Discussing strategies with peers or mentors can reveal additional insights and common pitfalls to avoid.

Enhancing Accuracy Under Time Constraints

- **Building Confidence**: As you become more adept at using elimination methods, your confidence in handling complex questions will grow, reducing exam-day anxiety and improving your overall performance.

- **Strategic Guessing**: When you're unable to identify the correct answer conclusively, a well-informed guess among the remaining options is better than leaving a question unanswered. The process of elimination increases the odds in your favor.

- **Final Review Strategy**: Use any remaining exam time to revisit questions where you've applied elimination. A fresh look might reveal new insights or reinforce your initial choice.

Conclusion: Mastering elimination methods is more than a test-taking tactic; it's a reflection of your depth of understanding and application of project management principles. By systematically practicing and refining your approach to eliminating incorrect answers, you not only enhance your efficiency but also deepen your comprehension of the PMBOK Guide's core concepts. This strategic mastery ensures you're well-prepared to tackle the PMP exam's challenges, making efficient use of your knowledge and time to achieve success.

Scenario-based Question Tactics - The PMP exam extensively tests your ability to apply project management principles in practical, real-world situations through scenario-based questions. These questions challenge your understanding and application of the PMBOK Guide's concepts, requiring not just memorization, but deep comprehension and critical thinking. Here's an advanced approach to excel in these questions:

Comprehensive Understanding of Scenarios:

1. **Initial Assessment:**

   - **Careful Reading:** Start by reading the scenario attentively. Understand the main issue and the specific project management context.

   - **Key Elements Identification:** Pinpoint critical information such as project stage, stakeholders involved, and the main conflict or decision point.

2. **Contextual Analysis:**

   - **Project Phase Recognition:** Determine which phase of the project lifecycle the scenario pertains to. Each phase may require different approaches and considerations.

   - **Stakeholder Perspectives:** Consider the interests and influences of different stakeholders mentioned in the scenario.

Application of PMBOK Principles:

1. **Theoretical Integration:**

   - **Relevant Processes and Knowledge Areas:** Link the scenario to relevant processes and knowledge areas from the PMBOK Guide. Understand which principles are being tested.

   - **Best Practices and Guidelines:** Apply best practices and guidelines appropriate to the situation. Ensure your chosen solution aligns with PMBOK standards.

2. **Solution Evaluation:**

   - **Option Analysis:** Evaluate each response option through the lens of PMBOK methodologies and your understanding of effective project management practices.

   - **Logical Deduction:** Use logical reasoning to eliminate options that don't comply with PMBOK principles or don't suit the scenario's specifics.

Critical Thinking and Problem Solving:

1. **Underlying Issues Identification:**

- **Root Cause Analysis**: Identify underlying issues within the scenario that may not be immediately apparent.

- **Impact Assessment**: Consider the potential impacts of different decisions, particularly in terms of project scope, time, cost, quality, and stakeholder satisfaction.

2. **Decision-Making Process**:

- **Prioritization**: Determine which issues or objectives should be prioritized based on the scenario and PMBOK guidelines.

- **Outcome Prediction**: Anticipate possible outcomes of different courses of action, considering risk and change management principles.

Effective Practice and Improvement:

1. **Practice with Variety**:

- **Diverse Scenarios**: Engage with a wide range of practice questions to cover various situations, project phases, and problem types.

- **Self-Reflection**: After answering, reflect on your thought process and rationale. Compare your approach to best practices outlined in the PMBOK Guide.

2. **Feedback and Adaptation**:

- **Peer Review**: Discuss challenging scenarios with peers or mentors to gain different perspectives and insights.

- **Continuous Learning**: Incorporate feedback and new understanding into your approach for continuous improvement.

Time Management in Scenario Analysis:

1. **Pacing Strategies**:

- **Allocated Time**: Develop a sense of how long to spend on scenario-based questions, balancing thorough analysis with time constraints.

- **Checkpoint System**: Create mental or physical checkpoints to ensure you remain on track without spending excessive time on any single question.

2. **Review and Adjustment**:

- **Flagging for Review**: Mark questions you are uncertain about for later review, ensuring you have time to address all questions.

- **Final Review**: Use remaining time to revisit flagged questions, applying fresh insights or reconsiderations.

Conclusion: Scenario-based questions are a critical component of the PMP exam as they reflect real challenges faced in project management. By thoroughly understanding scenarios, applying PMBOK principles judiciously, engaging in critical thinking, and practicing effectively, you enhance your ability to navigate complex problems and make informed decisions. This comprehensive approach not only prepares you for the PMP exam but also equips you with valuable skills for practical project management, ensuring that you're ready to tackle real-world challenges with confidence and expertise.

Stress Management during the Exam - Managing stress effectively is crucial for achieving success in the PMP exam. The ability to stay calm under pressure not only enhances your focus and performance but also reflects core competencies of an adept project manager. Here is an in-depth guide to mastering stress management techniques tailored for the PMP exam.

Understanding Stress and Its Impacts:

Before delving into specific strategies, it's important to recognize how stress manifests during exams. Symptoms can range from physical (e.g., headaches, tension) to psychological (e.g., anxiety, fear). Understanding that these reactions are normal can help you approach stress management more practically and compassionately.

Deep Breathing Techniques:

Breathing exercises are a powerful tool to mitigate stress. Here's how to integrate them into your exam routine:

- **4-7-8 Breathing**: This technique involves breathing in for four seconds, holding the breath for seven seconds, and exhaling for eight seconds. It's effective for calming nerves and refocusing your mind.

- **Box Breathing**: Inhale, hold, exhale, and hold again, each for four seconds. This method is beneficial for maintaining calm and steadiness in stressful situations.

Practicing these techniques daily leading up to the exam will make them more instinctive to use when stress levels rise.

Effective Use of Scheduled Breaks:

Utilize scheduled breaks strategically during the exam to prevent burnout and mental fatigue:

- **Plan Your Breaks**: Familiarize yourself with the exam's structure and plan your breaks accordingly. Even brief mental pauses can significantly rejuvenate your cognitive clarity.

- **Engage in Relaxation Activities**: Use break times for stretching, mindfulness, or other relaxation techniques. Avoid overthinking exam questions during these periods to truly mentally recharge.

Maintaining a Positive Mindset:

Cultivating a positive mindset is essential for navigating the exam confidently:

- **Visualization**: Regularly visualize yourself successfully navigating the exam. This mental rehearsal can enhance self-confidence and reduce exam-day anxiety.

- **Positive Affirmations**: Develop and repeat affirmations that bolster your confidence and readiness. Reminding yourself of your preparation and abilities can keep negative thoughts at bay.

Handling Difficult Questions:

Approach challenging questions with a structured strategy to avoid panic and time wastage:

- **Mark and Move On**: If a question seems particularly daunting, mark it for review and proceed. Concentrate on questions that you are more confident about to secure those points first.

- **Time Management**: Allocate a maximum time limit for each question to prevent any single problem from consuming too much of your exam time.

- **Emotional Control Techniques**: Practice quick stress-relief strategies such as taking three deep breaths or briefly closing your eyes to refocus if you start to feel overwhelmed.

Advanced Preparation and Mindset Techniques:

- **Simulate Exam Conditions:** Regularly practice under exam-like conditions to become accustomed to the pressure. Time yourself, sit in a quiet, exam-like environment, and follow the same break schedule you plan for the actual exam.

- **Build Resilience:** Engage in activities that build your resilience and stress tolerance, such as regular exercise, meditation, or yoga.

- **Pre-Exam Routine:** Establish a calming pre-exam routine that might include light reading, breathing exercises, or a brief walk. Arrive at the exam center early to avoid any last-minute stressors.

Conclusion: Effective stress management for the PMP exam encompasses more than just day-of tactics; it involves comprehensive preparation and mindset strategies that begin well before the exam date. By adopting these practices, you not only enhance your ability to perform optimally on the exam but also equip yourself with valuable skills for managing stress in your professional and personal life.

Implement these strategies to approach your PMP exam with confidence, calm, and clarity. Remember, your ability to manage stress is indicative of your readiness to tackle not just the exam, but the challenges of project management in real-world scenarios. Good luck, and remember, every step you take in preparation, including stress management, brings you one step closer to achieving your PMP certification.

Chapter-End Questions for Knowledge Areas

Introduction - Welcome to a crucial segment of your PMP exam preparation journey. The "Chapter-End Questions for Knowledge Areas" are designed to solidify your understanding and application of the core project management principles outlined in A Guide to the Project Management Body of Knowledge (PMBOK® Guide). These questions are not just a test of memory but a bridge connecting theoretical knowledge with practical project management skills.

The PMBOK® Guide, recognized globally as a fundamental resource for effective project management, organizes project management into distinct knowledge areas. Each area covers a different aspect of project management, ensuring a comprehensive approach to delivering successful projects. These areas encompass integration, scope, schedule, cost, quality, resource, communications, risk, procurement, and stakeholder management. The depth and breadth of these topics reflect the dynamic and multifaceted nature of project management.

Reflecting the evolution of the project management profession, the PMBOK® Guide's latest editions emphasize the value delivery spectrum, including predictive, agile, and hybrid approaches. As the PMP Examination Content Outline January 2021 indicates, modern project management practitioners operate across this spectrum, employing different approaches depending on the project's context. This shift is mirrored in the PMP exam structure, ensuring it remains relevant and challenging.

Your journey through these chapter-end questions will involve multiple-choice, matching, and scenario-based queries that mirror the PMP exam format. These questions are crafted to challenge your understanding, stimulate critical thinking, and enhance your ability to apply project management principles in real-life situations.

Each knowledge area is introduced with a summary that encapsulates its key components, followed by questions designed to probe your comprehension and application of these elements. The questions range from straightforward to complex, testing various aspects of project management knowledge and skills.

Here's what you can expect in this section:

1. **Integration Management**: Questions will explore your ability to identify and coordinate project elements, ensuring consistency and coherence across the project lifecycle.

2. **Scope Management**: You'll encounter scenarios testing your proficiency in defining and controlling what is and is not included in the project.

3. **Schedule Management**: Expect questions on your ability to manage project timelines, ensuring timely completion of project milestones.

4. **Cost Management**: Queries will assess your skills in planning, estimating, budgeting, and controlling costs to complete the project within the approved budget.

5. **Quality Management**: Challenges will focus on your understanding of quality planning, assurance, and control to meet project requirements.

6. **Resource Management**: Look for questions on planning, estimating, acquiring, developing, managing, and controlling project resources.

7. **Communications Management**: You'll be tested on your ability to ensure timely and appropriate planning, collection, creation, distribution, storage, retrieval, management, control, monitoring, and the ultimate disposition of project information.

8. **Risk Management**: This section will probe your ability to identify, analyze, and respond to project risks, ensuring project success despite uncertainties.

9. **Procurement Management**: Questions will evaluate your skills in purchasing or acquiring products, services, or results needed from outside the project team.

10. **Stakeholder Management**: You'll face scenarios testing your ability to effectively engage stakeholders, considering their needs and expectations, and ensuring their support throughout the project.

After completing the questions for each knowledge area, detailed explanations and references to the PMBOK® Guide sections will guide your review process, helping you understand why each answer is correct or incorrect. This approach is not just about testing your knowledge; it's about deepening your understanding and equipping you with the insight to apply project management principles effectively.

This structured approach ensures that you gain a comprehensive grasp of each knowledge area essential for the PMP exam. As you progress, you'll not only prepare for the exam but also build a solid foundation for a successful career in project management.

Remember, these chapter-end questions are more than just exam preparation; they are an opportunity to reflect, learn, and grow as a project manager. Embrace this challenge with an open mind and a commitment to excellence. The insights and skills you gain here will serve you well beyond the exam, throughout your project management career.

Integration Management

As we revisit the realm of Integration Management, let's encapsulate the key elements and concepts that were covered in detail earlier. This section is not merely a test of memory but an opportunity to reaffirm your understanding of how various processes and activities are woven together to ensure project success.

Integration Management is the backbone of project management, entailing the coordination of all elements of the project. This includes the harmonization of processes, tasks, and activities across the Project Management Process Groups. It's where strategic decision-making meets operational execution, ensuring that project objectives are achieved with efficiency and cohesion.

Remember, the essence of Integration Management lies in the synthesis of:

- **Project Charter Development**: The initiation of any project, laying the groundwork and giving authority to the project manager.

- **Project Management Plan Creation**: The blueprint guiding all project activities, from inception through to completion, adaptable to project needs and changes.

- **Directing and Managing Project Work**: The active phase where plans are executed and deliverables are created and monitored.

- **Monitoring and Controlling Project Work**: This involves tracking the project's progress, making adjustments as necessary to keep it aligned with the plan.

- **Performing Integrated Change Control**: A critical component, dealing with how changes are managed and controlled throughout the project lifecycle.

- **Closing the Project or Phase**: The formal conclusion, ensuring all work is completed satisfactorily and stakeholders are in agreement.

As you approach the following questions, reflect on how each element of Integration Management interplays within the project's lifecycle. The upcoming questions are structured to delve into your grasp of these principles, focusing on their practical application and strategic importance. This is your chance to connect theory with practice, showcasing your ability to integrate and manage diverse project elements seamlessly.

Approach these questions with a holistic view, considering not only the 'what' but also the 'why' and 'how' of Integration Management. Your responses will illuminate your readiness to tackle real-world project challenges and to steer projects towards their successful completion.

Questions:

    a. **Multiple-Choice Questions:**

1. **What is the primary purpose of a Project Charter?**

    a) To formally authorize a project or a phase

    b) To list the project's deliverables

    c) To assign team members to the project

    d) To outline the project's budget

2. **Which document establishes the total scope of a project?**

    a) Project Scope Statement

    b) Project Management Plan

    c) Project Charter

    d) Scope Management Plan

3. **During which process would a project manager assess and integrate all change requests?**

    a) Direct and Manage Project Work

    b) Monitor and Control Project Work

    c) Perform Integrated Change Control

    d) Close Project or Phase

b. Matching Questions:

1. Match the following Integration Management processes with their primary purpose:

1. Develop Project Charter

2. Develop Project Management Plan

3. Monitor and Control Project Work

4. Perform Integrated Change Control

a) Authorizes the project

b) Documents how the project will be executed, monitored, and controlled

c) Tracks, reviews, and regulates the progress and performance of the project

d) Reviews all change requests and manages changes to the project deliverables

2. Match the following terms related to Project Integration Management with their correct descriptions:

1. Close Project or Phase

2. Direct and Manage Project Work

3. Develop Project Charter

4. Perform Integrated Change Control

a) Involves tracking, reviewing, and orchestrating the changes to the project and its deliverables.

b) Authorizes the start of the project or a project phase and gives the project manager the authority to use organizational resources.

c) Involves completing the work defined in the project management plan to satisfy the project specifications.

d) Formalizes the completion of project deliverables and the handover to others or closure of a project phase.

3. Match the following terms related to Project Integration Management with their correct descriptions:

1. Develop Project Management Plan

2. Monitor and Control Project Work

3. Create Project Charter

4. Direct and Manage Project Execution

a) Involves overseeing the actual execution and implementation of the project's activities to create project deliverables.

b) Establishes the total combined baseline plans for how the project will be executed, monitored, controlled, and closed.

c) Formalizes the authorization to start a new project or a new phase of a project, providing the project manager with the authority to commit organizational resources.

d) Involves tracking, reviewing, and reporting the progress to meet the performance objectives defined in the project management plan.

c. Scenario-Based Questions:

1. **You are managing a project when a major stakeholder requests a significant change that could affect the project scope and timeline. What should be your first course of action?**

a) Implement the change immediately to please the stakeholder.

b) Evaluate the impact of the change on the project's scope, schedule, and cost.

c) Reject the change to keep the project on schedule.

d) Request additional funds from the sponsor to cover the change.

2. **While executing a project, you realize that the integration of a new technology will significantly benefit the project outcome but was not included in the initial plan. What is the best action to take?**
   a) Proceed with the integration without informing the stakeholders.
   b) Discuss the integration with the project team but decide independently.
   c) Document the change and submit it for approval through the project's change control process.
   d) Inform the stakeholders about the benefits and bypass the formal change control process.

3. **You are the project manager for an international construction project when sudden regulatory changes in the host country impact several project compliance requirements. The changes necessitate alterations to construction materials and methods, which could delay the project and increase costs. What should be your first course of action?**

a) Ignore the regulatory changes and continue with the planned materials and methods.

b) Inform the project team and stakeholders about the regulatory changes and their potential impacts.

c) Proceed to make the necessary changes to the construction materials and methods immediately.

d) Seek advice from legal and regulatory advisors before taking any action.

Answers:

a1. Correct Answer: a) To formally authorize a project or a phase.
Explanation: The Project Charter is crucial for formally authorizing a project or phase, providing the

project manager with the authority to utilize organizational resources. This is specifically highlighted in the PMBOK® Guide as its main purpose.

- **Why not b, c, or d?** The charter's primary role is not listing deliverables (b), which is more aligned with the scope management tasks, nor is it specifically for assigning team members (c) or outlining the budget (d). While it might touch on these areas, its formal authorization of the project is the key function.

a2. Correct Answer: b) Project Management Plan.
Explanation: The Project Management Plan is a comprehensive document that details how the project will be executed, monitored, and controlled, integrating all subsidiary plans and baselines, including scope.

- **Why not a, c, or d?** While the Project Scope Statement (a) details what is and is not included in the project, and the Scope Management Plan (d) outlines how scope will be managed, neither establishes the total scope like the Project Management Plan does. The Project Charter (c) authorizes the project but doesn't establish its total scope.

a3. Correct Answer: c) Perform Integrated Change Control.
Explanation: The Perform Integrated Change Control process is dedicated to reviewing all change requests, approving changes, and managing changes to deliverables, organizational process assets, and the project management plan.

- **Why not a, b, or d?** Direct and Manage Project Work (a) involves executing the project plan, not assessing changes. Monitor and Control Project Work (b) involves tracking project progress but not the integration of changes. Close Project or Phase (d) finalizes all project activities but doesn't assess change requests.

b1. Correct Answers:

- **Develop Project Charter** (1) matches with (a) Authorizes the project – The charter provides formal authorization, as outlined in the PMBOK® Guide.

- **Develop Project Management Plan** (2) aligns with (b) Documents how the project will be executed, monitored, and controlled – This plan outlines all aspects of project execution and oversight.

- **Monitor and Control Project Work** (3) corresponds to (c) Tracks, reviews, and regulates the progress and performance of the project – It involves measuring project performance against the management plan.

- **Perform Integrated Change Control** (4) pairs with (d) Reviews all change requests and manages changes to the project deliverables – This process ensures all changes are appropriately reviewed and implemented.

Why other matches are incorrect? Each process has a specific purpose within the framework of project integration management, and swapping any for another would misrepresent their defined roles in the PMBOK® Guide.

b2. Correct Answers:

1. **Close Project or Phase** matches with (d) Formalizes the completion of project deliverables and the handover to others or closure of a project phase – It signifies the formal end of project phases or the project itself.

2. **Direct and Manage Project Work** aligns with (c) Involves completing the work defined in the project management plan to satisfy the project specifications – It represents the execution phase where the project plan is implemented.

3. **Develop Project Charter** pairs with (b) Authorizes the start of the project or a project phase and gives the project manager the authority to use organizational resources – The charter provides the initial documentation and authority required to start the project.

4. **Perform Integrated Change Control** corresponds to (a) Involves tracking, reviewing, and orchestrating the changes to the project and its deliverables – It is the process where all requests for changes are processed and decided upon.

Why other matches are incorrect?

1. **Close Project or Phase** matching with anything other than (d) is incorrect because its primary purpose is not to initiate or manage ongoing work, but rather to conclude or terminate project activities and processes, signifying the project's or a phase's formal closure.

2. **Direct and Manage Project Work** matching with other options like (a) or (b) is incorrect as this process does not deal directly with change control or project initiation but rather with the implementation of the project plan and the creation of project deliverables.

3. **Develop Project Charter** matching with options other than (b) is incorrect because the main objective of the project charter is to initiate the project by formally authorizing its start, not to manage its changes (a) or define its completion (d).

4. **Perform Integrated Change Control** should not match with options other than (a) because its exclusive function is to oversee all changes in the project, including deliverables, documents, and project plans, ensuring they are reviewed and approved properly. It's not about starting the project (b), executing the work (c), or closing the project (d).

b3. Correct Answers:

1. **Develop Project Management Plan** matches with (b) Establishes the total combined baseline plans for how the project will be executed, monitored, controlled, and closed – It's the foundational document that guides the execution and control of the project.

2. **Monitor and Control Project Work** aligns with (d) Involves tracking, reviewing, and reporting the progress to meet the performance objectives defined in the project management plan – This process is crucial for ensuring that project objectives are met by monitoring project variables.

3. **Create Project Charter** corresponds to (c) Formalizes the authorization to start a new project or a new phase of a project, providing the project manager with the authority to commit organizational resources – It's the initial document that defines the project at a high level.

4. **Direct and Manage Project Execution** matches with (a) Involves overseeing the actual execution and implementation of the project's activities to create project deliverables – This

process is about executing the work defined in the project management plan to achieve project objectives.

Explanation of Incorrect Matches:

1. **Develop Project Management Plan** matching with any other descriptions is incorrect because it is specifically concerned with the integration and consolidation of all other project plans and baselines, not with initiating, monitoring, or executing the project.

2. **Monitor and Control Project Work** is incorrectly matched with any description other than (d) because its sole focus is on overseeing project execution against the project management plan and making necessary adjustments, not on planning, initiating, or executing.

3. **Create Project Charter** should not be matched with descriptions other than (c) because its unique role is to initiate the project by providing formal authorization, not to oversee its planning, execution, or monitoring.

4. **Direct and Manage Project Execution** incorrectly paired with other options diverges from its primary function, which is the enactment of project plans and creation of deliverables, distinct from planning, initiating, or monitoring and controlling the project.

c1. Correct Answer: b) Evaluate the impact of the change on the project's scope, schedule, and cost.
Explanation: Evaluating the impact is crucial for informed decision-making.

- **Why not a, c, or d?** Implementing changes immediately (a) can disrupt project plans without understanding their implications. Rejecting changes outright (c) might miss opportunities for project improvement. Requesting additional funds (d) without impact analysis may not be justified.

c2. Correct Answer: c) Document the change and submit it for approval through the project's change control process.
Explanation: Documenting and following the formal change control process ensures that all changes are thoroughly evaluated and approved, maintaining project integrity.

- **Why not a, b, or d?** Proceeding without informing stakeholders (a) can lead to issues with transparency and trust. Deciding independently (b) undermines the collaborative project management approach. Informing stakeholders without formal approval (d) misses critical steps for change evaluation.

c3. Correct Answer: b) Inform the project team and stakeholders about the regulatory changes and their potential impacts.

Explanation: Communication is key in project management, especially when facing unexpected changes that could affect project scope, timeline, and costs. Informing the team and stakeholders ensures transparency and allows for collaborative decision-making regarding the next steps.

- **Why not a, c, or d?** Ignoring regulatory changes (a) can result in legal issues and project failure. Immediately making changes (c) without team input or stakeholder agreement can lead to misalignment and further complications. While seeking legal advice (d) is important, the initial step should be to ensure all parties are informed and prepared to contribute to the solution process.

Scope Management

Scope Management is a fundamental aspect of project management, ensuring that the project includes all the work required, and only the work required, to complete the project successfully. This crucial balance prevents scope creep, controls what is and is not included in the project, and aligns with stakeholders' expectations and requirements.

In this section, we will recap the primary components of Scope Management as outlined in your previous studies and detailed within the PMBOK® Guide. This summary will serve as a foundational review to solidify your understanding and assist in the efficient preparation for the PMP examination.

Defining Scope: This step involves developing a detailed description of the project and its deliverables, setting the foundation for the project's success. Understanding how to accurately define the scope is critical to ensure the project's objectives are met while adhering to constraints such as time and cost.

Creating the Work Breakdown Structure (WBS): The WBS is a hierarchical decomposition of the total scope of work to be carried out by the project team. It organizes and defines the total scope of the project, ensuring nothing is overlooked and making the project manageable and measurable.

Validating and Controlling Scope: These processes ensure the project's deliverables meet the requirements specified by the stakeholders and manage changes to the project scope. Validation involves formal acceptance of the completed project deliverables, while control involves monitoring the project's status and managing changes to the scope baseline.

By thoroughly understanding and applying the principles of Scope Management, project managers can ensure that the project remains focused, deliverables meet stakeholder requirements, and changes are properly managed, all critical elements for the successful completion of the project.

Now, let's proceed with some practice questions to assess your understanding and readiness for the Scope Management portion of the PMP exam.

Questions:

a. Multiple-Choice Questions:
1. **What is the primary purpose of creating a Work Breakdown Structure (WBS) in project scope management?**

a) To allocate the project budget across tasks.

b) To define and organize the total scope of the project.

c) To identify and analyze project risks.

d) To establish communication channels within the project team.

2. **Which document formally authorizes the existence of a project and provides a summary of the project's objectives and management?**

a) Project Management Plan.

b) Project Scope Statement.

c) Project Charter.

d) Scope Management Plan.

   3. **Which process ensures that the project work delivers the outcomes specified in the Project Scope Statement?**

a) Develop Project Management Plan.

b) Validate Scope.

c) Control Scope.

d) Define Scope.

   b. **Matching Questions:**
   1. **Match the following Scope Management activities with their descriptions:**

   2. Collect Requirements

   3. Define Scope

   4. Create WBS

   5. Validate Scope

   6. Control Scope

a) Ensures that the project includes all and only the work required.

b) Formal acceptance of the completed project deliverables by stakeholders.

c) Determining, documenting, and managing stakeholder needs and requirements.

d) Developing a detailed description of the project and product.

e) Breaking down project deliverables into smaller, more manageable parts.

   2. **Match the following Scope Management terms with their correct descriptions:**

   1. Scope Baseline

   2. Scope Creep

   3. Work Package

   4. Scope Verification

   5. Change Log

a) The process of obtaining formal acceptance of the completed project deliverables.
b) Uncontrolled changes or continuous growth in a project's scope without proper adjustments to time, cost, and resources.
c) A document used to record all changes that have been requested and their current status.
d) The approved version of a scope statement, WBS, and its associated WBS dictionary, against which the project performance can be compared.
e) The smallest unit of work in the WBS that can be scheduled and cost estimated.

   3. **Match the following Scope Management processes with their correct descriptions:**

1. Plan Scope Management

2. Collect Requirements

3. Define Scope

4. Create WBS

5. Control Scope

a) Establishes the policies, procedures, and documentation for planning, managing, executing, and controlling the project scope.
b) Involves documenting the project and product requirements necessary to meet stakeholder needs and expectations.
c) Describes in detail the project's deliverables and the work required to create those deliverables.
d) Breaks down project deliverables into smaller, more manageable components.
e) Monitors the status of the project and scope and manages changes to the scope baseline.

   c. Scenario-Based Questions:
   1. **During a project status meeting, a team member suggests an additional feature that could enhance the project's end product. However, this feature was not included in the initial scope. As a project manager, what is your best course of action?**

a) Approve the addition immediately to keep the team member motivated.

b) Discuss the feature's benefits and impacts with the team, then decide.

c) Document the suggestion and submit it to the change control board for a decision.

d) Ignore the suggestion to avoid scope creep.

   2. **You discover an error in a project deliverable that has already been approved. This error could lead to increased costs if not corrected. What should you do first?**

a) Correct the error immediately without informing anyone to save time.

b) Inform the client or stakeholder about the error and discuss potential impacts.

c) Document the issue and refer it to the change control board for action.

d) Charge extra to the client for any corrections to maintain profit margins.

   3. **Your project is ahead of schedule but suddenly, a key supplier announces a delay in delivering critical components. This delay will likely cause your project to miss its next milestone. As the project manager, what is your first course of action?**

a) Update the project schedule to reflect the delay and inform the stakeholders.

b) Request the team to work overtime to compensate for the delay.

c) Assess the impact of the delay and explore alternative solutions, such as finding another supplier or adjusting the project plan.

d) Blame the supplier and demand they expedite shipping at their cost.

Answers:

a1. Correct Answer: b) To define and organize the total scope of the project.

Explanation: The WBS is designed to break down the project's total scope into more manageable components, ensuring all aspects are covered.

Why not a, c, or d? The primary purpose of the WBS is not to allocate budget (a), which is part of cost management, nor to identify risks (c), which falls under risk management. While communication (d) is crucial, it's not the function of the WBS.

a2. Correct Answer: c) Project Charter.

Explanation: The Project Charter formally authorizes the project, giving the project manager authority to utilize resources.

Why not a, b, or d? The Project Management Plan (a) is a document created after the project is authorized, detailing how the project is executed. The Project Scope Statement (b) outlines what is included in the project scope, not the project itself. The Scope Management Plan (d) details how the scope will be managed, not the project authorization.

a3. Correct Answer: c) Control Scope.

Explanation: Control Scope is the process of monitoring the status of the project and managing changes to the scope baseline.

Why not a, b, or d? Developing the Project Management Plan (a) is about how to execute and oversee the entire project, not just ensuring specific outcomes. Validate Scope (b) is concerned with formalizing acceptance of completed project deliverables. Define Scope (d) involves creating a detailed project scope statement, not ensuring the project work meets it.

b1. Correct Answers: 1 - c, 2 - d, 3 - e, 4 - b, 5 - a.

Why other matches are incorrect:

- Collect Requirements (1) specifically deals with identifying stakeholder needs, not with accepting deliverables (b) or controlling the project scope (a).

- Define Scope (2) is about developing a detailed project description, not about collecting requirements (c) or validating scope (b).

- Create WBS (3) involves breaking down deliverables, not defining the project scope (d) or controlling scope changes (a).

- Validate Scope (4) is aimed at obtaining stakeholder acceptance, not at collecting requirements (c) or breaking down deliverables (e).

- Control Scope (5) ensures only necessary work is included, not about accepting deliverables (b) or defining the project scope (d).

b2. Correct Answers: 1 - d, 2 - b, 3 - e, 4 - a, 5 - c.

Why other matches are incorrect:

- Scope Baseline (1) is meant to be a standard or reference, not a record of changes (c) or a process (a).

- Scope Creep (2) represents the gradual expansion of scope without approvals, not a controlled documentation process (c) or a completion validation process (a).

- Work Package (3) defines a task at its lowest level, not the process of formal acceptance (a) or the documentation of changes (c).

- Scope Verification (4) is about formal acceptance, not about tracking uncontrolled changes (b) or defining the work breakdown (e).

- Change Log (5) is specifically for tracking changes, not for detailing work packages (e) or defining the project's approved scope (d).

b3. Correct Answers: 1 - a, 2 - b, 3 - c, 4 - d, 5 - e.

Why other matches are incorrect:

- Plan Scope Management (1) is the process that outlines how the scope will be defined, validated, and controlled, not the detailing of specific deliverables (c) or the collection of requirements (b).

- Collect Requirements (2) specifically deals with understanding what stakeholders need and expect from the project, not with establishing management plans (a) or creating smaller work components (d).

- Define Scope (3) provides a detailed description of the project and its products, distinguishing it from the initial planning of scope procedures (a) or the monitoring of scope (e).

- Create WBS (4) refers to breaking down the deliverables into smaller parts, different from collecting requirements (b) or defining the overall management plan (a).

- Control Scope (5) involves ensuring the project remains within its planned scope, distinctly different from planning how scope is managed (a) or defining what constitutes the scope (c).

c1. Correct Answer: c) Document the suggestion and submit it to the change control board for a decision.

Explanation: Proper scope management requires all changes to be assessed for their impact on the project's time, cost, and quality.

Why not a, b, or d? Instant approval (a) risks uncontrolled scope creep. Simply discussing (b) is insufficient without formal assessment and decision-making. Ignoring (d) could miss potential improvements.

c2. Correct Answer: c) Document the issue and refer it to the change control board for action.

Explanation: The change control board should assess all project changes or issues to decide on the appropriate action.

Why not a, b, or d? Immediate correction (a) bypasses necessary project management protocols. While informing the client (b) is part of good communication, formal procedures must be followed. Charging extra (d) without formal approval and assessment could breach contract terms and damage stakeholder relationships.

c3. Correct Answer: c) Assess the impact of the delay and explore alternative solutions, such as finding another supplier or adjusting the project plan.

Explanation: It's important to first assess the overall impact and then look for viable solutions to mitigate the delay.

Why not a, b, or d? Simply updating the schedule (a) without exploring solutions is passive. Requesting overtime (b) might be a premature action before exploring all options. Blaming the supplier (d) does not constructively address the problem or lead to a viable solution.

Schedule Management

Schedule Management is essential in project management, ensuring projects are completed on time. Here's a condensed overview:

- **Activity Identification**: Break down project goals into specific tasks, utilizing clarity to avoid overlooking crucial details.

- **Activity Sequencing**: Organize these tasks based on dependencies, employing methods like:

  - Precedence Diagramming Method (PDM) for visual task sequencing.

  - Critical Path Method (CPM) to identify key task sequences affecting project duration.

- **Duration Estimation**: Assess time needed for each task by:

  - Evaluating resource availability and historical project data.

  - Applying Three-Point Estimating to balance optimistic, pessimistic, and most likely durations.

- **Schedule Development**: Combine identified activities, their sequence, and durations into a coherent timeline. Tools such as Gantt charts are typically used here for visual representation and easier management.

- **Schedule Control**: Continuously monitor and adjust the schedule to reflect actual project progress. This step is crucial for maintaining project alignment with planned timelines.

Integration is key: Schedule Management interacts closely with other project areas like Cost and Risk Management. Changes in the schedule can significantly impact the budget and introduce new risks, requiring a well-coordinated approach to manage effectively.

Questions:
  a. **Multiple-Choice Questions:**
  1. **What is the main purpose of the Critical Path Method (CPM) in project management?**

a) To identify project risks

b) To allocate project resources

c) To estimate project costs

d) To determine the longest path of tasks in a project

  2. **Which scheduling technique allows for flexibility by identifying early start, late start, and float for activities?**

a) Milestone Chart

b) Gantt Chart

c) Critical Path Method (CPM)

d) Resource Leveling

3. What does 'float' represent in project scheduling?

a) The total cost for a project

b) The minimum resources required for a task

c) The amount of time a task can be delayed without affecting the project end date

d) The number of days a project has been delayed

b. Matching Questions:
1. Match the following terms related to Schedule Management with their correct descriptions:

1. Gantt Chart

2. Float

3. Milestone

4. Lead

5. Lag

a) A point in time representing a major achievement or critical event in the project.

b) The graphical representation of a project's timeline.

c) The amount of time a task can be delayed without delaying the project.

d) Time added between tasks.

e) Time fast-forwarded between tasks.

2. Match the following scheduling techniques and concepts with their correct descriptions:

1. Fast Tracking

2. Resource Leveling

3. Critical Chain Method

4. Baseline Schedule

5. PERT (Program Evaluation and Review Technique)

a) A schedule adjustment method that involves performing tasks in parallel that were originally planned in sequence.

b) Balancing the demand for resources against the available supply without altering the project's critical path.

c) A method that takes into account resource constraints and project uncertainties, focusing on the resources required to complete the tasks.

d) The approved version of a schedule model that can be changed only through formal change control procedures.

e) A statistical tool used to analyze the tasks involved in completing a project, particularly the time needed to complete each task and identifying the minimum time needed to complete the total project.

3. **Match the following terms with their appropriate definitions in the context of Schedule Management:**

1. Slack Time

2. Milestone Chart

3. Simulation

4. Crashing

5. Activity Duration Estimates

a) A technique to shorten the project schedule without reducing project scope by adding resources to critical path activities.

b) Visual representation highlighting major events and phases in the project timeline.

c) The amount of time that a task can be delayed without causing a delay to subsequent tasks or the project finish date.

d) The process of calculating and applying probable project durations based on various scenarios and variables.

e) Approximations concerning how many work periods are needed to complete individual activities with

c. **Scenario-Based Questions:**
1. **You are managing a software development project when you realize a key integration task is taking longer than expected. To avoid delaying the project, what should you do?**

a) Increase the project budget.

b) Fast-track the project by overlapping tasks.

c) Extend the project deadline immediately.

d) Add more resources to earlier tasks.

2. **During a project status update, you notice that several tasks are ahead of schedule. What is the best use of this time advantage?**

a) Extend the deadlines for all remaining tasks.

b) Begin subsequent tasks earlier, if possible.

c) Allocate more tasks to the team.

d) Take no action; continue as planned.

3. **Your project is running behind schedule. In your next team meeting, what should be the primary focus to bring the project back on track?**

a) Assigning blame to team members for delays.

b) Revising the schedule to reflect realistic progress and constraints.

c) Canceling the project due to time overruns.

d) Decreasing the quality standards to save time.

Answers:

a1. Correct Answer: d) To determine the longest path of tasks in a project.

Explanation: The Critical Path Method is utilized to identify the sequence of dependent tasks that determine the project's duration.

Why not a, b, or c? CPM is specifically designed for time analysis rather than risk identification (a), resource allocation (b), or cost estimation (c).

a2. Correct Answer: c) Critical Path Method (CPM).

Explanation: CPM helps in identifying critical and non-critical activities, providing information on early and late starts, and calculating float.

Why not a, b, or d? Milestone charts (a) and Gantt charts (b) help in visualizing the schedule but don't specifically offer flexibility regarding start times and float. Resource Leveling (d) is a technique used to balance resource demand with supply.

a3. Correct Answer: c) The amount of time a task can be delayed without affecting the project end date.

Explanation: Float, or slack, is the measure of flexibility in starting and completing a task without impacting the project's overall timeline.

Why not a, b, or d? Total cost (a) is unrelated to scheduling flexibility. Minimum resources (b) refer to resource management, not time management. The number of days a project has been delayed (d) is a status metric, not a planning tool.

b1. Correct Answers: 1 - b, 2 - c, 3 - a, 4 - e, 5 - d.

Why other matches are incorrect:

- Gantt Chart (1) is known for its timeline visualization (b), not for marking significant project events (a) or showing task delays (c).

- Float (2) defines scheduling flexibility (c), not a visual tool (b) or a time interval between tasks (d, e).

- Milestone (3) signifies key project events (a), not delay flexibility (c) or a scheduling representation (b).

- Lead (4) accelerates task succession (e), differing from slack time (c) or project achievements (a).

- Lag (5) introduces a delay between tasks (d), which is not about project visualization (b) or crucial achievements (a).

b2. Correct Answers: 1 - a, 2 - b, 3 - c, 4 - d, 5 - e.

Why other matches are incorrect:

- Fast Tracking (1) specifically refers to the strategy of overlapping tasks (a), not to resource allocation (b) or project evaluation techniques (e).

- Resource Leveling (2) is aimed at evenly distributing resources (b), not accelerating project timelines (a) or defining initial schedule models (d).

- Critical Chain Method (3) emphasizes managing resources for project execution (c), distinct from scheduling evaluations (e) or baseline settings (d).

- Baseline Schedule (4) is the original project schedule which serves as a standard for comparison (d), not a method for managing resources (b) or analyzing project timelines (e).

- PERT (5) is used for project time analysis (e), not for overlapping activities (a) or resource constraint management (c).

b3. Correct Answers: 1 - c, 2 - b, 3 - d, 4 - a, 5 - e.

Why other matches are incorrect:

- Slack Time (1) is specifically the buffer or leeway in a schedule (c), not a strategy for accelerating project tasks (a) or a method for projecting durations (d).

- Milestone Chart (2) provides a high-level overview of key project events (b), not detailed resource estimations (e) or schedule reduction techniques (a).

- Simulation (3) involves creating various project "what-if" scenarios (d), which is different from showing progress through charts (b) or estimating the time for activities (e).

- Crashing (4) is the act of expediting project timelines through increased resources or shifting priorities (a), not a description of slack or buffer time (c) or a visual scheduling tool (b).

- Activity Duration Estimates (5) concern the time necessary to accomplish tasks (e), not the visualization of project milestones (b) or the analysis of time flexibility (c).

c1. Correct Answer: b) Fast-track the project by overlapping tasks.

Explanation: Fast-tracking involves starting tasks earlier than planned, even when others haven't finished, to keep the project on schedule.

Why not a, b, or c? Increasing the budget (a) does not directly address time constraints. Extending the deadline (c) should be a last resort. Adding resources to earlier tasks (d) may help but doesn't directly address the current delay like fast-tracking does.

c2. Correct Answer: b) Begin subsequent tasks earlier, if possible.

Explanation: Advancing the start of subsequent tasks can maintain or increase the project's lead time, offering a buffer for future uncertainties.

Why not a, c, or d? Extending deadlines (a) wastes the time gained. Allocating more tasks (c) could overload the team unnecessarily. Taking no action (d) misses the opportunity to utilize the time saved effectively.

c3. Correct Answer: b) Revising the schedule to reflect realistic progress and constraints.

Explanation: Updating the schedule allows the team to realign with achievable deadlines and identify areas for recovery.

Why not a, c, or d? Blaming team members (a) is counterproductive. Canceling the project (c) may be premature without exploring recovery options. Decreasing quality (d) can have long-term negative impacts and should be avoided.

Cost Management

Cost Management is a critical discipline in project management, focusing on the planning, estimation, budgeting, and control of project costs to ensure project completion within the approved budget. It intertwines with other project management domains, impacting and influenced by scope and schedule management, to ensure financial resources are used effectively and efficiently.

At the heart of effective Cost Management lies:

1. **Cost Planning**: Developing a detailed Cost Management Plan sets the foundation. This plan outlines how project costs will be estimated, budgeted, financed, and controlled. It's essential for guiding all cost-related activities and decisions throughout the project lifecycle.

2. **Cost Estimation**: This step involves determining the monetary resources necessary for project activities. Accurate cost estimation is vital to prevent budget overruns and forms the basis for the project budget. Techniques such as bottom-up estimating provide detailed insights, ensuring comprehensive coverage of all expected expenses.

3. **Budgeting**: Here, costs are allocated to project components, forming the Cost Baseline. This baseline serves as a yardstick for measuring financial performance and controlling expenses, ensuring that the project stays within budget while achieving its objectives.

4. **Cost Control**: This ongoing process involves monitoring and managing changes to the project budget. Tools like Earned Value Management (EVM) integrate cost, scope, and schedule measures to give project managers a clear view of project performance and financial health. By tracking key metrics such as the Cost Performance Index (CPI) and Schedule Performance Index (SPI), managers can make informed decisions to steer the project back on track financially.

In real-world applications, Cost Management proves to be indispensable. From handling unforeseen cost increases due to market fluctuations to navigating budget constraints while maintaining project quality, mastering this area is essential for project success. Effective Cost Management ensures that projects deliver value while staying within financial boundaries, making it a key area for PMP candidates to understand and apply in their project management practices.

In summary, Cost Management is not just about counting pennies but about ensuring that every dollar spent contributes to the ultimate project goals. Understanding and applying the principles of Cost Management is crucial for passing the PMP exam and for the successful financial governance of projects in any industry.

Questions:

a. Multiple-Choice Questions:

1. What is the primary purpose of developing a Cost Management Plan?

a) To determine the project's profit margin.

b) To outline how costs will be estimated, budgeted, financed, and controlled.

c) To list all possible expenses in the project.

d) To allocate tasks to project team members.

2. Which tool or technique is especially useful for cost control in project management?

a) Work Breakdown Structure (WBS)

b) Gantt Chart

c) Earned Value Management (EVM)

d) Precedence Diagramming Method (PDM)

3. What does the Cost Performance Index (CPI) represent in project management?

a) The estimated cost of work scheduled.

b) The actual cost of work performed.

c) The ratio of earned value to actual cost.

d) The financial value of completed work.

b. Matching Questions:

1. Match the following cost management elements with their descriptions:
1. Cost Baseline
2. Contingency Reserve
3. Budget At Completion (BAC)
4. Actual Cost (AC)
5. Variance Analysis

a) The total budgeted project cost at the start.

b) The original budget plus or minus approved changes.

c) Funds set aside for unforeseen changes.

d) The examination of deviations from the budget.

e) The total costs incurred for the work completed.

2. Match the cost-related terms to their correct definitions:

1. Fixed Costs
2. Variable Costs
3. Direct Costs
4. Indirect Costs
5. Life Cycle Costing

a) Costs that do not change with the level of production or project scope.

b) Costs that vary in proportion to the level of production or project activity.

c) Costs directly attributable to a specific work package or task.

d) Costs not directly tied to a specific project activity or work package.

e) The total cost of ownership of a project's product, service, or result over its lifespan.

3. Match the following cost management concepts with their correct definitions:

1. Budget At Completion (BAC)

2. Estimate At Completion (EAC)

3. Estimate To Complete (ETC)

4. To-Complete Performance Index (TCPI)

5. Reserve Analysis

a) The estimated total cost of completing all work expressed as the sum of the actual cost to date and the estimate to complete.

b) An analysis used to determine the amount of contingency and management reserves needed for the project.

c) The original total budget of the project.

d) The expected cost needed to complete all the remaining project work.

e) The calculated performance measure needed to achieve a specific management goal with the remaining resources.

c. Scenario-Based Questions:

1. You are managing a project with a tight budget. Halfway through, you realize that material costs have increased significantly, threatening to exceed the Cost Baseline. What should be your first action?

a) Request additional funds from the sponsor without any analysis.

b) Cut project scope to reduce costs immediately.

c) Perform a variance analysis to understand the impact of increased costs.

d) Ignore the increase as these fluctuations are common.

2. **During a project status meeting, it's reported that the project's actual expenses are significantly lower than the planned budget due to unexpected resource availability. How should you proceed?**

a) Immediately reduce the project scope to match the lower costs.

b) Reallocate savings to areas of the project with higher risk.

c) Report the under-spending as project savings without further action.

d) Ignore the variance as it might change in the future.

3. **Your project is behind schedule, but under budget. You're considering fast-tracking to catch up. What should you analyze first regarding costs?**

a) Determine if there is enough budget to handle potential rework costs.

b) Immediately allocate all remaining budget to speed up all tasks.

c) Reduce the project scope to balance the schedule and costs.

d) Ignore cost implications and proceed with fast-tracking.

Answers:

a1. Correct Answer: b) To outline how costs will be estimated, budgeted, financed, and controlled.

Explanation: The Cost Management Plan serves as a guide for managing project costs throughout its lifecycle, ensuring all financial aspects are handled systematically.

Why not a, c, or d?: Determining profit margin (a) is not the primary focus of project cost management, listing all expenses (c) is part of budgeting but not the sole purpose of the plan, and task allocation (d) relates more to resource management than cost management.

a2. Correct Answer: c) Earned Value Management (EVM).

Explanation: EVM integrates scope, schedule, and cost data to provide a comprehensive view of project performance and financial health, making it crucial for cost control.

Why not a, b, or d?: WBS (a) is used for breaking down project work, Gantt Chart (b) is a scheduling tool, and PDM (d) helps in task sequencing rather than cost control.

a3. Correct Answer: c) The ratio of earned value to actual cost.

Explanation: CPI is a key performance index in EVM used to measure cost efficiency by comparing the value of work completed to the actual cost incurred.

Why not a, b, or d?: Estimated cost of work scheduled (a) is related to the planned value, actual cost of work performed (b) defines the actual expenses without performance context, and financial value of completed work (d) is more aligned with earned value, not a performance index.

b1. Correct Answers:

1 - b, 2 - c, 3 - a, 4 - e, 5 - d.

Why other matches are incorrect:

The Cost Baseline (1) is defined as the original budget (b), not just total budgeted cost (a) or a measure of costs incurred (e).

Contingency Reserve (2) is for unexpected changes (c), not the total budgeted cost (a) or actual expenditure (e).

BAC (3) represents the total initial budgeted cost (a), not the reserve for unforeseen events (c) or the actual expenditure (e).

AC (4) refers to actual expenditures (e), not a financial reserve (c) or budget analysis method (d).

Variance Analysis (5) is the process of examining budget deviations (d), not defining total project costs (a) or actual expenditures (e).

b2. Correct Answers:

1 - a, 2 - b, 3 - c, 4 - d, 5 - e.

Why other matches are incorrect:

Fixed Costs (1) remain constant regardless of activity levels (a), not varying with production (b) or directly attributable to tasks (c).

Variable Costs (2) change with activity levels (b), unlike fixed (a) or indirect costs (d).

Direct Costs (3) can be directly linked to specific activities (c), as opposed to variable (b) or indirect costs (d).

Indirect Costs (4) are not tied to specific activities (d), different from direct (c) or variable costs (b).

Life Cycle Costing (5) considers all costs over the product's lifetime (e), not just initial or specific task costs (a-d).

b3.

Correct Answers: 1 - c, 2 - a, 3 - d, 4 - e, 5 - b.

Why other matches are incorrect:

- Budget At Completion (BAC) is the initial budget, not the forecasted completion cost (a) or the analysis method (b).

- Estimate At Completion (EAC) forecasts the project's total cost, differing from the original budget (c) or the remaining work cost (d).

- Estimate To Complete (ETC) reflects the expected future spending, not the total project budget (c) or a performance index (e).

- To-Complete Performance Index (TCPI) measures the cost performance required to meet a specific objective, not associated with initial estimates (c) or total forecasts (a).

- Reserve Analysis evaluates funds needed beyond the estimate, unlike total budget (c) or cost to complete the project (d).

c1. Correct Answer: c) Perform a variance analysis to understand the impact of increased costs.

Explanation: Variance analysis helps in understanding how the increased costs affect the overall budget and what measures can be taken to mitigate the impact.

Why not a, b, or d?: Requesting additional funds (a) without analysis is premature, cutting scope (b) may affect project deliverables, and ignoring cost increases (d) can lead to budget overrun.

c2. Correct Answer: b) Reallocate savings to areas of the project with higher risk.

Explanation: Reallocating savings to higher-risk areas can provide a buffer and enhance project success without compromising scope or quality.

Why not a, c, or d?: Reducing scope (a) may compromise project goals, reporting as savings (c) misses an opportunity for risk mitigation, and ignoring (d) neglects potential strategic reallocation.

c3. Correct Answer: a) Determine if there is enough budget to handle potential rework costs.

Explanation: Before fast-tracking, it's crucial to assess whether the budget can accommodate the risks associated with expedited activities, including potential rework.

Why not b, c, or d?: Allocating all remaining budget (b) is reckless without specific strategy, reducing scope (c) might not address the schedule issue, and ignoring costs (d) can lead to financial overrun.

Quality Management

Quality Management in project management is a comprehensive approach that goes beyond simply meeting specified requirements; it's about achieving excellence and ensuring stakeholder satisfaction. This essential aspect of project management is integrated throughout the project lifecycle to ensure that deliverables not only meet but surpass expected standards.

Key Concepts in Quality Management:

- **Defining Quality Policies and Objectives**: Establish clear and concise quality policies aligned with the project's vision and stakeholder expectations. Set SMART (Specific, Measurable, Achievable, Relevant, Time-bound) objectives as benchmarks for assessing project success.

- **Planning for Quality**: Identify relevant quality standards and strategies for achieving them. Utilize techniques such as Failure Mode and Effects Analysis (FMEA) and Six Sigma to anticipate and address potential quality issues. Develop a Quality Management Plan that complements the overall project plan.

- **Performing Quality Assurance**: Conduct systematic activities to ensure project processes meet defined quality standards. This preventive approach involves regular assessments and adherence checks to foster confidence in the project's quality procedures.

- **Controlling Quality**: Apply operational techniques to fulfill quality requirements. This includes inspecting deliverables, identifying defects, and taking corrective action. Utilize tools like Control Charts and Pareto Diagrams for defect monitoring and cause identification.

- **Integration with Other Knowledge Areas**: Recognize the interconnectedness of Quality Management with Scope, Schedule, and Cost Management to ensure quality is maintained despite project variations. Changes in scope, for instance, should prompt a revision of the quality plan to meet new project demands without compromising standards.

Effective Quality Management ensures projects exceed stakeholder expectations. By weaving quality processes, planning, and continuous improvement into the project fabric, managers secure not only the project's success but also heightened stakeholder satisfaction.

Questions:

a. Multiple-Choice Questions:
1. What is the primary goal of Quality Management in project management?

a) To ensure the project is completed within budget.

b) To ensure the project meets or exceeds stakeholder expectations.

c) To ensure the project is completed on time.

d) To ensure the project uses all available resources.

2. Which tool is commonly used in Quality Management to identify the causes of defects?

a) Gantt Chart

b) Fishbone (Ishikawa) Diagram

c) Pareto Chart

d) WBS (Work Breakdown Structure)

3. What does a Control Chart primarily monitor in a project's Quality Management process?

a) Project Budget

b) Staff Performance

c) Quality Variance

d) Scope Changes

b. Matching Questions:
1. Match the following Quality Management tools to their correct descriptions:

1. Pareto Chart

2. Control Chart

3. Fishbone Diagram

4. Benchmarking

a) Identifies the root causes of a problem.

b) Monitors the stability and variability of a process.

c) Helps prioritize problem-solving efforts by identifying the most significant issues.

d) Compares project practices against the best in the industry.

2. **Match the following Quality Management concepts with their correct definitions:**

1. Total Quality Management (TQM)

2. Cost of Quality (CoQ)

3. Root Cause Analysis

a) A method used to identify the underlying reasons for defects or problems.

b) The approach that involves everyone in the organization in improving processes, products, services, and culture.

c) The total amount of costs incurred by the implementation of quality throughout the project lifecycle.

3. **Match the following tools to their Quality Management applications:**

1. Six Sigma

2. Quality Audit

3. Statistical Sampling

a) A systematic process to check whether project activities comply with organizational and project policies, procedures, and processes.

b) A technique that employs mathematical analysis to measure and improve a company's operational performance by identifying and eliminating 'defects.'

c) The method of selecting a part of a population to represent the whole population, used to conduct quality control tests.

c. **Scenario-Based Questions:**
1. **You have noticed a pattern of defects in the project output. What is your first step according to Quality Management principles?**

a) Reassign project team members to different tasks.

b) Conduct a root cause analysis using tools like the Fishbone Diagram.

c) Immediately inform the stakeholders about potential project failure.

d) Reduce the project scope to focus on fewer quality issues.

2. **During project execution, you find that the quality metrics are not meeting the standards defined in the Quality Management Plan. What should you do next?**

a) Ignore the metrics and continue with the planned activities.

b) Review and adjust the Quality Management Plan and processes based on the metrics.

c) Disband the quality control team and form a new one.

d) Increase the project budget to cover additional quality control measures.

3. **A key stakeholder is not satisfied with the quality of the project deliverables despite them meeting the specifications outlined in the Quality Management Plan. What is the most appropriate action?**

a) Ignore the stakeholder's concerns since the specifications were met.

b) Review the stakeholder's concerns and compare them against the Quality Management Plan.

c) Change the project specifications to align with the stakeholder's expectations without a review.

d) Terminate the project due to stakeholder dissatisfaction.

Answers:

a1. Correct Answer: b) To ensure the project meets or exceeds stakeholder expectations.

Explanation: Quality Management focuses on meeting and surpassing the quality standards expected by stakeholders.

Why not a, c, or d? While budget, time, and resource utilization are important, they pertain more to Cost, Schedule, and Resource Management respectively. Quality Management specifically targets stakeholder satisfaction through quality deliverables.

a2. Correct Answer: b) Fishbone (Ishikawa) Diagram

Explanation: Fishbone diagrams help trace back the root causes of defects or problems in processes.

Why not a, c, or d? Gantt Charts and WBS are primarily scheduling and task breakdown tools, respectively, while Pareto Charts focus on identifying the most significant factors.

a3. Correct Answer: c) Quality Variance

Explanation: Control Charts are used to monitor the variance in quality performance and detect trends outside of control limits.

Why not a, b, or d? Budget, staff performance, and scope changes are not the primary focus of Control Charts within Quality Management.

b1. Correct Answers:

1-c, 2-b, 3-a, 4-d

Why other matches are incorrect:

- 1: The Pareto Chart does not directly monitor process stability (b) nor identify root causes (a), nor is it used primarily for comparing against industry standards (d).

- 2: The Control Chart is not used for prioritizing problems (c), identifying root causes (a), or benchmarking (d).

- 3: The Fishbone Diagram is not designed for monitoring variability (b), prioritizing issues based on their impact (c), or benchmarking (d).

- 4: Benchmarking does not monitor process stability (b), identify root causes (a), or prioritize issues (c).

b2. Correct Answers: 1-b, 2-c, 3-a

Why other matches are incorrect:

- TQM is not just about identifying reasons for problems (which would be Root Cause Analysis) nor just about financial implications (which would be Cost of Quality).

- CoQ is not about organizational culture or problem-solving methods; it specifically deals with financial aspects related to quality.

- Root Cause Analysis is a problem-solving method, not an overarching management approach like TQM or a financial assessment like CoQ.

b3.

Correct Answers: 1-b, 2-a, 3-c

Why other matches are incorrect:

- Six Sigma is not directly a method for policy compliance (Quality Audit) or a method of selecting population samples (Statistical Sampling).

- Quality Audit is not about improving operational performance through defect reduction (Six Sigma) or about sample-based testing (Statistical Sampling).

- Statistical Sampling does not aim to eliminate operational defects (Six Sigma) or ensure compliance with policies (Quality Audit).

c1. Correct Answer: b) Conduct a root cause analysis using tools like the Fishbone Diagram.

Explanation: Root cause analysis helps identify the underlying reasons for defects, which is fundamental for effective quality improvement.

Why not a, c, or d? Reassigning team members (a) does not address the root cause of defects. Informing stakeholders about failure (c) is premature without understanding the problem. Reducing scope (d) may neglect essential quality aspects.

c2.

Correct Answer: b) Review and adjust the Quality Management Plan and processes based on the metrics.

Explanation: Adjusting plans and processes based on actual performance metrics is a core principle of quality improvement.

Why not a, c, or d? Ignoring metrics (a) disregards quality management principles. Disbanding the team (c) does not address systemic issues. Increasing the budget (d) may not solve the underlying quality problems without a plan review.

c3. Correct Answer: b) Review the stakeholder's concerns and compare them against the Quality Management Plan.

Explanation: Addressing stakeholder concerns and verifying them against the plan ensures that quality objectives align with stakeholder expectations.

Why not a, c, or d? Ignoring concerns (a) can lead to dissatisfaction and project failure. Changing specifications without review (c) can cause scope creep. Terminating the project (d) is an extreme action without attempting resolution.

Resource Management

Resource Management is an integral part of project management that emphasizes the efficient and effective utilization of organizational resources to fulfill project objectives and ensure successful outcomes. It involves a comprehensive process that includes planning, estimating, acquiring, developing, and managing both human and physical resources.

Effective Resource Management ensures that the right resources are available at the right time and are used in the most efficient way possible. This includes identifying the specific skills, materials, equipment, and other resources required for the project and determining how to acquire them, allocate them, manage their use, and when to release them.

Key components of Resource Management include:

- **Strategic Planning:** Determining the types and quantities of resources required to complete the project successfully.

- **Resource Estimation:** Assessing the needs for each activity and aggregating them to determine the overall resource requirements.

- **Team Development:** Building a cohesive team with the necessary skills and fostering a productive working environment.

- **Physical Resource Management:** Ensuring materials, equipment, and supplies are available as needed and used efficiently.

- **Resource Monitoring and Control:** Tracking resource utilization, making adjustments as necessary, and managing changes effectively.

This strategic approach to Resource Management helps to avoid resource shortages, minimize costs, and ensure that project activities are completed on time. Additionally, it involves collaborating closely with other areas of project management, such as cost and schedule management, to ensure a holistic approach to project execution.

Through effective Resource Management, project managers can optimize resource allocation, enhance team performance, manage costs effectively, and ultimately achieve project objectives more efficiently.

Questions:

a. Multiple-Choice Questions:

1. What is the primary objective of resource leveling in project management?

a) To enhance team skills through training

b) To address resource overallocation

c) To increase the project budget

d) To reduce the project scope

2. **Which of the following best describes the purpose of a Resource Breakdown Structure (RBS)?**

a) To define project tasks and activities

b) To organize and categorize project resources

c) To outline the project budget

d) To schedule project timelines

3. **Effective team acquisition in Resource Management involves:**

a) Procuring the cheapest available resources

b) Matching skills and competencies with project requirements

c) Assigning tasks based solely on availability

d) Prioritizing resources from preferred vendors

b. **Matching Questions:**
1. **Match the following terms related to Resource Management with their definitions:**

1. Resource Leveling

2. Resource Allocation

3. Resource Aggregation

4. Human Resource Plan

a) Adjusting the start and finish dates based on resource limitations.

b) Distribution of resources across project tasks.

c) Summarizing the types, quantities, and durations of resources required.

d) Document outlining how project HR resources are defined, staffed, managed, and eventually released.

Correct Answers: 1-a, 2-b, 3-c, 4-d.

Explanation: Each term corresponds to specific actions within Resource Management to ensure efficient and effective use of resources.

Why other matches are incorrect: The definitions are unique to each term and not interchangeable, reflecting distinct aspects of resource management.

2. **Match the following Resource Management activities with their descriptions:**

1. A hierarchical representation of resources by category and type used in planning and controlling project work.

2. Adjusting the start and finish dates in the project schedule to balance the demand for resources with the available supply.

3. Cataloging the skills and competencies of available team members to aid in resource planning and team assembly.

4. The process of bringing together the people needed to complete the project, aligning their skills with project requirements.

a) Resource Leveling

b) Acquiring Team Members

c) Resource Breakdown Structure (RBS)

d) Skills Inventory

3. Match the following Resource Management terms with their corresponding descriptions:
1. Resource Leveling
2. Resource Smoothing
3. Acquisition
4. Team Development
5. Conflict Resolution

a) Process to ensure that resources are allocated efficiently, often requiring the adjustment of the project schedule.

b) Techniques aimed at improving team performance and dynamics, such as training sessions and team-building activities.

c) The procedure for obtaining the team members and necessary equipment or materials for the project.

d) Approaches to manage and mitigate interpersonal and group conflicts within the project team.

e) Techniques used to reduce the intensity of resource usage, usually without affecting the project timeline.

Correct Answers:

1 - a) 2 - e) 3 - c) 4 - b) 5 - d)

Why other matches are incorrect:

1 - Resource Leveling cannot be matched with techniques that do not alter the project schedule significantly (e).

2 - Resource Smoothing does not deal directly with acquiring resources or developing the team (c, b).

3 - Acquisition is specifically related to gathering resources, not to scheduling techniques or conflict resolution (a, d).

4 - Team Development focuses on improving team relations and performance, not on acquiring resources or adjusting schedules (c, a).

5 - Conflict Resolution is about resolving differences, not about the logistical aspects of resources or their optimization (c, e).

c. Scenario-Based Questions:

1. **You are leading a project to develop a new software application. Halfway through, one of your key developers resigns unexpectedly. Your project is already tight on schedule and budget. What is your first course of action?**

a) Immediately hire a new developer, regardless of costs.

b) Reallocate existing team members to cover the key developer's tasks while seeking a replacement.

c) Pause the project until a suitable replacement is found.

d) Reduce the project scope to accommodate the reduced resources.

2. **During a project, you discover that the tasks assigned to your team are being completed much slower than anticipated, causing delays. Upon investigation, you find that many team members lack certain technical skills. What should you do next?**

a) Reassign all work to the most skilled team members.

b) Organize immediate training sessions to upskill the team.

c) Ignore the issue and hope the team catches up over time.

d) Increase the number of team members to spread out the workload.

3. **Your project is running behind schedule, and a key team member has just resigned. What is your first step according to best Resource Management practices?**

a) Immediately hire a replacement regardless of fit

b) Reallocate remaining team members to cover the gap

c) Assess the impact on the project and identify the skills required for replacement

d) Pause the project until a new team member is found

Correct Answer: c) Assess the impact on the project and identify the skills required for replacement.

Explanation: Before making changes, assess the impact and understand what skills are needed to ensure a proper fit.

Why not a, b, or d? a) Hiring without assessing fit can lead to issues; b) Reallocating without assessment may overburden other team members; d) Pausing the project might not be feasible and could delay it further.

Answers:

171

a1. Correct Answer: b) To address resource overallocation.

Explanation: Resource leveling is used to address the issue of overallocation of resources, ensuring that no resource is overburdened.

Why not a, c, or d? a) Training enhances skills but doesn't directly address overallocation; c) Increasing the budget does not resolve resource distribution issues; d) Reducing scope is a different approach to solving resource constraints.

a2. Correct Answer: b) To organize and categorize project resources.

Explanation: An RBS is used to categorize project resources in a hierarchical structure.

Why not a, c, or d? a) Project tasks are outlined in the Work Breakdown Structure; c) Budget outlines are found in cost management plans; d) Timelines are managed through schedule management.

a3. Correct Answer: b) Matching skills and competencies with project requirements.

Explanation: Effective team acquisition ensures that the skills and competencies of team members align with project needs.

Why not a, c, or d? a) Cheapest resources may not meet project needs; c) Assignments should also consider skills, not just availability; d) Vendor preference doesn't ensure resource suitability.

b1. Correct Answers: 1-a, 2-b, 3-c, 4-d.

Explanation: Each term corresponds to specific actions within Resource Management to ensure efficient and effective use of resources.

Why other matches are incorrect: The definitions are unique to each term and not interchangeable, reflecting distinct aspects of resource management.

b2. Correct Answers: 1-C, 2-A, 3-D, 4-B

Why Other Matches Are Incorrect:

- A is not associated with cataloging skills (3) or directly assembling the team (4), it deals with adjusting schedules.

- B is not about creating hierarchical structures (1) or adjusting schedules (2), but about forming the project team.

- C does not directly involve adjusting project schedules (2) or acquiring team members (4), it categorizes resources.

- D is specifically for cataloging team member skills, not for structuring resources (1) or acquiring team members (4).

b3. Correct Answers:

1 - a) 2 - e) 3 - c) 4 - b) 5 - d)

Why other matches are incorrect:

1 - Resource Leveling cannot be matched with techniques that do not alter the project schedule significantly (e).

2 - Resource Smoothing does not deal directly with acquiring resources or developing the team (c, b).

3 - Acquisition is specifically related to gathering resources, not to scheduling techniques or conflict resolution (a, d).

4 - Team Development focuses on improving team relations and performance, not on acquiring resources or adjusting schedules (c, a).

5 - Conflict Resolution is about resolving differences, not about the logistical aspects of resources or their optimization (c, e).

c1. Correct Answer: b) Reallocate existing team members to cover the key developer's tasks while seeking a replacement.

Explanation: This option allows the project to continue moving forward without immediate additional costs and without compromising the project scope. It's a balanced response to an unexpected resource loss.

Why Not a, c, or d? Immediately hiring a new developer (a) might exceed budget constraints and requires time for onboarding. Pausing the project (c) delays all progress, potentially harming the schedule and stakeholder satisfaction. Reducing the project scope (d) should be a last resort and requires stakeholder agreement.

c2. Correct Answer: b) Organize immediate training sessions to upskill the team.

Explanation: By investing in the team's development, you address the root cause of the delays and improve productivity.

Why Not a, c, or d? Reassigning all work (a) could lead to burnout in skilled members and neglects the development of others. Ignoring the issue (c) will likely result in continued delays and does not solve the underlying problem. Increasing the team size (d) without addressing the skill gap may not improve efficiency and can add to project costs.

c3. Correct Answer: c) Assess the impact on the project and identify the skills required for replacement.

Explanation: Before making changes, assess the impact and understand what skills are needed to ensure a proper fit.

Why not a, b, or d? a) Hiring without assessing fit can lead to issues; b) Reallocating without assessment may overburden other team members; d) Pausing the project might not be feasible and could delay it further.

Communications Management

Communications Management stands as a cornerstone in project management, focusing on ensuring the precise and prompt flow of project information. It underpins every aspect of a project, facilitating the strategic dissemination of information to all stakeholders. By managing how information is generated, shared, and understood, project managers can significantly improve project outcomes and stakeholder satisfaction.

Key Components of Effective Communications Management:

1. **Strategic Planning**: At the heart of robust Communications Management is a comprehensive plan. This outlines the communication objectives, stakeholder information needs, and the channels and technologies for disseminating information. A well-crafted plan ensures targeted and timely delivery of crucial project updates.

2. **Execution and Engagement**: Beyond mere information dissemination, executing the Communications Plan requires engaging stakeholders through active feedback mechanisms, status updates, and customized communication channels. This dynamic approach caters to varied stakeholder preferences and project environments, ensuring effective and inclusive information exchange.

3. **Monitoring and Adaptation**: Constant evaluation of communication strategies is essential to remain effective. This involves tracking the success of communication initiatives, adapting to stakeholder feedback, and swiftly addressing any misunderstandings or gaps in information.

Practical Considerations and Integration:

- Consider the challenges of a globally distributed project team: employing diverse communication methods, respecting cultural sensitivities, and ensuring seamless collaboration are key to overcoming geographical and cultural barriers.

- Addressing common communication challenges involves recognizing and mitigating potential barriers such as language differences, technological hurdles, and cultural disparities. Solutions include employing straightforward language, providing reliable technology, and fostering a culture of openness and inclusivity.

- Communications Management interlocks with all project management areas, ensuring cohesive project tracking and informed decision-making. It's essential for transmitting vital changes and updates, facilitating a collaborative project environment.

In summary, effective Communications Management is critical for the success of any project. It not only ensures that information is shared accurately and timely but also supports stakeholder engagement and project alignment. A strategic approach, coupled with attentive execution and continuous monitoring, equips project managers with the tools to navigate complex communication landscapes, ultimately driving project success.

Questions:

a. Multiple-Choice Questions:

1. What is the primary goal of the Communications Management Plan?

a) To document the project's timelines

b) To outline the project's budget

c) To ensure effective generation, collection, and dissemination of project information

d) To track the project's performance metrics

2. Which method is best for ensuring a project manager understands the cultural differences among international team members?

a) Earned Value Management

b) Cross-cultural training

c) Critical Path Method

d) Gantt charts

3. **What should a project manager do when a stakeholder misunderstands a project report?**

a) Revise the project budget.

b) Update the project schedule.

c) Reissue the report without changes.

d) Clarify the report and engage in a feedback loop.

b. Matching Questions:

1. **Match the communication methods with their most suitable scenarios:**

   1. Informal Written Communication
   2. Formal Written Communication
   3. Informal Verbal Communication

a) Discussing project changes in an informal team meeting.

b) Sending a project status report to stakeholders.

c) Writing a quick update to a team member on a task status.

2. **Align the following Communication Management processes with their primary functions:**

   1. Identify Stakeholders
   2. Plan Communications Management
   3. Manage Stakeholder Engagement

a) Defining the approach for disseminating information to stakeholders.

b) Interacting with stakeholders to satisfy their needs and resolve issues.

c) Recognizing all people or organizations impacted by the project and documenting their interests.

3. **Match the following terms with their definitions:**

   1. Communication Channels
   2. Feedback Loops
   3. Communication Constraints

a) Restrictions that impact the flow of information.

b) The paths through which information is transmitted.

c) Systems in place to capture responses and reactions.

c. Scenario-Based Questions:

1. You are managing a project with teams in four different countries. What is the best approach to manage communications effectively?

a) Send out weekly emails in English only.

b) Hold daily stand-up meetings at a time that suits only the head office.

c) Develop a communication plan that includes multilingual support and flexible meeting times.

d) Use only text messages for communication to avoid time-zone conflicts.

2. Your project is behind schedule, and you need to communicate this to stakeholders. How should you proceed?

a) Wait until the next scheduled meeting to bring it up.

b) Update the project schedule and send it without explanation.

c) Organize an urgent meeting to discuss the delays, potential impacts, and mitigation plans.

d) Send an email blaming the responsible team members.

3. Your project team is spread across different time zones, leading to challenges in scheduling meetings. What strategy would best facilitate effective communication?

a) Schedule all meetings during the project manager's working hours.

b) Rotate meeting times to accommodate different time zones.

c) Send email updates instead of holding meetings.

d) Only hold meetings during the client's business hours.

Answers:

a1. Correct Answer: c) To ensure effective generation, collection, and dissemination of project information.

Explanation: The Communications Management Plan aims to facilitate effective and efficient communication among all project stakeholders. It's not primarily about timelines, budgets, or performance metrics.

Why not a, b, or d?: These choices relate to other management plans within project management, such as Schedule Management, Cost Management, and Performance Measurement.

a2. Correct Answer: b) Cross-cultural training.

Explanation: Cross-cultural training is designed to help understand and respect cultural differences, crucial in international projects.

Why not a, c, or d?: These are tools for project performance, scheduling, and planning, not for understanding cultural differences.

a3. Correct Answer: d) Clarify the report and engage in a feedback loop.

Explanation: Clarification and feedback are essential to resolving misunderstandings and ensuring clear communication.

Why not a, b, or c?: These actions do not directly address the misunderstanding or improve communication.

b1. Correct Answers: 1-c, 2-b, 3-a.

Explanation: Informal written communication suits quick updates among team members; formal written communication is needed for structured, official information like status reports; and informal verbal communication fits casual discussions.

Why other matches are incorrect: Each communication method has a specific context where it is most effective, and mixing these contexts can lead to miscommunication or inefficiency.

b2. Correct Answers: 1-c, 2-a, 3-b.

Explanation: Identifying stakeholders is about understanding who is affected by the project; planning communications outlines how to provide information; managing stakeholder engagement is about actively working with stakeholders.

Why other matches are incorrect: The processes have specific goals within the project's communication framework, ensuring targeted and effective interactions.

b3. Correct Answers: 1-b, 2-c, 3-a.

Explanation: Communication channels refer to the means through which information is sent; feedback loops are mechanisms for receiving responses; communication constraints are barriers to effective communication.

Why other matches are incorrect: Each term has a distinct role within the realm of Communications Management, affecting how information is shared and received.

c1. Correct Answer: c) Develop a communication plan that includes multilingual support and flexible meeting times.

Explanation: This approach caters to the diverse needs of an international team, considering language barriers and different time zones.

Why not a, b, or d?: These methods could exclude or misunderstand some team members due to language and time differences.

c2. Correct Answer: c) Organize an urgent meeting to discuss the delays, potential impacts, and mitigation plans.

Explanation: Direct communication about issues, along with collaborative problem-solving, is key in project management.

Why not a, b, or d?: Waiting could worsen the situation, sending updates without context may lead to confusion, and blaming individuals is not constructive.

c3.

Correct Answer: b) Rotate meeting times to accommodate different time zones.

Explanation: Rotating meeting times ensures all team members can participate at convenient times, fostering inclusivity and effective communication.

Why not a, c, or d? These approaches could lead to exclusion, miscommunication, or dependency on written updates, which may not be as effective as direct discussions.

Risk Management

Risk Management is essential in project management, focusing on identifying, analyzing, and responding to potential risks. This proactive approach helps in minimizing the impact of unforeseen events and ensures smoother project execution.

Key Steps in Risk Management:

1. **Risk Identification:** Utilize methods such as brainstorming and SWOT analysis to uncover potential risks.

2. **Risk Analysis:** Prioritize risks using qualitative and quantitative techniques to assess their impact and likelihood.

3. **Risk Response Planning:** Develop strategies to avoid, mitigate, transfer, or accept identified risks based on their severity.

4. **Risk Monitoring and Control:** Regularly review and update risk management strategies to adapt to project changes and new risks.

Effective Risk Management integrates with other project areas like Scope, Schedule, and Cost Management to create a comprehensive project plan. By anticipating and preparing for potential issues, project managers can steer their projects towards successful completion, even in the face of challenges. This brief overview sets the stage for understanding how to apply Risk Management practices effectively in project settings.

Questions:

  a. **Multiple-Choice Question:**
  1. **What is the primary purpose of risk identification in project management?**

a) To create a risk management plan

b) To list all potential events that might affect the project

c) To assign risks to project team members

d) To calculate the project's budget

Correct Answer: b) To list all potential events that might affect the project.

Explanation: Risk identification aims to create a comprehensive list of potential risks that could impact the project, allowing for better preparation and response strategies. It's the foundational step in the risk management process.

Why not a, c or d? a) is incorrect because the primary purpose is to identify risks, not to create a plan. c) is incorrect because risks are not assigned to team members; they are identified and then managed. d) is incorrect as risk identification is not directly for budgeting but for recognizing potential issues that could impact the project.

2. **Which of the following best describes a risk response strategy known as 'Mitigation'?**

a) Transferring the impact of the risk to a third party

b) Reducing the probability or impact of the risk

c) Accepting the consequences of the risk

d) Avoiding the risk by changing the project plan

Correct Answer: b) Reducing the probability or impact of the risk.

Explanation: Mitigation refers to actions taken to reduce the likelihood and/or impact of a risk, thereby lessening its potential negative effects on the project.

Why not a,c or d? a) describes 'Transfer', not Mitigation. c) describes 'Acceptance', where the risk consequences are accepted. d) describes 'Avoidance', which involves changing the project to eliminate the risk.

3. **In risk management, what does the term 'Risk Appetite' refer to?**

a) The total cost of all identified risks

b) The level of risk that an organization is willing to accept

c) The speed at which risk responses are implemented

d) The amount of time allocated to risk management activities

Correct Answer: b) The level of risk that an organization is willing to accept.

Explanation: Risk appetite is the degree of uncertainty an organization is prepared to tolerate, reflecting its willingness to take on risks in pursuit of its objectives.

Why not a, c or d? a) is incorrect as it describes potential risk impacts, not appetite. c) is incorrect because it concerns the implementation speed of responses, not the willingness to accept risk. d) is incorrect as it relates to time management, not the organizational stance on risk acceptance.

b. **Matching Questions:**
1. **Match the risk management terms to their correct descriptions.**

1. Risk Appetite

2. Qualitative Risk Analysis

3. Risk Register

4. Risk Mitigation

5. Risk Transfer

a) A document that contains details of identified risks, including their descriptions, impacts, and response strategies.

b) The strategy of reducing the probability or impact of an adverse risk event to an acceptable threshold.

c) The process of prioritizing risks for further analysis or action by assessing their probability of occurrence and impact.

d) The amount of uncertainty or potential financial loss an organization is willing to accept in pursuit of its objectives.

e) The strategy of shifting the impact of a risk and the responsibility for managing it to a third party.

Correct Answers: 1 - d), 2 - c), 3 - a), 4 – b, 5 - e)

Why other matches are incorrect:

- Risk Appetite (1) is not about documenting risks (a) or directly about prioritizing or transferring them.

- Qualitative Risk Analysis (2) is specifically about assessing and prioritizing risks, not documenting them in a register (a) or engaging in risk transfer (e).

- Risk Register (3) serves as a documentation tool, not a process for assessment (c) or a strategy like mitigation (b) or transfer (e).

- Risk Mitigation (4) aims to reduce risks, not to document (a), assess (c), or transfer them (e).

- Risk Transfer (5) is about shifting risk responsibility, not about appetite for risk (d), analyzing risk (c), or documenting them (a).

2. **Match the following risk management processes with their primary functions:**
1. Identify Risks
2. Perform Qualitative Risk Analysis
3. Plan Risk Responses
4. Monitor and Control Risks

a) Evaluates the impact and likelihood of identified risks

b) Tracks identified risks, identifies new risks, and evaluates risk process effectiveness throughout the project

c) Develops options and actions to enhance opportunities and reduce threats to project objectives

d) Determines which risks might affect the project and documents their characteristics

Correct Answers: 1-d, 2-a, 3-c, 4-b.

Why other matches are incorrect:

- Identify Risks does not evaluate impact and likelihood, that's the purpose of Perform Qualitative Risk Analysis.
- Perform Qualitative Risk Analysis doesn't create response plans, that's for Plan Risk Responses.
- Plan Risk Responses doesn't monitor ongoing risks; it's about planning, not tracking, which is the role of Monitor and Control Risks.

- Monitor and Control Risks isn't about identifying initial risks, it's about the ongoing oversight of risks.

3. **Match the risk response strategies with their appropriate scenarios:**
   1. Avoid
   2. Mitigate
   3. Transfer
   4. Accept

a) Assigning the financial impact of a risk to a third party, such as purchasing insurance

b) Deciding to no longer engage in the action that generates the risk

c) Implementing actions to reduce the probability or impact of a risk

d) Acknowledging the risk but not taking any action unless it occurs

Correct Answers: 1-b, 2-c, 3-a, 4-d.

Why other matches are incorrect:

- Avoid doesn't mean accepting or transferring the risk, it means changing plans to prevent the risk.
- Mitigate is not about transferring or accepting but about reducing the impact or likelihood of the risk.
- Transfer does not involve accepting or avoiding but passing the risk consequences to another party.
- Accept is not about reducing, transferring, or avoiding, but about recognizing and preparing to deal with the consequences.

c. **Scenario-Based Question:**

1. **You are the project manager of an IT upgrade project. During the planning phase, a key stakeholder expresses concern about the potential for data breaches. Which risk response strategy should you consider first?**

a) Accept the risk and do nothing.

b) Transfer the risk by purchasing insurance.

c) Mitigate the risk by implementing additional security measures.

d) Exploit the risk by using it to add new features.

Correct Answer: c) Mitigate the risk by implementing additional security measures.

Explanation: Mitigating risks involves taking action to reduce their likelihood or impact. Implementing additional security measures addresses the concern directly.

Why not a, b, or d?: Accepting the risk is not proactive in this high-stakes context; transferring the risk doesn't eliminate the possibility of a data breach; exploiting the risk doesn't apply here as it's about turning a potential threat into an opportunity, not applicable for security breaches.

2. **Your construction project is delayed due to an unexpected government regulation change. What risk response strategy should you implement to handle potential future regulatory changes?**

a) Mitigation by lobbying against the regulation.

b) Acceptance, since regulatory changes are beyond control.

c) Contingency planning to prepare for possible changes.

d) Transfer, by making the contractor responsible for delays.

Correct Answer: c) Contingency planning to prepare for possible changes.

Explanation: Contingency planning prepares the project to respond quickly to changes, minimizing disruption.

Why not a, b, or d?: Lobbying is not a direct project management strategy; acceptance does nothing to address future risks; transferring does not manage the actual risk of regulatory changes and may not be feasible or ethical.

3. **Halfway through a project, a critical piece of equipment fails, threatening to delay the project. What should be your immediate action according to risk management practices?**

a) Accept the delay and inform the stakeholders.

b) Use reserve funds to expedite the repair or replacement.

c) Reassign team members to other tasks until the issue is resolved.

d) Cancel the project due to unforeseen circumstances.

Correct Answer: b) Use reserve funds to expedite the repair or replacement.

Explanation: Reserve funds are set aside for unforeseen events, and using them can prevent delays.

Why not a, c, or d?: Accepting the delay without action disregards proactive management; reassigning team members may be inefficient without addressing the main issue; canceling the project is an extreme response not aligned with effective risk management.

Procurement Management

Procurement Management involves the processes necessary for acquiring external resources crucial to a project's success. This includes everything from identifying needs and soliciting vendor bids to managing contracts and ensuring that vendors meet their obligations.

1. **Plan Procurement Management:** Develop a detailed Procurement Management Plan, identifying what needs to be procured and the best methods for doing so. This plan sets the foundation for successful procurement activities, including selection of appropriate contract types and establishing procurement protocols.

2. **Conduct Procurements:** This stage is about executing the procurement plan by inviting, assessing, and choosing vendors based on pre-set criteria. It emphasizes transparency and fairness throughout the bidding and selection process.

3. **Control Procurements:** Manage relationships with vendors and oversee contractual obligations. This ensures that vendors are meeting their commitments and that any changes or disputes are handled effectively.

4. **Close Procurements:** Ensure that all procurement activities are completed, contracts are closed, and all parties are satisfied with the results. This final step involves confirming that all work has been properly completed and resolving any remaining issues.

Procurement Management's integration with other project management areas like Cost, Risk, and Schedule Management ensures that external procurements are aligned with the overall project objectives and contribute positively to its success. Proper Procurement Management is vital for maintaining project integrity, managing external vendor relationships, and ensuring project deliverables are met within the agreed upon timelines and budgets.

Questions:

a. **Multiple-Choice Questions:**

1. **What is the primary purpose of developing a Procurement Management Plan?**

a) To outline the project's budget constraints

b) To document how procurement processes will be executed and controlled throughout the project

c) To list potential vendors for the project

d) To define the project's scope

2. **Which document formalizes the purchase of products, services, or results from an external source?**

a) Project Charter

b) Procurement Statement of Work (SOW)

c) Purchase Order

d) Vendor Contract

3. **Which of the following best describes the Conduct Procurements process?**

a) Monitoring the status of procurement activities and making changes as needed

b) Completing and settling each procurement contract, including resolution of any open items

c) Obtaining seller responses, selecting a seller, and awarding a contract

d) Identifying which project needs can be best met by procuring products or services outside the project organization

b. **Matching Questions:**
1. **Match the following procurement management processes with their correct descriptions:**

1. Plan Procurement Management

2. Conduct Procurements

3. Control Procurements

4. Close Procurements

a) Involves completing and settling each contract, including the resolution of any open items and closing each contract applicable to the project or project phase.

b) Involves the process of documenting project procurement decisions, specifying the approach, and identifying potential sellers.

c) Entails managing procurement relationships, monitoring contract performance, and making changes and corrections as needed.

d) Involves obtaining seller responses, selecting a seller, and awarding a contract.

2. Match the following terms related to Procurement Management with their correct descriptions:

1. Request for Proposal (RFP)

2. Contract Closure

3. Procurement Audits

4. Sole Source Procurement

a) A formal process to review all procurement activities, identifying successes and failures to improve future procurement practices.

b) A procurement method used when only one supplier is capable of providing the required goods or services.

c) The formal process of completing and settling the contract, including resolving any open items.

d) A document used to solicit proposals from potential suppliers, detailing the project and procurement requirements.

3. Match the following terms related to Procurement Management with their correct descriptions:

1. Procurement Audits

2. Make-or-Buy Analysis

3. Procurement Negotiations

4. Supplier Selection

a) The process of reviewing and evaluating the procurement processes from plan to contract administration.

b) The systematic approach to deciding whether to purchase a product or service externally or produce it internally.

c) The final step in the procurement process where the buyer and seller discuss terms and conditions, and finalize contractual agreements.

d) The method used to assess, compare, and choose among potential vendors based on predetermined criteria.

 c. Scenario-Based Question:

 1. Your company is working on a new construction project, and you are responsible for procuring high-quality concrete. Two suppliers submit proposals: Supplier A offers a lower price, but there have been quality concerns in the past. Supplier B is more expensive, but they have a stellar reputation for quality and reliability. What should be your primary consideration when making your decision?

a) Choose Supplier A to reduce costs and increase profit margins.

b) Choose Supplier B to ensure quality and reduce potential future risks.

c) Select Supplier A and perform additional quality checks during delivery.

d) Negotiate with Supplier B for a lower price without compromising quality.

 2. During a software development project, a key component needs to be outsourced. After receiving bids from several vendors, you notice that the lowest bid comes from a new vendor with limited track record. What should be your next step before making a decision?

a) Automatically select the lowest bid to save costs.

b) Conduct a risk assessment on the new vendor including reference checks.

c) Reject all bids and reissue the procurement request.

d) Choose a known vendor even if their bid is higher.

 3. You are managing a project that requires the procurement of specialized IT equipment. Halfway through the procurement process, a change in project scope necessitates different equipment specifications. What is the most appropriate action to take?

a) Continue with the current procurement process to avoid delays.

b) Update the procurement documents and reissue the request for quotations with the new specifications.

c) Cancel the procurement process and absorb the costs internally.

d) Order the original equipment and try to modify it to meet the new requirements.

Anwers:

a1. Correct Answer: B) To document how procurement processes will be executed and controlled throughout the project.

Explanation: The Procurement Management Plan is essential for defining how procurement should be managed from the planning stage through to contract closure. It ensures that all procurement activities are aligned with the project's needs and executed efficiently.

Why not A, C, or D? a) While managing costs is important, it's not the primary purpose of the Procurement Management Plan. c) Listing potential vendors is a part of the procurement process but not the main goal of the plan. d) Defining the project's scope is not the objective of the Procurement Management Plan.

a2. Correct Answer: d) Vendor Contract.

Explanation: A Vendor Contract is a formal agreement between the project and the external vendor, specifying the products, services, or results to be provided, terms, and conditions.

Why not A, B, or C? a) The Project Charter authorizes the project itself, not purchases. b) The SOW describes the procurement's work requirements but is not the formal purchase agreement. c) A Purchase Order is a common procurement document but does not formalize purchases in the context of project management like a contract does.

a3. Correct Answer: c) Obtaining seller responses, selecting a seller, and awarding a contract.

Explanation: Conduct Procurements encompasses the process of receiving bids or proposals from potential sellers, evaluating these, and then selecting a vendor and awarding the contract.

Why not A, B, or D? a) This describes the Control Procurements process. b) This is more aligned with the Close Procurements process. d) Identifying needs is part of the Plan Procurement Management process.

b1. Correct Answers: 1 - b, 2 - d, 3 - c, 4 - a.

Why other matches are incorrect:

- Plan Procurement Management (1) is not about awarding contracts (d) or managing relationships (c); it's about setting up the procurement approach.

- Conduct Procurements (2) doesn't involve the management or closing of procurements; it focuses on obtaining bids and choosing a seller.

- Control Procurements (3) is not about the initial planning (b) or the final closing (a) but about managing ongoing contracts.

- Close Procurements (4) does not deal with the planning (b), conducting (d), or day-to-day control (c) of procurements.

b2. Correct Answers: 1-d, 2-c, 3-a, 4-b

Why other matches are incorrect:

- Request for Proposal (RFP) is not about auditing procurement processes (3), completing contracts (2), or selecting a single source without competition (4).

- Contract Closure does not involve soliciting proposals (1), conducting audits (3), or choosing suppliers without competition (4).

- Procurement Audits are not for soliciting bids (1), closing contracts (2), or selecting a single supplier (4).

- Sole Source Procurement is not about requesting proposals from multiple suppliers (1), finalizing contractual terms (2), or auditing procurement practices (3).

b3. Correct Answers: 1-a, 2-b, 3-c, 4-d.

Why other matches are incorrect:

- Procurement Audits (1) are not about choosing suppliers or making buy or lease decisions; they are about evaluating the effectiveness of the procurement process.

- Make-or-Buy Analysis (2) doesn't directly deal with the negotiation or the audit process but rather with the decision-making process regarding production.

- Procurement Negotiations (3) are distinct from supplier selection as negotiations typically occur after a supplier has been preliminarily selected but before the contract is finalized.

- Supplier Selection (4) is a process that leads to negotiations; it is not about auditing procurement processes or deciding whether to make or buy a component.

c1. Correct Answer: b) Choose Supplier B to ensure quality and reduce potential future risks.

Explanation: In procurement management, ensuring the quality and reliability of procured materials is crucial, especially for critical components like concrete in construction projects. While Supplier A is less expensive, past quality concerns can lead to increased risks and costs in the long term. Supplier B, despite being more expensive, provides better assurance of quality and reliability, which are paramount in project management to avoid delays and additional costs.

Why not a, c, or d?: Option a) ignores the importance of quality, which can result in higher costs later. Option c) may still risk project quality and incur additional costs for quality checks. d) is a valid strategy, but not the primary consideration; the quality should come first before negotiating prices.

c2. Correct Answer: b) Conduct a risk assessment on the new vendor including reference checks.

Explanation: In procurement management, while cost is an important factor, it's essential to assess the risks associated with new vendors, especially those with limited track records. Conducting a comprehensive risk assessment and checking references can provide insights into the vendor's capability and reliability, helping to make an informed decision.

Why not a, c, or d?: Selecting the lowest bid without assessment (a) can lead to quality issues and project delays. Rejecting all bids and restarting the process (c) can cause unnecessary delays. Automatically choosing a known vendor (d) may result in higher costs without exploring potentially beneficial new partnerships.

c3.

Correct Answer: b) Update the procurement documents and reissue the request for quotations with the new specifications.

Explanation: When there's a change in project scope that affects procurement requirements, it's essential to update the procurement documents to reflect the new specifications and reissue the request for quotations. This ensures that the procured items will meet the project's updated needs and objectives.

Why not a, c, or d?: Continuing with the current process (a) may result in acquiring unsuitable equipment. Cancelling the procurement process (c) wastes resources and time already invested. Ordering the original equipment and modifying it (d) can lead to increased risks and additional costs.

Stakeholder Management

Stakeholder Management is crucial in guiding a project towards success by effectively engaging with individuals and groups impacted by or interested in the project. Here's how to succinctly approach it:

1. **Stakeholder Identification**: Begin with a comprehensive identification of all stakeholders using methods like stakeholder analysis matrices. This step is vital to ensure no potential influencer or affected party is overlooked.

2. **Stakeholder Analysis**: Delve deeply into understanding the needs, interests, and the influence of each stakeholder. This detailed analysis helps in tailoring strategies to manage different stakeholder groups effectively.

3. **Engagement Planning**: Develop a clear, detailed Stakeholder Engagement Plan that outlines the approach for engaging with each stakeholder or stakeholder group throughout the project. This plan should detail the frequency, mode, and content of communications.

4. **Engagement Execution**: Execute the engagement strategies diligently, ensuring open, clear, and continuous communication. Adapt strategies as needed based on project evolution and stakeholder feedback.

5. **Monitoring and Management**: Keep a constant check on stakeholder engagement levels and relationship dynamics. Adjust strategies as required to ensure ongoing support and cooperation.

Consider real-world applications and challenges, and remember that effective Stakeholder Management is intertwined with other project management aspects like Communications, Risk, and Change Management. This integrated approach ensures that stakeholder needs and project goals remain aligned, promoting project success and stakeholder satisfaction.

Questions:

a. Multiple-Choice Questions:
1. What is the primary purpose of Stakeholder Analysis in project management?

a) To determine the project schedule

b) To identify all individuals or groups affected by the project and understand their interests

c) To allocate the project budget

d) To establish the project's deliverables

Correct Answer: b) To identify all individuals or groups affected by the project and understand their interests.

Explanation: Stakeholder analysis is a technique used to identify and assess the importance of key people, groups of people, or institutions that may significantly influence the project's success. It is crucial for understanding their interests, influences, and potential impact on the project.

Why not a, c, or d? Answer a is incorrect because stakeholder analysis does not determine the project schedule; that is the role of schedule management. Answer c is incorrect because stakeholder analysis does not allocate the project budget; that falls under cost management. Answer d is incorrect because stakeholder analysis aims to understand stakeholders' needs and expectations, not to establish project deliverables.

2. Which of the following strategies is NOT typically used in Stakeholder Engagement Planning?

a) Tailoring communication to stakeholder needs and expectations

b) Excluding less influential stakeholders from communication plans

c) Developing a feedback loop to address concerns and adapt strategies

d) Identifying the frequency, mode, and content of communications

Correct Answer: b) Excluding less influential stakeholders from communication plans.

Explanation: Stakeholder engagement planning involves tailoring communication strategies to meet the needs of all stakeholders, not excluding them based on their influence level. Every stakeholder can have an impact on the project, directly or indirectly.

Why not a, c, or d? Answer a is incorrect because tailoring communication to stakeholders' needs is a key part of stakeholder engagement planning. Answer c is incorrect because developing a feedback loop is essential for effective stakeholder engagement. Answer d is incorrect because identifying communication details is part of creating an effective stakeholder engagement plan.

3. In Stakeholder Management, what does the term 'Power/Interest Grid' represent?

a) A tool to track project expenses and stakeholder financial interests

b) A matrix to categorize project risks based on their impact and likelihood

c) A visualization tool to classify stakeholders based on their level of authority and interest in the project

d) A scheduling method for stakeholder meetings and communications

Correct Answer: c) A visualization tool to classify stakeholders based on their level of authority and interest in the project.

Explanation: The Power/Interest Grid, also known as a stakeholder matrix, is a tool used in stakeholder analysis to categorize stakeholders by their power over and interest in the project. It helps in determining the strategy for stakeholder engagement.

Why not a, b, or d? Answer a is incorrect because the Power/Interest Grid does not track financial interests or expenses. Answer b is incorrect because it is used for stakeholder categorization, not risk categorization. Answer d is incorrect because it is not a scheduling method, but rather a classification tool.

b. Matching Questions:
1. Match the stakeholder management activities with their descriptions:
1. Identify Stakeholders
2. Plan Stakeholder Engagement
3. Manage Stakeholder Engagement
4. Monitor Stakeholder Engagement

a) Regularly reviewing and adjusting strategies for engaging stakeholders based on their engagement levels and project changes.

b) Determining the best ways to involve stakeholders in the project based on their needs, expectations, influence, and potential impact.

c) Recognizing all individuals, groups, or organizations that could affect or be affected by the project and documenting relevant information about them.

d) Actively working with stakeholders to meet their needs/expectations, addressing issues as they occur, and fostering appropriate stakeholder involvement.

Correct Answers: 1 c), 2 b), 3 d), 4 a)

Why other matches are incorrect:

- Identify Stakeholders is specifically about finding out who the stakeholders are, not about planning engagement strategies, managing actual engagement, or monitoring their involvement.
- Plan Stakeholder Engagement is about strategizing rather than the actual identification, direct management, or monitoring of stakeholder engagement.
- Manage Stakeholder Engagement is not about identifying, planning, or monitoring but about the active involvement and management of stakeholders in the project.
- Monitor Stakeholder Engagement does not involve identifying, planning, or directly managing stakeholders but rather tracking and assessing the effectiveness of engagement strategies and interactions.

2. **Match the following terms related to stakeholder management with their definitions:**
   1. Stakeholder Satisfaction
   2. Power/Interest Grid
   3. Stakeholder Register
   4. Engagement Levels

a) A tool used to classify stakeholders based on their authority (power) and concern (interest) regarding project outcomes.

b) A document that lists all identified stakeholders, providing information such as their interests, involvement, and potential impact on the project.

c) The extent to which stakeholders are supportive, neutral, or resistant regarding the project.

d) The degree to which stakeholders' needs and expectations are met by the project.

Correct Answers: 1 d), 2 a), 3 b), 4 c)

Why other matches are incorrect:

- Stakeholder Satisfaction is specifically related to how well stakeholders' needs and expectations are fulfilled, not their classification, documentation, or engagement state.
- Power/Interest Grid is a classification tool, not a measure of satisfaction, a list, or a measure of engagement depth.
- Stakeholder Register is a documentation tool, not a tool for measuring satisfaction, classifying stakeholders based on power/interest, or detailing their engagement levels.

- Engagement Levels indicate the degree of stakeholder involvement and support, not their satisfaction, classification, or listing details.
3. **Match the stakeholder management process with the appropriate action:**
1. Engage Stakeholders
2. Analyze Stakeholders
3. Collect Stakeholder Requirements
4. Update Stakeholder Register

a) Determining stakeholder needs, wants, and expectations for the project.

b) Involving stakeholders through effective communication and consultation to gain their support and address their concerns.

c) Reviewing and updating information on stakeholders as the project progresses and as new stakeholders are identified.

d) Evaluating the interest, influence, and potential impact of stakeholders on the project.

Correct Answers: 1 b), 2 d), 3 a), 4 c)

Why other matches are incorrect:

- Engage Stakeholders is about active interaction and communication with stakeholders, not about analyzing them, collecting their requirements, or documenting their information.
- Analyze Stakeholders involves understanding stakeholders' characteristics and influence, not engaging with them, collecting their requirements, or updating their records.
- Collect Stakeholder Requirements is focused on understanding what stakeholders expect from the project, not on engaging, analyzing, or updating records.
- Update Stakeholder Register is about maintaining current stakeholder information, not about engaging them, analyzing their influence, or gathering their requirements.

c. **Scenario-Based Question:**
1. **You are leading a new infrastructure project that has garnered significant attention from local communities, environmental groups, and local government. Despite your efforts in stakeholder engagement, there's rising opposition due to environmental concerns. As the project manager, what should be your first step in managing this situation effectively?**

a) Cancel all upcoming project activities until the opposition subsides.

b) Engage directly with the opposition groups to understand their concerns and discuss potential mitigation strategies.

c) Increase the project budget to cover potential legal disputes with stakeholders.

d) Ignore the opposition, assuming it will decrease over time.

Correct Answer: b) Engage directly with the opposition groups to understand their concerns and discuss potential mitigation strategies.

Explanation: Effective stakeholder management involves actively engaging with all stakeholders, especially those with concerns or opposition, to understand their perspectives and work towards mutually beneficial solutions. Ignoring or avoiding stakeholder concerns can lead to increased resistance and can jeopardize project success.

Why not a, c, or d? a) Cancelling project activities without addressing the underlying concerns does not resolve stakeholder issues and can lead to further distrust. c) Increasing the budget for legal disputes does not address stakeholders' environmental concerns and could escalate conflicts. d) Ignoring opposition can lead to increased resistance and potential project delays or failures.

2. **During the execution phase of a software development project, you realize that the key stakeholders, including the client, are not fully engaged and have missed several critical meetings. What is the best approach to improve stakeholder engagement in this scenario?**

a) Continue the meetings without the key stakeholders' presence.

b) Update the Stakeholder Engagement Plan to include more suitable communication methods and schedules for the key stakeholders.

c) Postpone the project until all stakeholders agree to be more involved.

d) Reduce the frequency of the meetings to lessen the burden on stakeholders.

Correct Answer: b) Update the Stakeholder Engagement Plan to include more suitable communication methods and schedules for the key stakeholders.

Explanation: Modifying the engagement plan to accommodate the preferences and schedules of key stakeholders can improve engagement and ensure that critical project decisions are communicated effectively.

Why not a, c, or d? a) Continuing without key stakeholders can lead to decisions that don't align with their needs or expectations, risking project outcomes. c) Postponing the project can lead to delays and increased costs without guaranteeing improved engagement.d) Reducing the frequency of meetings without addressing the specific reasons for disengagement might not solve the underlying issues.

3. **You are managing an international project and have stakeholders from different cultural backgrounds. You notice that there are misunderstandings arising from these cultural differences, affecting project communication and progress. What should be your immediate action to address the cultural misunderstandings among project stakeholders?**

a) Dismiss the misunderstandings as minor and focus on the project deliverables.

b) Arrange for cultural sensitivity training for the project team and stakeholders.

c) Only communicate in writing to avoid any further misunderstandings.

d) Assign a team member from each cultural background to handle communications.

Correct Answer: b) Arrange for cultural sensitivity training for the project team and stakeholders.

Explanation: Providing cultural sensitivity training helps in understanding and respecting different cultural perspectives, which can reduce misunderstandings and improve communication among stakeholders.

Why not a, c, or d? a) Ignoring cultural misunderstandings can lead to worsening communication issues and stakeholder disengagement. c) Relying solely on written communication may not resolve existing misunderstandings and could lead to further misinterpretations. d) While having representatives can be helpful, it does not ensure that all team members and stakeholders will understand or respect cultural differences.

Navigating Professional and Ethical Responsibilities

Understanding the PMI Code of Ethics

Navigating Professional and Ethical Responsibilities

In the realm of project management, adherence to a set of ethical principles is not just a matter of professional compliance; it's the cornerstone of building trust, credibility, and integrity in every project undertaken. The PMI Code of Ethics and Professional Conduct serves as a beacon, guiding project managers across industries to navigate the complex ethical challenges they might encounter in their professional journey.

Understanding the PMI Code of Ethics

The PMI Code of Ethics is articulated around four fundamental values that set the standard for professional behavior in the field of project management. These values – Responsibility, Respect, Fairness, and Honesty – are not mere suggestions. They are imperative to fostering an environment where trust thrives, and project outcomes are not just successful but are achieved through honorable means.

1. **Responsibility**

Responsibility is the backbone of ethical conduct. It emphasizes the importance of project managers owning their decisions and actions, being accountable for the outcomes of their projects, and fulfilling their commitments. This principle encourages project managers to:

- Acknowledge and correct mistakes promptly.

- Make decisions based on the best interests of society, public safety, and the environment.

- Adhere to all applicable laws and regulations, ensuring every project action is defensible and justifiable.

- Recognize the need for continuous improvement, committing to personal and professional growth to enhance their capability to produce value.

2. **Respect**

Respect within the PMI Code of Ethics underscores the importance of valuing others and honoring their rights and feelings in all project interactions. This principle guides project managers to:

- Listen to diverse viewpoints, fostering an inclusive environment that encourages collaboration and trust.

- Acknowledge the contributions of others, showing appreciation for their efforts and insights.

- Treat everyone with courtesy and understanding, regardless of personal differences, promoting a culture of mutual respect that transcends professional boundaries.

3. **Fairness**

Fairness in the PMI Code of Ethics highlights the importance of making decisions impartially and objectively. Project managers are urged to:

- Act without bias, ensuring equal treatment and opportunities for all stakeholders and team members.

- Manage conflicts of interest transparently, maintaining the integrity of project decisions.

- Base decisions and actions on fair and just considerations, ensuring an environment of trust and respect where ethical dilemmas can be navigated with integrity.

4. **Honesty**

Honesty, as outlined in the PMI Code of Ethics, emphasizes the significance of being truthful in all project communications and actions. This principle requires project managers to:

- Accurately represent themselves, their intentions, and their actions.

- Ensure transparency and integrity in their professional conduct, fostering a culture of trust among team members, stakeholders, and clients.

- Promote ethical problem-solving and decision-making, ensuring that honesty guides every step of the project management process.

Real-World Application and Ethical Decision-Making

Understanding and living by these principles require more than just theoretical knowledge. It demands practical application and the development of ethical decision-making skills that can navigate the gray areas and the complex, often challenging situations that arise in project management. Project managers are encouraged to:

- Engage in continuous learning, seeking out resources, training, and professional development opportunities that deepen their understanding of ethical principles in practice.

- Participate in community discussions, forums, and professional groups that explore ethical dilemmas and share experiences and strategies for maintaining ethical standards in challenging situations.

- Develop a personal code of ethics, a set of guiding principles that complements the PMI Code of Ethics and serves as a personal compass in professional decision-making.

Conclusion

The PMI Code of Ethics is not just a set of rules; it's a commitment to a way of professional life that elevates the practice of project management. By embedding these ethical principles into every aspect of their work, project managers not only contribute to the success of their projects but also advance the profession as a whole, building a legacy of integrity, trust, and excellence.

Professional and Social Responsibility

Professional and Social Responsibility in Project Management

Professional and social responsibility in project management encompasses a spectrum of ethical practices, sustainable development, social impact considerations, and continuous improvement. This section elaborates on these principles, offering guidance to project managers on upholding professional standards and contributing positively to society and the environment.

Ethical Practice in Project Management: Ethical practice forms the cornerstone of professionalism and trust in project management. It requires commitment to the PMI Code of Ethics and Professional Conduct, emphasizing:

- **Integrity:** Maintaining honesty, fairness, and impartiality in all project activities and decisions. This includes avoiding conflicts of interest and ensuring transparency in communications.

- **Respect:** Valuing diverse viewpoints and treating all individuals with dignity and fairness. This involves creating an inclusive project environment where every team member feels valued.

- **Accountability:** Taking ownership of one's decisions and actions, acknowledging mistakes, and committing to continuous improvement.

Project managers can demonstrate ethical practice by leading by example, fostering a culture of ethical behavior within their teams, and addressing unethical conduct promptly and effectively.

Sustainability and Social Impact: Modern project management extends beyond meeting project objectives to encompass broader impacts on society and the environment. Project managers play a pivotal role in:

- **Promoting Sustainability:** Integrating sustainable practices into project planning and execution, considering environmental, economic, and social factors to ensure long-term benefits.

- **Assessing Social Impact:** Evaluating how projects affect various stakeholders and the community, striving to maximize positive impacts while mitigating negative ones.

Incorporating sustainability and social impact considerations into projects not only enhances their value but also aligns them with global sustainability goals and corporate social responsibility initiatives.

Contribution to the Profession: Project managers contribute to the growth and development of the profession through:

- **Knowledge Sharing:** Participating in professional communities, writing articles, giving presentations, and sharing best practices and lessons learned.

- **Mentorship:** Guiding and mentoring emerging professionals, helping them develop their project management skills and ethical understanding.

- **Continuous Learning:** Engaging in professional development opportunities to stay updated with the latest trends, tools, and methodologies in project management.

Advocacy for Ethical Practices: Advocating for ethical practices involves promoting and adhering to high ethical standards within project teams and the wider organization. This includes:

- **Setting Clear Expectations:** Communicating ethical guidelines and expectations to project teams and stakeholders.

- **Creating Ethical Awareness:** Providing training and resources to enhance understanding and application of ethical principles.

- **Addressing Ethical Dilemmas:** Establishing mechanisms for reporting and resolving ethical issues discreetly and effectively.

Continuous Improvement and Learning: A commitment to continuous improvement and lifelong learning ensures project managers remain effective and relevant. This involves:

- **Self-Assessment:** Regularly reflecting on personal and project performance to identify areas for improvement.

- **Professional Development:** Pursuing certifications, attending workshops, and engaging in other learning activities.

- **Adaptability:** Embracing change and staying flexible to adapt to new challenges and environments.

In summary, professional and social responsibility in project management is about leading with integrity, considering the broader impacts of projects, contributing to the profession, advocating for ethical practices, and committing to continuous improvement. By embodying these principles, project managers not only ensure the success of their projects but also contribute to a more ethical, sustainable, and responsible practice of project management.

Additional Resources and Continuing Education

Further Reading and Study Materials

Core PMBOK® Guide and Agile Practice Guide: The PMBOK® Guide is essential for mastering traditional project management practices, outlining key processes and areas necessary for effective project execution. The companion Agile Practice Guide provides essential insights into adopting agile methodologies, emphasizing adaptability and customer-centric frameworks. Together, these guides offer a holistic view of project management, catering to a wide array of project types and environments.

Key Areas to Focus:

1. Integration of agile practices with traditional project management.

2. Understanding of lifecycle phases: Initiation, Planning, Execution, Monitoring and Controlling, and Closure.

3. Roles and responsibilities within project and agile teams.

Recommended Approach:

- Study both guides comprehensively, noting differences and complementarities between traditional and agile methodologies.

- Apply concepts through case studies or project simulations.

- Regularly review key terms and processes for reinforcement.

Advanced Project Management Books: Expand your knowledge beyond foundational concepts through specialized literature focusing on risk management, leadership, and strategic alignment. Select books that provide in-depth analyses and case studies to enhance practical understanding and application.

Recommended Strategy:

- Create a reading list prioritizing areas where you seek deeper insight.

- Summarize key concepts and apply them to real-world scenarios or your current projects.

- Engage with online forums or study groups to discuss and debate complex topics.

Academic Journals and Articles: Staying updated with the latest research in project management can provide innovative solutions and enhance decision-making. Scholarly articles often present new methodologies, performance analyses, and theoretical advancements.

Action Points:

- Subscribe to reputable academic journals and online libraries.

- Set aside regular time for reading and reflecting on new studies.
- Apply new findings to your project management practice, evaluating effectiveness and efficiency.

Online Resources and Blogs: The internet offers a vast array of up-to-date project management resources. Engaging with reputable blogs, forums, and websites can keep you informed about industry trends and peer solutions.

Utilization Tips:

- Follow thought leaders and professional bodies on social media.
- Participate in webinars and online discussions.
- Share insights and experiences, contributing to the knowledge base.

Professional Development Workshops and Webinars: Interactive learning through workshops and webinars provides practical insights and networking opportunities. These platforms often feature industry experts discussing the latest project management trends, tools, and strategies.

Engagement Recommendations:

- Identify workshops and webinars that align with your career goals and knowledge gaps.
- Actively participate and network with other professionals.
- Implement learned strategies in your projects to gauge their impact.

Integration with PMP ECO and PMIstandards+: The PMP Examination Content Outline and PMIstandards+ are invaluable for aligning your study and practice with current exam standards and real-world demands.

Study Integration:

- Map study topics and practical experiences to the ECO's domains and tasks.
- Use PMIstandards+ for up-to-date case studies and templates that illustrate PMBOK® principles in action.
- Regularly review these resources to ensure your knowledge remains current and comprehensive.

By integrating these resources into your study plan, you're not only preparing for the PMP exam but also enhancing your capabilities as a project manager. Continuous learning, application, and engagement with the project management community are key to both exam success and career advancement.

Maintaining PMP Certification

In the dynamic field of project management, maintaining a PMP certification is crucial for staying relevant and demonstrating continued competence. The Continuing Certification Requirements (CCR) Program by

PMI ensures that PMP credential holders remain committed to professional development and up-to-date with evolving industry standards.

Continuing Certification Requirements (CCR) Program

The CCR Program is designed to promote lifelong learning among PMP certification holders. To retain the PMP credential, individuals must accrue a specified number of Professional Development Units (PDUs) within a three-year renewal cycle. This commitment supports the ongoing professional growth and sustains the global recognition of PMP holders.

Earning PDUs: PDUs can be earned through various activities categorized under Education and Giving Back. Education PDUs are achieved by engaging in learning activities that enhance one's project management knowledge and skills. Giving Back PDUs are earned by contributing to the profession, such as volunteering, creating new project management knowledge, or working as a practitioner.

Professional Development Units (PDUs)

PDUs serve as the metric for tracking professional development activities. They are divided into two main categories:

1. **Education**: Activities under this category aim to expand a project manager's competency. These can include formal courses, workshops, webinars, and self-directed learning. Topics should be relevant to project management, agile methodologies, strategic and business management, or leadership.

2. **Giving Back**: This category allows PMPs to share their knowledge and contribute to the growth of the profession. Activities include volunteering, mentoring, creating content related to project management, or applying professional skills in a practical setting.

Each PMP must earn at least 60 PDUs to fulfill the CCR requirements within the three-year cycle.

Education and Giving Back

The distribution of PDUs between Education and Giving Back is flexible, yet there are minimum requirements for each to ensure a balanced approach to professional development. Education PDUs must constitute at least two-thirds of the total required PDUs, equating to a minimum of 35 PDUs. The remaining one-third, up to 25 PDUs, can be earned under the Giving Back category.

PDU Reporting and Tracking

Maintaining accurate records of PDUs is essential. The PMI's online Continuing Certification Requirements System facilitates PMPs in reporting new PDUs, reviewing certification status, and ensuring compliance with the CCR program. Timely and accurate reporting helps in the smooth renewal of the PMP credential.

Renewal Process and Fees

The renewal process is initiated by submitting the recorded PDUs through the PMI's CCR system before the end of the three-year certification cycle. A renewal fee is applicable, with different rates for PMI members and non-members. Renewing the PMP certification validates the credential holder's commitment to the profession and their continuous skill development.

Conclusion

Final Tips and Motivation for the Exam

Review Strategy

Embarking on your PMP exam preparation journey necessitates a strategic and focused approach. Delve deeply into the core elements of the PMBOK® Guide, concentrating on its foundational principles and methodologies. Identify areas that have posed challenges and allocate additional time to convert weaknesses into strengths.

Incorporate insights from the Agile Practice Guide, understanding the flexibility and responsiveness of agile methodologies, and how they can be integrated within traditional project management frameworks. This comprehension is vital in today's dynamic project environments.

Utilize active recall and practice questions to reinforce learning and ensure concepts are not only understood but can be applied in practical scenarios. This method solidifies knowledge and builds confidence.

Exam Mindset

The mindset with which you approach the PMP exam can significantly influence your performance. Cultivate a mindset of success and confidence. Visualize passing the exam and the opportunities this achievement will unlock. Regularly practicing relaxation and stress-management techniques will help maintain focus and alleviate anxiety.

Adopt a positive outlook, viewing the exam as an opportunity to showcase your dedication and knowledge. A constructive attitude can dramatically impact your exam experience, transforming it from a hurdle into a milestone of your professional journey.

Stress Management

Effective stress management is crucial for peak performance. Maintain physical well-being through regular exercise, rest, and nutrition. These elements are foundational to mental clarity and energy levels.

Implement mindfulness and meditation to enhance focus and reduce exam anxiety. Establishing a routine that includes short, focused study sessions with regular breaks can prevent burnout and keep your mind sharp.

Success Visualization

Practice success visualization to reinforce confidence and positivity. Imagine each step of the exam process, from entering the testing center to completing the exam confidently. Envision the success that awaits beyond the exam – the doors it will open and the professional validation it provides.

Long-term Perspective

Understand that the PMP certification is more than an exam; it's a step towards broader professional achievement. It represents a commitment to the field of project management and a pledge to continue growing and contributing to the community.

The certification opens avenues for career advancement, increases your marketability, and enhances your credibility among peers and organizations. It's a testament to your dedication and expertise in project management.

Conclusion: Building Your Professional Legacy

As you conclude this preparation journey, remember that obtaining your PMP certification is not merely the end goal but a significant milestone in your professional development. It's a commitment to excellence, continuous improvement, and a pledge to uphold the highest standards of ethical and professional conduct.

Let this manual not only be a guide for passing the exam but also a blueprint for a rewarding and impactful career in project management. Your journey doesn't end with certification; it's just beginning. Embrace the challenges, celebrate the successes, and continue to grow and contribute to your field.

Every project you lead, every team you inspire, and every challenge you overcome contributes to your legacy as a project manager. The PMP certification is your stepping stone towards shaping a career that not only achieves goals but also drives change, fosters innovation, and makes a lasting impact.

Carry forward the knowledge, skills, and best practices you've learned, and use them to navigate the complexities of modern projects. Be a mentor to others, sharing your insights and experiences, and contribute to the ever-evolving tapestry of project management.

In closing, the path to PMP certification is rigorous, but it is also immensely rewarding. It equips you with the tools to manage projects more effectively, lead teams more efficiently, and contribute to your profession at a higher level. Remember, the ultimate measure of your success is not just passing the exam, but in applying these principles to become a leader in the field of project management. Good luck, and may your professional journey be fulfilling and impactful.

Bonus Study Resources

Congratulations on Completing "PMP Exam Prep"!

You're now one step closer to mastering your PMP exam. To further enhance your preparation, we've included exclusive bonus content, accessible through the QR code below.

Your Bonus Content Includes:

- **Full-Length Mock Exam:** Test your knowledge under real exam conditions.

- **300 Additional Q&A:** Deepen your understanding with detailed questions and answers.

- **300 Key Flashcards:** Quick review tools to sharpen recall and test your grasp of crucial concepts.

- **Formulas Cheat Sheet:** All the essential formulas you need in one place.

- **Real-World Scenario Case Studies:** Apply what you've learned in practical, complex scenarios.

- **40+ Hours of E-Learning Videos:** Comprehensive video lessons covering PMBOK essentials and exam strategies.

How to Access Your Bonus Content:

Scan the QR Code: Use your smartphone's camera or a QR code scanner app to scan the code below. This will direct you to the download page.

Need Help?

If you encounter any issues accessing or downloading your bonus content, please don't hesitate to contact us at **nexusprepeditions@gmail.com** for assistance.

Thank you for choosing us for your exam preparation, and we wish you the best of luck on your PMP exam!

Made in the USA
Las Vegas, NV
17 October 2024

97019078R00111